CW01651993

WILDERNESS LONG-TERM SURVIVAL GUIDE

FORGOTTEN SKILLS TO MAKE THE WILD YOUR HOME

Nicole Apelian, Ph. D.

The European Edition

Published by GLOBAL BROTHER.

Dedication

For all of us who love being in nature; here's to our wild side.

Acknowledgements

I want to thank my friends, family, and chosen family, who have always supported and embraced my love of the wild.

Thank you to the many mentors I have had over the years – we do not learn these skills in a bubble; we learn from others and by spending a lot of time in the wild ("dirt time").

Deep gratitude for my sons Colton and Quinn, for the joy, love, laughter, and perspective they bring to my life.

Thank you to my bestie John, who is always there to remind me what is truly important in life, and deep gratitude to my partner; his love of the wild runs as deeply as mine.

Great appreciation to Elena for her behind-the-scenes work putting this book together, to my publisher and dear friend Claude, and to the rest of my incredible publishing team – I am blessed to have each and every one of them.

A huge shout out to you for your desire to learn more about wilderness living and how to survive and thrive in nature. I hope that every reader of this book will form a deeper connection to the natural world, and experience the great joy that comes from being in nature.

Disclaimer

This book, "Wilderness Long-Term Survival Guide. Forgotten Skills to Make the Wild Your Home" is dedicated to providing information about living in the wild and mastering survival skills. It is important to note that this publication is sold with the understanding that the author, editor, and publisher do not offer legal, financial, medical, or other professional advice. Laws and practices vary from state to state and country to country, and if legal or expert assistance is required, readers are advised to seek the services of a professional, whether that be an herbalist or other certified expert in the relevant domain.

This book does not encompass all the information available on the subject of wilderness survival and is not tailored to specific individual or organizational situations or needs. Readers should be aware that the information contained within this document is for educational and entertainment purposes only. No warranties of any kind are declared or implied, and the author is not engaging in the rendering of legal, financial, medical, or professional advice.

While efforts have been made to ensure accuracy, currency, and reliability, typographical and content errors may exist. Consequently, this book should serve as a general guide rather than the ultimate source of information on wilderness survival. The authors, editor, and publisher disclaim any liability or responsibility for losses or damage incurred, directly or indirectly, by the information contained in this book. Readers agree that the authors, editors, and publishers are not responsible for any losses resulting from errors, omissions, or inaccuracies.

Furthermore, there is no warranty, expressed or implied, regarding the safety of the final products or methods described in the book. Undertaking any projects outlined in this book, including building and using the described methods, is done at the reader's own risk. The author, editor, and publisher hold no responsibility for the misuse or misidentification of plants, and readers are cautioned against consuming any plant without proper knowledge of its edibility.

The information contained in this book is intended for informational purposes only and should not be construed as legal advice. Readers are cautioned against acting or refraining from acting based on any content included in this book without seeking legal or other professional advice. Additionally, the information is not presented with the intention of diagnosing or prescribing, but rather as information for maintaining and promoting health in cooperation with a physician.

In summary, readers should approach the content within this document with caution and acknowledge that they are bound by this disclaimer. If unsatisfied, the book can be returned within the guarantee time period for a full refund.

Table of Contents

LOCATION

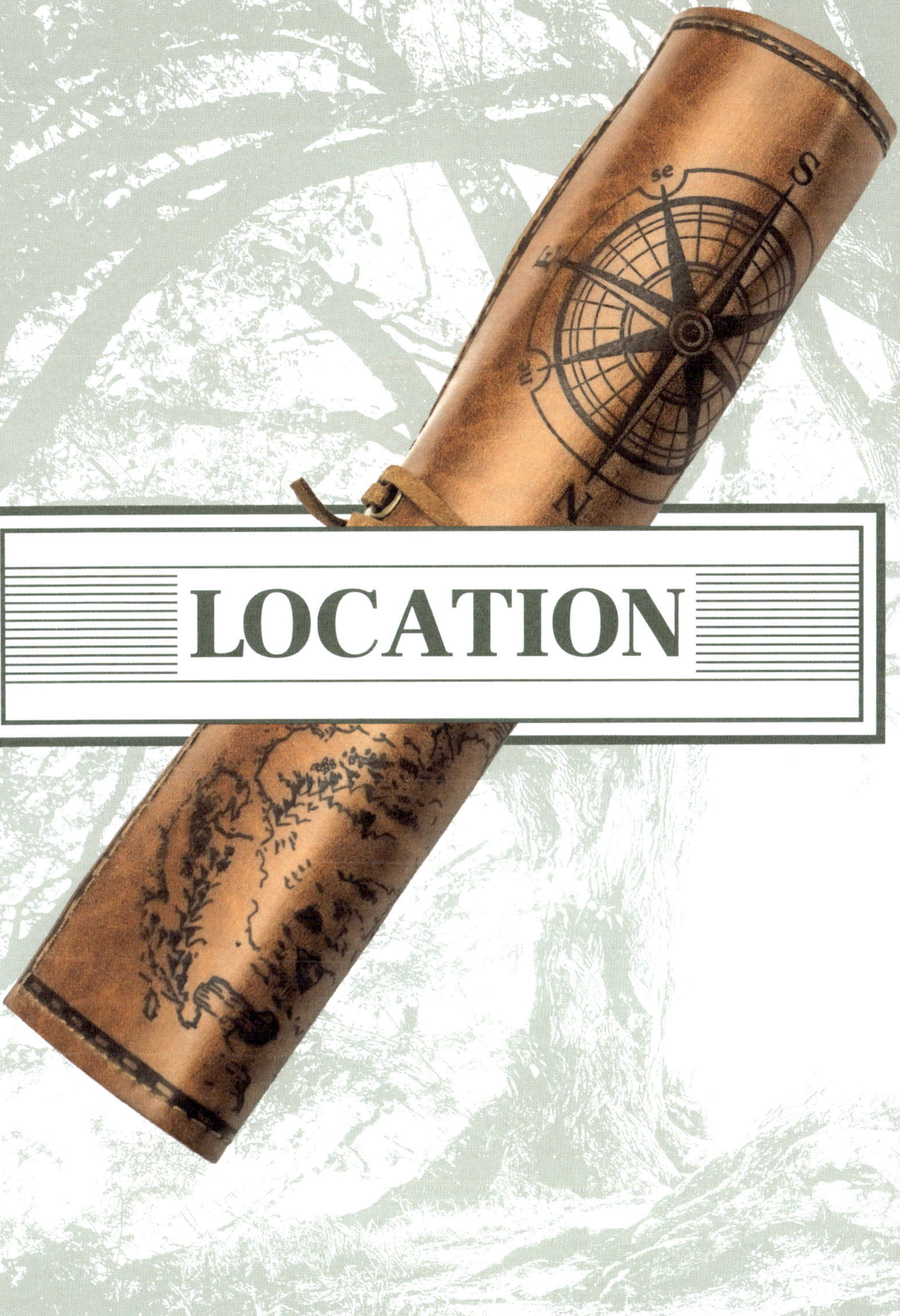

THE BEST PLACES TO LIVE IN THE WILD IN EUROPE

The diverse landscapes in Europe, from the rugged Scandinavian wilderness to the verdant forests of the Alps, offer great opportunities for off the beaten path living.

However, there are substantial challenges. Harsh weather conditions, difficulty in finding food, and the necessity of building shelters are a few of the hurdles to overcome. This chapter will outline the best areas that you can choose for living in the wild in Europe.

What to Look for in a Wilderness Survival Location

When venturing into the wild anywhere in Europe, several key factors should inform your choice of survival location.

- **Water availability:** Proximity to a natural water source like a river or lake.
- **Food sources:** While you may bring supplies, the ability to forage or hunt extends your survival time. Look for areas rich in edible plants, with a known presence of game.
- **Shelter:** Seek areas where natural shelter is available, or where materials for creating a shelter, such as wood, are plentiful.
- **Safety:** Avoid locations known for dangerous wildlife or unstable weather conditions. While seclusion may be desirable, ensure you're within a reasonable distance of civilization or known hiking routes for emergencies.
- **Terrain and climate:** Some areas may be too harsh for survival, especially for beginners. Select an area that matches your skill level.

Wilderness Survival Locations in Western Europe

The Alps

The Alps are a mountain range extending across eight countries in Europe. These include France, Switzerland, Italy, Monaco, Liechtenstein, Austria, Germany, and Slovenia. Each of these nations offers a unique perspective on the majestic alpine landscapes, making the Alps a versatile and challenging locale for wilderness survival.

Geographic Map of The Alps

The region is rich in water sources from melting snow and ice. The terrain is rugged, posing both a challenge and providing natural shelter options. Two significant challenges are the extreme winter weather and altitude sickness.

While the Alps may seem barren at first glance, they are home to a variety of wildlife that can serve as potential sources of food for wilderness survival. The challenging alpine terrain is frequented by chamois, a type of goat-antelope native to the region, and marmots, a large type of rodent.

Chamois

The forests located at the lower altitudes often shelter roe deer and wild boar. Birds such as grouse may be encountered, but catching them can be difficult without the right equipment or experience. Use a bow and approach with caution to be successful.

The bilberry is a common edible plant found throughout the Alps. This hardy shrub thrives in the acidic soils of the region's high-altitude heathlands, producing small, dark blue berries that can be consumed raw or used in cooking.

The Black Forest, Germany

The Black Forest, a mountainous region in southwest Germany, extends across the states of Baden-Württemberg and Rhineland-Palatinate. This vast forest is a challenging but rewarding environment for wilderness survival, offering a different perspective on Germany's natural landscapes.

The region is dotted with rivers and lakes, providing an ample supply of fresh water. Edible plants such as wood sorrel, elderberry, and stinging nettle can be harvested throughout the region. The dense woodland offers both a challenge for navigation and an abundant source of materials for shelter (please see our chapters on how to build a shelter on page 17, 21, and 29) and fuel.

The Black Forest, Germany_location_map.svg NordNordWest, CC BY-SA 3.0

While the damp conditions can be a challenge for maintaining warmth, building a well-insulated shelter can help overcome this. The Black Forest may seem eerily quiet at first, but it teems with wildlife that serve as potential food sources. Roe deer, wild boar, red foxes, badgers, and ibex make their home in these woods.

Birds such as wood grouse, partridge, pheasant, and quail can be hunted as a food source all year-round.

The Scottish Highlands

The Scottish Highlands, a rugged region in the northern part of the United Kingdom, stretches across the mainland and includes a multitude of islands.

The area has many lochs and burns, providing a plentiful supply of fresh water. Edible plants, such as nutritious bilberries, nettles, and wild garlic, are abundant.

The tough, fibrous branches of heather can be used as a sturdy framework for a shelter in the Scottish Highlands. Peat, when dried, can act as a good insulating material, effectively protecting against the often harsh and unpredictable weather conditions in the region.

The Scottish Highlands are filled with wildlife that serve as potential food sources. Red deer and wild goats inhabit these highlands. Birds such as ptarmigan and grouse can be captured and eaten for a small meal.

A pair of Rock Ptarmigan, Jan Frode Haugseth - Own work, CC BY-SA 3.0

Wilderness Survival Locations in Eastern Europe

The Carpathian Mountains

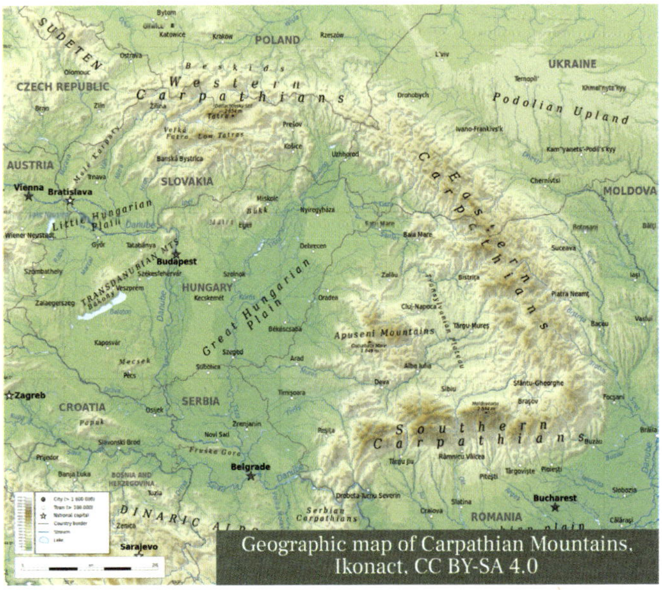

Geographic map of Carpathian Mountains, Ikonact, CC BY-SA 4.0

The Carpathian Mountains, a series of rugged ranges extending across Central and Eastern Europe, offer a unique blend of terrain, stretching from the Czech Republic to Romania.

The region is filled with reliable water sources. Edible plants, including nutritious wild berries, nettles, and dandelions, are widespread.

In the Carpathian Mountains, the dense forests offer abundant wood and foliage, which can be used to construct a robust and well-insulated shelter, while rocky outcrops can provide a natural framework or windbreak.

The Carpathian Mountains are teeming with wildlife that may be used for sustenance. Animals such as roe deer and chamois roam these mountains. Birds such as grouse and the Eurasian jay can be trapped for food.

The Taiga Forest, Russia

The Russian Taiga Forest, also known as the Siberian wilderness, is the world's largest terrestrial biome. Encompassing a vast, cold, and dense forest, the Taiga is one of the best places to live in the wild if you can handle the climate.

The climate here is distinguished by long, harsh winters and short, mild summers, making survival a testament to resilience and adaptability. During winter, temperatures can plummet to -50 degrees Celsius, making it crucial to prioritize shelter and warmth. A traditional shelter, like a lean-to (please see "How to Build a One-Month Shelter on page 21) built with fallen branches and insulated with snow, can help retain heat.

The forest is abundant with coniferous trees like spruce, pine, and fir, which not only provide material for shelter construction and firewood, but their resin can be used as a fire starter, even in damp conditions. The inner bark of these trees can serve as an emergency food source, while the needles from pine trees can be made into a vitamin C-rich tea.

Wildlife such as Siberian roe deer, brown bears, and snowshoe hares thrive in the Taiga. Fish, including Northern pike and perch, are found in the region's lakes and rivers, offering an alternative food source.

Snowshoe Hare

Despite its harsh conditions, the Taiga offers edible berries, herbs, and mushrooms during the short summer months. Look for lingonberries, blueberries, morels, chanterelles, and cattail as good supplements to your diet.

Wilderness Survival Locations in Southern Europe

Southern Europe, famed for its diverse landscapes and temperate climate, presents its own set of survival challenges and resources. The terrain varies from rocky coastal areas to dense inland forests, each offering unique resources.

The Mediterranean Sea provides an abundant source of fish, while the land offers a rich variety of edible plants and game. However, survival is not without its challenges. The dry, hot summers increase the risk of wildfires, while the mountainous regions present treacherous terrain.

The Apennine Mountains, Italy

The Apennine Mountains, a rugged spine of rock running the length of Italy, is an ideal survival area. These mountains consist mainly of deciduous and coniferous trees, providing ample firewood and shelter materials. The streams teeming with trout offer a source of fresh water and food, supplementing the plentiful game, such as deer and wild boar, that inhabit these forests.

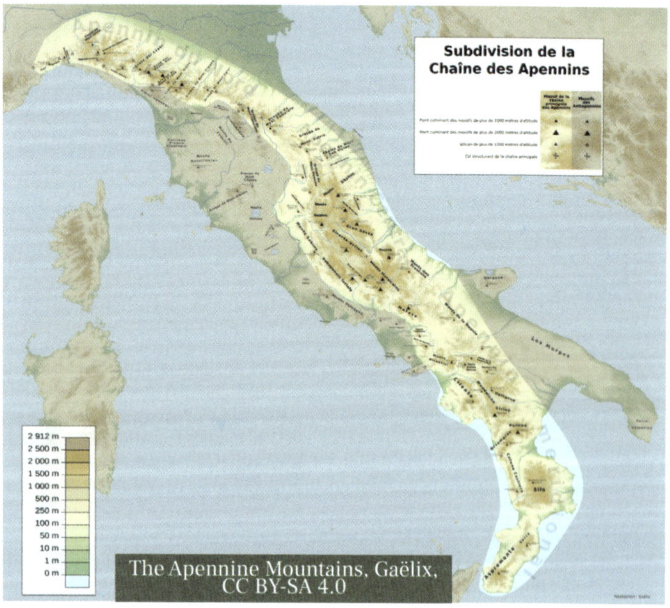

The Apennine Mountains, Gaëlix, CC BY-SA 4.0

This is in contrast to the sharp and unpredictable terrain filled with cliffs and valleys. Additionally, weather conditions can change abruptly, with temperatures plummeting in the higher altitudes even in summer. Winter survival can be particularly harsh due to heavy snowfall and freezing temperatures.

Among the edible plants found here, wild asparagus and various species of mushrooms are available during the warmer months. Porcini, field, and oyster mushrooms can be found during the wetter seasons of spring and fall.

Pleurotus ostreatus, Oyster Mushrooms, Stephen Sikes, CC BY-SA 3.0

Porcini mushroom, Giacomo Eupizi - Own work, CC BY-SA 4.0

THE SURVIVAL FORAGING MAP
Cornflower
Marsh Marigold
Bedstraw
Horsetail
15
Chamomile
Dewberry
Salsify
Plantain
Cattail
Horsetail
Dock
DENMARK
16
Marsh Marigold
Chamomile
Horsetail
Lady Fern
Creeping Bellflower
Salsify
SLOVAKIA
17
Pipsissewa/ Prince's Pine
Milk Thistle
Plantain
Cattail
Salsify
Chamomile
Dandelion
Deadnettle
CROATIA
18
Chamomile
Salsify
Creeping Bellflower
Dock
Stinging Nettle
Dandelion
Plantain
SLOVENIA
Chicory
Cranberry
Cattail
Pipsissewa/ Prince's Pine
Dandelion
Yellowcress
Salsify
Plantain
Raspberry
Chamomile
Wild Mint
Lady Fern
Chicory
Bearberry
Thistle (Plume)
Yellowcress
Salsify
Marsh Marigold
Dock
Bearberry
Cranberry
Wild Mint
Stinging Nettle
Dewberry
Goldenrod
Cranberry
Chamomile
Cattail
Salsify
Chicory
Dock
Lady Fern
Dandelion
Yellowcress
Creeping Bellflower
15
Cranberry
Thistle (Plume)
Pipsissewa/ Prince's Pine
Marsh Marigold
5
Bearberry
Daylily
Chicory
Purslane
14
Salsify
Chamomile
Milk Thistle
Horsetail
7
Chicory
Lady Fern
Pipsissewa/ Prince's Pine
Milkweed
Purslane
Cranberry
Chamomile
16
Milk Thistle
Bearberry
Purslane
Dewberry
Goldenrod
Wild Mint
12
Cranberry
18
Cranberry
Thistle (Plume)
17
Marsh Marigold
Yellowcress
Chicory
9
Cattail
Lady Fern
Wild Mint
Salsify
Horsetail
Yellowcress
Daylily
Plantain
Salsify
Wild Mint
Milk Thistle
19
Lady Fern
London Rocket
Bearberry
Chicory
Thistle (Plume)
Passion-flower
Purslane

Bearberry
Wild Mint
Burdock
Salsify
Cornflower
Fleabane
Cranberry
Raspberry
London Rocket
Stinging Nettle
Cattail
Wild Leek
Bracken Fern
Bittercress
Chicory
Deadnettle
Pipsissewa/ Prince's Pine
Horsetail
Bearberry
Deadnettle
Marsh Marigold
Milk Thistle
Reishi
Mullein
Chamomile
Hazelnut
Chicory
6
Elderberry
Creeping Bellflower
Salsify
Dewberry
Chamomile
Dewberry
London Rocket
Pipsissewa/ Prince's Pine
Dewberry
Thistle (Plume)
Yellowcress
Horsetail
Bedstraw
Lady Fern
Salsify
Chicory
Plantain
Goldenrod
Cranberry
Dandelion
Raspberry
Thistle (Plume)
Salsify
Cranberry
Kudzu
Horsetail
Bearberry
Lady Fern
Pipsissewa/ Prince's Pine
Milkweed
Marsh Marigold
Raspberry
1
Purslane
Dock
Chamomile
Sumac
Dock
Lady Fern
Yarrow
Stinging Nettle
Chicory
Cattail
Raspberry
Catnip
Dock
4
Chicory
Salsify
8
2
Cattail
Purslane
Wild Mint
Creeping Bellflower
Dewberry
Milk Thistle
Yellowcress
Stinging Nettle
Horsetail
Lady Fern
Sumac
1
Dandelion
Chamomile
Milk Thistle
Mullein
MOLDOVA
2
Daylily
Chamomile
Creeping Bellflower
Dewberry
Kudzu
Lady Fern
AZERBAIJAN
3
Lady Fern
Dandelion
Raspberry
Chamomile
ALBANIA
4
Dandelion
Salsify
Cattail
Chamomile
Kudzu
Daylily
Dewberry
Stinging Nettle
GEORGIA
19
Purslane
Milk Thistle
Lady Fern
Chamomile
Cattail
Wild Mint
Dock
Plantain
PORTUGAL
5
Salsify
Bedstraw
London Rocket
Lady Fern
NETHERLANDS
6
Dock
Cranberry
Marsh Marigold
Dandelion
Dewberry
Chamomile
ESTONIA
7
Salsify
Bedstraw
Raspberry
Dock
Cranberry
LUXEMBOURG
8
Salsify
Yellowcress
Chamomile
Daylily
Dewberry
Dandelion
MASSACHUSETTS
9
Cattail
Milk Thistle
Salsify
Yellowcress
BOSNIA AND HERZEGOVINA
10
Chamomile
Salsify
Marsh Marigold
Milk Thistle
Horsetail
Stinging Nettle
Lady Fern
NORTH MACEDONIA
11
Chamomile
Bedstraw
Lady Fern
Dandelion
MONTENEGRO
12
Wild Mint
Cranberry
Horsetail
Lady Fern
Chamomile
Salsify
Yellowcress
Dock
SWITZERLAND
13
Chamomile
Bedstraw
Cattail
Dock
Milk Thistle
KOSOVO
14
Chamomile
Yellowcress
Dewberry
Salsify
Wild Mint
Cattail
Marsh Marigold
BELGIUM

SHELTERS FOR LIVING IN THE WILD

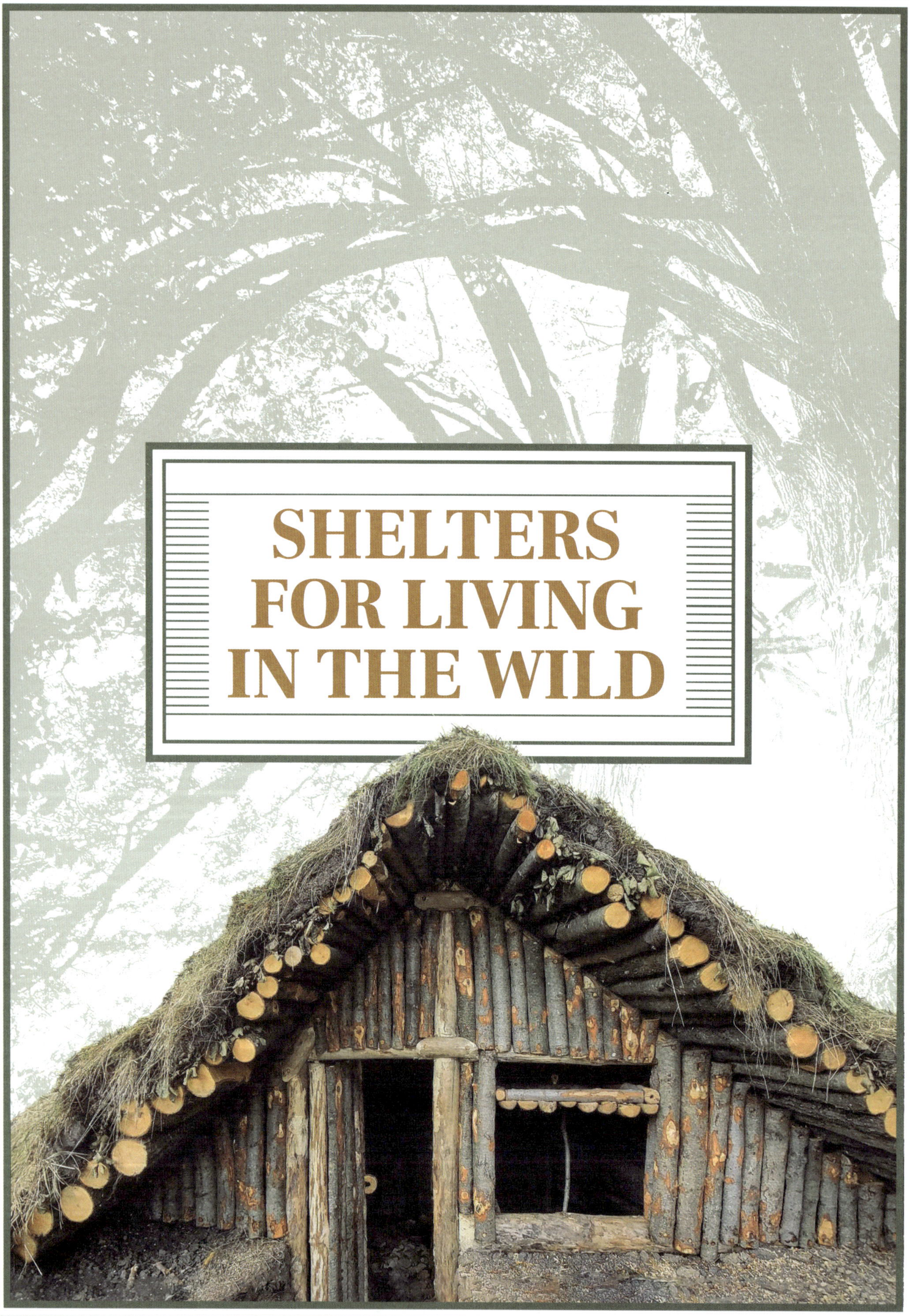

CHOOSING THE BEST LOCATION FOR YOUR SHELTER

Factors in Choosing the Best Shelter Location

While choosing the best location for your shelter can be narrowed down to a few different factors, small adjustments can be made to increase both safety and comfort.

These factors will help you choose the right spot, but it's important to remember that local knowledge will always come into play. For example, in certain landscapes, extreme winds can occur all the way from high elevations to low valleys. Knowing your environment will help you focus on the relevant and important factors for your shelter, and allow you to shift the design in order to prevent other hazards.

Elevation and Terrain

When looking for the right spot to start building, taking the elevation and terrain into consideration is the first step. No matter the length of time a shelter is being used, choosing the right elevation and placing it appropriately in the terrain is key.

Elevation plays a huge role in how the environment affects the shelter and the quality of sleep it can provide. Reading the terrain involves being able to look at the geography of the land, and use that information to choose the right placement along the elevation.

- **High Ground and Cold Wells**

Higher ground provides the opportunity to stay dry, which is important in any survival scenario. Choosing a location that provides higher ground can mean two completely different things when examining the terrain on a small and large scale.

On a small scale, choosing a location that is higher up than the surrounding ground will make for a well-placed shelter. Water will pool in the lower areas in the event of a flood or heavy rains, making a higher shelter the driest spot.

On a larger scale, choosing higher ground means staying out of valleys and lower pockets of land. Cold air sinks and collects in these "cold wells", which can be dangerous for colder nights and staying warm.

The flip side is choosing the top of a mountain. Exposed peaks tend to have high winds that can also bring a cold night's sleep and potential threats of hypothermia.

Different Types of Shelter

There are three main types of shelter in this section: a one-week shelter, a one-month shelter, and a long-term shelter.

One-Week Debris Shelter

A one-week debris shelter is going to be the simplest to choose a location for. Since the shelter isn't going to be used for a long period of time, it can be built with less consideration than a longer-term shelter. That doesn't mean it can be put up anywhere; I'll discuss below about what is important for a one-week shelter.

One-Month Shelter

One month can be an awkward middle ground for survival shelter building. It tiptoes into the longer-term category, and the shelter needs to accommodate certain changes that can happen over a month. Plus, making a shelter more comfortable for a month-long stay is much more important than when only staying in one spot for a week.

Long-Term Shelter

Long-term shelters tend to be the trickiest to find a spot for. In order to find the perfect location, each and every factor of the outdoors comes into play. Because you'll be out longer, the chances of dramatic weather shifts, animal encounters, and natural disasters increase. With the right consideration, all of these factors can be accounted for.

Usually the best spot for a shelter along an elevation profile is about three-quarters of the way to the top. This will keep the shelter safe from cold wells, extreme winds, large amounts of water drainage, and potential land, rock, or mudslides.

- **Utilizing the Terrain**

Natural structures such as caves and rock walls can be helpful forms of protection for a shelter. These structures can provide protection from wind and rain but they need to be carefully examined for any potential dangers of rockfall or flooding.

Placing a structure amongst a grove of trees provides a good level of protection from wind and rain, as well as additional structures to build off of. However, building a shelter in a grove of trees can bring about other issues that are discussed below.

When choosing the best location for a shelter, there are caveats. Pay attention to how to use the terrain and also how the terrain could be dangerous to you when staying in one place for a long time.

Orientation

The direction your shelter faces can play a huge role in the weather that can reach you inside of it. Even the slightest adjustment to a shelter can bring sunlight in, and a huge amount of warmth with it.

This tends to be most important for one-month and long-term shelters, but if the weather is more extreme, it will need to be accounted for in short-term shelters as well. The extra bit of sun and warmth can make a huge difference when cold temperatures are a major factor.

- **Wind**

Wind can come from all directions, but there is often a prevailing wind. If you know the area you're in well enough, this can be easy to predict.

If you're unfamiliar with the area, a decent rule of thumb is to account for winds that will blow from east to west. This is the simplest wind that is created by the rotation of the earth, so the rule tends to be universal.

That being said, certain geographical features and weather systems can have wind whipping in all directions. In this case, you may need to create a more elaborate shelter that includes a door to block wind coming from all directions.

Wind wall

Wind barrier

- **Sun**

In regards to shelter orientation, the sun is a major player. With the sun rising in the east and setting in the west, proper orientation can bring morning sunlight and warmth into the shelter after a long and cold night.

Access

The location of a shelter can determine your level of access to basic necessities throughout the day. When a shelter is built in an inconvenient spot, it can mean long trips out and more energy being exerted. The goal of survival tends to be energy conservation, which means you want to find prime and easy access.

For one-week shelters, access isn't as important. You can spare the energy to walk farther for a week, but those miles add up as time accumulates. One-month and long-term shelters require easy access to necessary resources.

- **Water**

Water is debatably the most important resource you need when in a survival scenario. You'll use it for almost everything throughout the day, and having it close by makes life a whole lot easier.

It can be tempting to build a shelter right next to the river for easy access. However, this brings up a lot of

Water source

different issues. From floods to competition with other animals, being creekside is more dangerous than it is beneficial.

The perfect spot is uphill from a water source, preventing flooding if the river overflows, and close enough to make the walk easy. It can be within sight, but if an animal spots you nearby its food and/or water source, there can be issues.

- **Wood**

Wood is a necessary resource to cook food, boil water, keep warm, and make any repairs or additions to your shelter. Some areas will be rich in wood, making it easy to find enough wood to burn, while others may have few trees that don't provide much downed wood for fuel.

The goal is to find an area where trees aren't dropping limbs on top of you, but nearby to a solid wood stash. For long-term shelters, this is more important as you will go through far more wood in a month than in a single week. Remember, as time goes on, your body will be more exhausted, and walking the extra distance to gather resources will become increasingly difficult.

Other Life

When out in a survival scenario, we're not the only ones trying to survive. Wildlife around us will be both beneficial and dangerous, depending on the species that we encounter.

While it's great to have an abundant resource to hunt and trap, many smaller critters threaten food caches and large animals could potentially see us as a threat or food source.

Living in tune with the other wildlife in any environment will help to determine where to place a shelter. Try to think like the other animals that are native to the area you're in. What do they like to eat? Where do they often sleep? What time of year do they have babies to protect?

All of these considerations come into play. For example, there are certain times of the year when moose are docile and barely notice you in their neck of the woods. When they are in rut, they can be incredibly dangerous and will see you as a threat no matter how calmly you move through their territory.

- **Game Trails**

One great way to avoid unwanted encounters with wildlife is to avoid game trails. Never place your shelter on a well-trodden game trail, as it's likely that some creature is using that path regularly.

The better thing to do is to locate game trails that can allow you to move around easily, set successful traps, and know where wildlife is likely to be. Then, build a shelter situated far enough to not deter the animals, but close enough to have access to the trails as resources.

Surroundings

One of the final, and most important things to look at when picking a shelter location is everything surrounding the spot. This applies for any shelter being put up for a single night or as a permanent home.

It's possible to find a shelter location at the perfect elevation, just close enough to water, away from animals, and on a nice flat chunk of ground that will stay dry, just to notice a huge limb lingering above you.

Hazards are everywhere in nature and checking your surroundings before starting to build a shelter will save effort and time. Don't start building just to notice a dangerous wasp nest feet away from where you're at or a bear den only a few yards off.

Moose scat

Hazard tree

Multiple hazards

Inspect the area and its surroundings thoroughly once you think you've found the perfect spot. There are certain things to be especially wary of.

- **Widowmakers and Deadfalls**

Widowmakers and deadfalls are two terms for trees that can easily fall on top of you and either leave you seriously injured or take your life.

The term "widowmaker" comes from the number of loggers who were killed by large branches and limbs hanging in another tree that can be easily dislodged by the wind and come falling down. These widowmakers are incredibly dangerous, and even smaller ones need to be taken into consideration when finding the right shelter spot.

Widowmaker

Deadfalls refer to standing dead trees that could fall at any time. In the winter, it can be difficult to distinguish between live trees and dead ones in deciduous forests, so it's important to learn how to tell the difference.

Dead trees can often be distinguished from live ones by the bark and branches in the winter. The bark will start to peel back and expose the core wood underneath. This process happens faster on the smaller branches but can take years to occur on the main trunk. Look for signs of dying limbs that are falling off, a large number of dead and brown needles (for conifers), or signs of insect infestation and large fungal growth.

Dead trunk

Setting up a shelter underneath a widowmaker or a deadfall is a serious mishap. Always look up and around before building a shelter.

- **Other Homes and Animals Signs**

All of the reasons that you found the perfect spot can also mean that other animals are already calling that place home. Imposing on another animal's home can be dangerous as you become a threat to their territory.

Look around your shelter site for animal signs and potential spots where larger animals may build long-term homes. If there are obvious signs that something is already living there, keep exploring and look for another site.

Collecting Material for Shelters

Once you've found the location for your shelter, it's time to start building. If an area is rich in debris, it will make building a well-constructed shelter much easier.

When collecting material for the shelter, always start by looking for debris that's already off the tree. It's perfectly doable to build a short-term shelter with dead, downed, and detached materials. A shelter for one month or longer may benefit from fresher materials.

Either way, there is often plenty of debris on the ground that can work for different protective layers of the shelter. Building a debris shelter requires collecting a large amount of downed leaves and evergreen conifer boughs to serve as insulation.

Collecting debris can help to clear a flat space for the shelter to lie on. This helps to clear out the area and ensure that you aren't building your home on top of any small burrows. Many mice and small critters call the duff layer home, so clearing it out and using it to provide insulation for your walls is beneficial in many ways.

ONE-WEEK SHELTER: How to Build a Debris Shelter

What Is a Debris Shelter?

In its simplest form, a debris shelter is a sturdy shelter consisting of a ridgepole, branches for walls, and various other natural materials for insulation and protection on top and below you. They are extremely easy to make and require no specialized tools to construct them.

Debris shelters are commonly used to teach beginner bushcraft skills since they show you how to utilize a lot of what's around you. Ensure you're using only dead material during the warmer months as you don't want to damage the forest.

When it is extremely cold out and a thick layer of snow is present, coniferous boughs are often used alongside whatever forest material can be found.

How to Choose a Good Location

Location is essential for a successful shelter as you want enough raw material around you to put together a makeshift roof, and you want to build your shelter in a safe location.

Start by searching for a place that has good drainage; no sense in building a structure only to find yourself swimming when you wake up. Signs of running water are an immediate red flag because if it rains you might find yourself in a wet situation. Do not build in a low-lying area as you want to avoid cold sinks (areas that hold the cold air).

When expecting stormy weather, it's best to build your shelter near a stand of low-reaching coniferous trees such as pine or spruce as they provide an excellent wind block.

Keep an eye out for widow-makers and falling branches from dead trees. Any windy weather can knock one of these loose and onto your shelter. The location you choose should have minimal branches above that could pose a risk of falling.

If you've ever noticed skinny paths throughout the forest that look more like someone trampled them than an actual trail, then you've stumbled upon a game trail. Avoid these areas as they will often encourage wandering critters to try and pilfer your much-needed food supplies.

The Best Materials for a Debris Shelter

You'll need to have a large number of leaves, grass, pine needles, and other debris to finish the job so keep an eye out for pockets of resources. The idea is to find the driest and most dense types of material so that it can withstand precipitation and retain the heat generated from your body.

How Much Insulation Will You Need?

To adequately maintain some level of warmth and fend off the elements you'll need at least an arm's length's worth of insulating material. If you are unsure if the amount of material is enough, stick your arm into it and grab the frame within. You should be at least arm deep into the dry material you used for the roof.

As important as the material on the outside, the material underneath your body should be just as insulating. This means filling your entire shelter floor with a layer of the driest debris you can find. Don't be surprised if you have to fill it almost the entire height of the shelter to get enough insulation.

The Tools You'll Need

While it is not necessary to use tools to build your debris shelter, construction is a lot easier if you have some basic items. Some tools that come in handy include:

- A good saw
- A hatchet or axe
- A sharp knife
- Paracord
- A tarp (to fill and carry/drag debris and for the top of your shelter)

Again, these items are optional and you can build a debris shelter without them. If you are an outdoor enthusiast, you more than likely already have these in your kit.

The Benefits of Making a Debris Shelter

While a debris shelter isn't the only option available out in the wilderness, it has some advantages. It can be built by anyone of any age and it is the easiest and warmest quick-build shelter, which is important if you're trying to conserve calories or are in a survival situation.

Easy Construction

Many, if not all of the components should be available on the ground, or at least readily accessible. The main idea is to layer on different thicknesses of debris and sticks to create a thermal layer between the interior and exterior.

Building it requires little strength and, as long as you can be outside working for at least 2-3 hours, you'll be able to accomplish this if you work quickly. When the decision to stay outside for the night is made that is when the debris shelter should be started and not a moment later. Gathering enough debris takes time.

Can Be Heated Easily

Debris shelters should be just large enough to fit you and the insulation, that's it. This means that your body heat should be sufficient to keep the small space toasty throughout the night. If the cavity inside is too big then your body won't be able to heat it properly and you'll have a very cold night.

Any drafts in the shelter will cause air to blow through it, negating any attempts at warming. Make sure to cover all of the gaps from within to maximize the effectiveness of the insulation. If you have a tarp with you use it for the build (carrying debris) and then cover the top in case of rain or snow.

Gathering the Materials Is Simple

Since you can pretty much use anything dead and dry that you find on the ground, it's relatively easy to find everything you need to make a debris shelter. If you find yourself without tools then you can still build this shelter as long as you can salvage the resources without having to cut them down.

Once you're done with the shelter you can take it down and discard the materials around the area. In terms of leaving a minimal footprint, a debris shelter is a great example of leaving no trace.

How to Build a Debris Shelter

Before you begin construction, take some time and clear out a space for your debris shelter. This includes lying down and "measuring" out where you'll be laying. Ensure that the shelter is not much longer than you are because the smaller the shelter the easier it will be for your body heat to keep it warm.

Make sure the entrance to your debris shelter is facing away from the wind. Spending all of that time building it properly only to have it become a funnel for the wind isn't a great way to use your energy.

Step 1:

Create a Ridgepole for Your Shelter

The first step is to source a ridgepole for your shelter. This will be the backbone of the entire operation and it needs to be sturdy enough to hold the weight of the debris you'll be piling up on it.

If you have a saw, you can cut down a 10-foot dead-standing tree, otherwise, look for a suitable piece on the ground. Avoid poles that have been in contact with the ground for a while as water can penetrate the wood, causing rot. It needs to be sturdy.

Check your ridgepole and make sure there aren't any weak sections. You'll often find rotting at the base of the pole if it spent too much time in the ground after it died.

Step 2:

Find Two "Y" Sticks (or Use a Tree)

One end of your ridgepole is going to be on the ground while the other will need to be suspended to create the entrance to your shelter. The easiest way is to find a tree with a suitable "Y" shaped branch that you can wedge the ridgepole into. The tree trunk will provide a great door that creates a windbreak and helps trap heat.

If you don't have a tree that will work then create your pseudo tent poles using sturdy branches about 3-4 feet long that have a "Y" at one end. The "Y" is where the branch splits off into separate shoots. If you have a knife, you can sharpen the end opposite the "Y" so that it's easier to drive into the ground.

Step 3:

Assemble the Frame and Interior Insulation

Push your "Y" sticks into the ground in a way where they will interlock. One "Y" stick will support the other as it supports the weight of the ridgepole you're going to rest on it.

Once you've interlocked the support sticks, you're going to rest one end of the ridgepole in between the "Y" while the other end will be angled downward into the ground. The result is a frame where you can now lay branches against the ridgepole to create the beginnings of the shelter.

Now is the best time to start piling your insulation on the floor of your shelter as it will get difficult when you put the support walls up. Try to get at least 1 meter of debris inside your shelter.

Step 4:

Add Your Support Walls

Gather sticks and lay them against the ridgepole to create the walls for your shelter. As you work from the entrance toward the back of the shelter, you'll need shorter and shorter sticks. Try to make the sticks as straight and durable as possible since they will be holding up the weight of the debris. If possible, use sticks that will be covered by the insulation (i.e. don't have long sticks protruding out of the top of the shelter as these can carry water down into your shelter if it starts to rain).

Step 5:

Add the First Layer of Insulation (Boughs)

The best source of boughs is a fallen spruce or pine tree. In a survival situation, cutting off some of the lower branches of nearby trees will suffice, but do not strip the tree completely of branches. Harvest ethically.

If you don't have any boughs near you, add a thicker layer of grasses, leaves, or sticks to the walls of your shelter.

Step 6:

Add a Second Layer of Insulation (Leaves/Sticks)

This is where the majority of the work is going to happen. Piling endless armfuls of leaves and other pieces of debris will slowly yield the fruits of thick insulation and protection from the elements. A tarp is useful for gathering leaves.

If it's a windy day then you can alternate leaves and stick layers to provide extra stability against layers being blown away.

To reiterate, you want at least an arm's length amount of material on the sides of your shelter. If you're questioning how much insulation you have, then you need to add more. Well-constructed debris shelters are difficult to spot as they tend to blend in with the scenery around them; you want a lot of debris on top.

Step 7:

Crawl Inside and Check for Light Leaking

Once you're certain you've put enough debris on the outside of the shelter, crawl inside and check for any light peeking through. These are spots that you need to fill in with more debris.

Step 8:

Add a Door (Optional)

A door is recommended if the temperature is going to be cold during the night. You don't have to make anything fancy; if you have a pack with you, use it to jam the entrance. Otherwise, gather excess debris from outside of your shelter and pile it at the entrance in an attempt to seal yourself in.

HOW TO BUILD A ONE-MONTH SHELTER

This shelter was built by survivalist Jacques Roos. It is a one-month shelter similar to one I made on the *Alone* show. I will let Jacques detail the step-by-step process he used for this build.

Tools, Materials, and Supplies

This basic toolkit should get you to the end of your build with enough essential items to craft basically anything you'll need for basic survival. Essential items that seem unimportant, like a pair of gloves, could save you a ton of energy and frustration down the line. Here are my go tools:

- Gloves
- Knife and multi-tool
- Cordage and wire
- Headlamp
- Handsaw
- Axe/ Hatchet
- Shovel
- Lighter/ Striker

Most materials and supplies, even tools, can be substituted or fashioned from nature. Here's an essential supply list you will need to prep or collect on your journey. Pay attention to your surroundings, taking advantage of what nature has to offer for items you couldn't bring with you or might not have access to.

- Water
- Container and cooking pot (bring if possible)
- Pan/ Plate/ Bowl/ Mug
- Sleeping Bag/ Mat (bring both if possible)
- Insulation

The Step-by-Step Process

1

Choosing Your Build-Site

They say location is key! In this case – two sturdy Blue-gum trees (*Eucalyptus globulus*). Not too close to each other, nor too far apart. It all depends on the final size of your build. In my case I went a little larger than necessary. Getting more than a few months good use was what I was looking for.

I found a clearing near the foot of a ravine between two blue-gum trees. Over the years these two trees have been chopped down a number of times, forcing new shoots to form from the original base, around 4 feet (1.2 m) in diameter. Think of these as vertical building columns that will serve as a foundation for the main cross-beam of the lean-to shelter.

In the Western Cape of South Africa, north-facing is the best choice when trying to get the most of the sun's heat (note this is the opposite for the southern hemisphere).

I made sure there was enough clearing towards the south side of the two trees where I'd attach my cross-beam. This allowed me to use poles of around 12 and 15 feet (4 and 5 m) in length for the roof (details below).

When searching your terrain for the perfect location, pay special attention to the seasonal elements.

Positioning the roof this way also serves as great protection against the prevailing South-Easter (note in Northern hemispheres this is the opposite). The strongest wind recorded in this region was measured at 116 miles/h (186km/h) - an absolute must to plan against.

Lastly, let us not forget about the element of seclusion, keeping your structure hidden from prying eyes or unwanted guests will reduce the amount of security measures that need to be taken into account.

Tips: Other important key factors are the distance to fresh water, not building on animal trails or in a cold sink, watching for widowmakers, and proximity to water gathering and building material sites.

2

Prepping Your Site

Begin by marking out the perimeter of your site. Remove any obstructions, leaves and debris. Then, level out the ground area. Start digging into highest point of your slope, filling the lower region using this dirt to get your ground as level as possible.

Dig a gutter around the base of your site and place four poles horizontally in these grooves to form a perimeter on the ground. I then added four vertical stakes, driving them in on either side of the rear ground log to secure this rear floor log. This will stop the leaning poles you will add from sliding backwards.

Next find the perfect crossbeam for your roof logs to lean-onto. The distance between my two trees is just over 12 feet (4 m). I chose a fallen straight section that was already dried out and hard as nails. The result was a monster log over 24 feet (8 m) long with a diameter of about 1 foot (30 cm).

I hauled the largest and straightest logs first, installing them first, only cutting them when needed down the line.

Remove all your bark, unless you enjoy the sound of bugs chewing away as you sleep.

Tip: Remember to remove the bark from your timber, unless you enjoy the sound of bugs chewing away at the structure while you sleep. This also keeps you safe from unexpected scorpions or spiders hiding in plain sight. If you are building a shorter-term shelter or if you're in a non-tropical area, this isn't as necessary.

3

Installing Your Cross-Beam

Place a thick pole against your support tree, use this to rest your cross-beam at the correct height, around 1 foot (30 cm) above your head, temporarily wedging it in place while you get your first knots in place.

Using 550 paracord, fasten the beam using a square lashing to secure it to the first tree. Repeat this on the opposite side.

Tip: Make use of a toggle (small diameter branch or knife handle) to get the best grip on your cordage by wrapping the working side around the branch a few times from opposite ends of the toggle.

Tighten using a toggle for the best grip on your cordage.

When you're done tying your two trees to the crossbeam, place weight onto the beam to seat everything in place.

4

Door-Frame

For the doorframe, I sized two poles 1 foot (30 cm) longer than the space between the crossbeam and the floor. I sharpened the bottom end into a stake and cut a v-notch into the top of the posts.

You'll want to drive the posts into the ground at a slight angle from topside until you clear the underside of the crossbeam. Then tap the column sideways until you hit a 90° angle.

Posts are positioned 3 feet (1m) apart to create the side-walls for your doorframe. We'll return to the doorframe crossbeam when we continue with the door construction.

5

Lean-To Roof Poles

The roof poles were the longest and thickest I could find. The thicker the better, reducing the number of poles needed to cover the distance from left to right.

Hoist each pole over the crossbeam. Once in place over the crossbeam, wedge the floor end to the inner side of the rear floor pole, which we secured in place earlier with our stakes.

This will keep the poles from slipping off the crossbeam. It's critical to secure the roof poles to the crossbeam to avoid injury from poles falling through while you're working below.

6

Roof Extension

(extra build - for a simpler shelter skip to section 8)

This was a design choice that added a little extra headroom over the bed area. It does come at the cost of quite a bit of additional labor. I'll leave it to you to keep it as simple as possible by skipping this step. In this case, simply lay your stack of roof poles across the entire width of your crossbeam (recommended for your first build).

If you have extra time on your hands, here's how I achieved the added headroom extension for the roof. Drive 4-6 stakes vertically into the ground to create a space to stack your logs horizontally on top of each other.

The idea is to create a wall by pinching the stacked logs between the stakes using cordage. This is a quick and effective method of creating a freestanding stacked wall without using too much cordage and with minimal effort. This same technique is used for making an outdoor windblock wall for your fire, blocking the wind and keeping the fire's warmth reflecting back to you.

Make a connection point on the top and bottom of each stake with cordage and tighten to pinch the wall in place securely. When you've reached the desired extension height - simply stack the remaining roof poles on top of your raised wall and secure in place with cordage to the top of your wall.

7

Adding Space to the Room

A quick way to gain around a foot of interior depth to your room is to secure the thickest off-cuts from your roofing poles to the outside of your crossbeam as upright columns.

When cladding up the outside, you'll end up with an opening below the crossbeam that you can use as either an exterior packing space or a flip up window frame for daytime airflow. Not entirely necessary, again I'll leave it up to your needs to decide if the extra space is worth the effort.

8

Building the Door

I decided to go with a hanging swing door. This doubles up as an extra rainproof cover at the entrance of the structure. It's also a great place to pack and dry lightweight items.

Start by measuring out a crossbeam slightly wider than the doorframe. Position it to create the top of your doorframe and tie it into place using a square lashing knot. We'll hang the door from this beam, so ensure that it's sturdy enough to handle the weight and repeated action of the door opening and closing.

Size up two vertical posts, these should be ½ foot (15 cm) smaller than the door opening top to bottom.

Lay the door posts on a flat surface and stack the thinner branches on top of the two posts horizontally completing the surface area, enough to cover the door frame from left to right.

Tying it all together. Start by tying your cordage to one of the vertical posts, a clove knot or slipknot will do (please see our chapter "Knots That Are Extremely Useful in the Wild" on page 133). Make a bite (loop) in your cordage, passing the bite over the top of the first horizontal pole, away from you, threading the bite under the vertical pole towards the outside. Now, place the bite over the end of the same pole and tighten.

You will have what looks like two vertical bindings around your first pole. Repeat this until you reach the opposite end, feeding only the bite throughout the process. This way, you can keep the rest of your cordage beside you without having to weave it through each pole and back. You can finish it off with a clove knot.

The door hinge is pretty simple; it's the same concept as the roof extension wall.

Cut four 1-foot (30-cm) poles. Fasten these at the top of the door both on the left and right side of the door, inside and outside of the door. Leave at least half of the length hanging over the door.

These will form a two-piece fork, becoming the hinge that the door will rest upon when opened. Tighten to set the right height and fasten by tying at least three fraps (lashings) between the door and frame. Finish with a clove knot and your door will swing open upwards using this makeshift hinge.

Finally, cut two poles to size and use these to rest the door against as vertical doorposts. You'll use these to lock the door from both inside and outside later on.

Tip: It's a good idea to clearly mark these loose doorposts, so as not to end up accidentally using them elsewhere.

9

Sidewall Construction

Here, we'll create another wall by driving stakes to the outside of the first pole we placed in the trench at the beginning of our build. Size, cut and stack the remaining poles on top of each other to form your wall.

As soon as you reach the top of the vertical stakes, tighten the vertical stakes to each other using cordage and a toggle. Fasten them at two separate points, top and bottom. This will straighten the entire structure up quite a bit. Continue all the way to the top to finish up your sidewall.

10

Insulation

Now for the most important part. Depending on your terrain, most forest woodlands provide an abundance of materials to use for insulation (leaves, grass, pine/spruce boughs, leaves, moss, etc.).

In cold locations you want this insulating layer to be 3 feet (1m) thick.

I started out with pine brush to fill large gaps between crooked poles. On top of that I packed a bit of moist ground to even out the surfaces and topped it off with moss above the sleeping area and a mixture of moss and forest turf for the rest of the roof. In cold locations you want this insulating layer to be 3 feet (1 m) thick.

11

Raising the Bed

Raising your bed is a great way to reduce the cold from creeping up from the ground as the evening temperatures drop throughout the night. It also serves as a moisture barrier for storms, and doubles as a stowaway space when needed.

I went with a 1-foot (30 cm) rise. I used stakes and stacked poles to build the sidewalls, cutting a square reduction into each cross section where they will fit/nest into each other.

To build your mattress platform, cut and place the vertical bed poles over the supporting structure and trim to size. This bed doubles as a handy bench to sit on when the weather is harsh. Add debris on top of this platform to form your mattress for both insulation and comfort. The colder the weather the more debris you want.

12

Stacking the Front Wall

You will need poles thick and long enough to span the entire width of your structure. I only went about 3 feet (1 m) high for the full-length poles. Use the same stake method to fix the wall securely in place against the posts we added earlier.

Leave a space to add your pop-out window (if wanted) and fasten the stakes as before. You can also secure these to the main vertical posts or trees on either side using a square lashing and clove knot. If necessary, you might need to add an extra post to the inside of the window frame to fasten the remaining shorter logs all the way up to the left and right of the window frame.

13

Pop-Out Window and Table

(if wanted)

Our pop-out window doubles up as a table by adding two vertical posts to your desired width above the front wall.

Cut two square reductions/notches onto each of these vertical posts, both top and bottom. Position these cuts so that they face each other. These will become the sides of the window frame that your window-door will squeeze into.

Use the same method as the door. Size up two horizontal poles as before and a few vertical poles to size. Ensure that the vertical poles are slightly longer than the window from top to bottom. Lash the structure together adding a diagonal cross brace to the back to stiffen it up. Test-fit the window before fastening the frames in place using cordage.

14

Front Hanging Window
(if wanted)

Here, I decided to cut and split short logs, using the same lashing method used for the door. I fastened a few split logs vertically to cover the opening above the door-frame from left to right. Attaching it just as we did for the door, swinging it open from the bottom then wedging the window in place with a short support stick.

This is what my shelter looked like after all these steps.

LONG-TERM SHELTER FOR LIVING IN THE WILD

Building a long-term shelter in the wild requires more than just survival instincts; it calls for practical skills and strategic planning. These shelters serve as a crucial refuge, protecting you from adverse weather conditions and potential threats, and providing the basic comfort needed for a prolonged stay in nature. Understanding how to construct a long-term shelter can be the difference between merely surviving and truly thriving in the wild. This shelter was built by Ionuț Păun.

Factors to Consider When Choosing a Location

When selecting a spot for your long-term shelter, many factors need to be taken into account.

- **Drainage:** Ensure that the area has good drainage to prevent water from accumulating near your shelter during heavy rains.
- **Storm Protection:** An ideal location should offer natural protection against storms, such as a clump of sturdy trees or a hillside.
- **Safety:** Be cautious of any potential hazards, such as falling branches from dead trees or widowmakers. Avoid areas near game trails to prevent unwanted encounters with wildlife.
- **Flat Ground:** A relatively flat surface will make it easier to build your shelter and create a comfortable living space.
- **Long Grasses**: Areas with long grasses can offer several benefits. Not only does long grass make digging easier, but it also often indicates the presence of clay, which is an excellent natural building material that can be used to construct and insulate your shelter. Additionally, long grass can be used as bedding material, providing a layer of insulation between you and the ground to help retain heat during cold nights.
- **Thick Trees:** Look for an area surrounded by lots of thick trees, as these can provide both materials for building your shelter and additional protection against the elements.

Tools for Building Your Shelter

Before embarking on your shelter-building project, it's crucial to be well-equipped with the right tools. These instruments will not only aid in the construction process, but also ensure efficiency and safety.

Here is the list of tools you should have:

- Shovel
- Machete or similar knife
- Draw knife
- Hatchet
- Large wood saw
- Manual wood drill
- Hammer or a large rock to use as a hammer

Benefits of a Long-Term Shelter

A long-term shelter is designed for extended stays, made with durable materials, and built to withstand various weather conditions. In contrast, a short-term shelter is typically rudimentary, constructed quickly for immediate protection, and used for a short period of time.

An underground or partially underground shelter offers several advantages over an above-ground structure:

- **Protection from the Elements:** Underground shelters are well-protected from harsh weather conditions, including extreme temperatures, heavy rainfall, strong winds, and snowstorms.
- **Insulation:** The ground naturally provides thermal insulation, helping to maintain a constant temperature inside the shelter, keeping it warm in winter and cool in summer.
- **Stealth:** An underground shelter is less visible, offering enhanced privacy and making it harder for other people to spot.
- **Security:** Being below or partially below ground level, these shelters offer superior protection against potential dangers or threats, including wildlife encounters and human conflicts.

Step-by-Step Guide to Building a Long-Term Shelter

1

Clear away the grasses from the area you want your shelter to be.

2

Dig a square trench, size it according to your preference, for instance, 15 ft. by 15 ft. (4.5 m by 4.5 m) wide and 2 ft. (0.6 m) deep, serving as your shelter's outline.

3

Next, excavate the interior of the square to a depth of 2 ft. (0.6 m) initially.

4

You now need to make the hole deeper. When it's done, it should be between shoulder and head height for yourself. The easiest way to do this is to dig it out in sections. For example, start digging out the middle of the hole by using your shovel to slice and dig. Move your way back until you have dug down another 2-3 feet (0.6-1m). Repeat this process until you have dug down to the appropriate depth. Be sure to keep a ledge a couple of feet up off the bottom of the hole so that you can climb out. This will also serve as the bed for your dwelling.

5

Identify sturdy trees with a minimum diameter of 10 inches (25 cm) to serve as supports for the roof. If necessary, cut them down unless they are already fallen. The length of the trees should be based on the size of your hole, ensuring they are long enough to be angled up from the side of the pit and meet in the middle.

6

If the trees are already on the ground, ensure they are not decaying internally. Use a draw knife to strip the bark off the trees, as this will help retain moisture within the wood. In case you encounter difficulty removing the bark, utilize a hatchet to carefully hack away at the ends, exposing the bark for easy stripping using the draw knife.

7

Once you have prepared five supports, bring them to the hole and begin assembling them. Start by placing two support poles opposite each other at an angle where they can rest upon one another. The angle should be approximately 5-6 ft. (1.5-1.8 m) above the top of the hole. If there is any overlapping wood, trim off the excess using a folding saw.

8

To complete the roof supports, position the third support diagonally from the back corner to align with the two previously installed supports. Utilize the fourth support to bridge the gap, providing a stable surface to stand on while securing the third support. Just like before, trim any excess wood. Angle the fourth support outward from the opposite rear corner, ensuring it applies pressure against the other three supports.

9

The fifth and final roof support should be slanted downward, serving as one of the entrance pillars. The tops of each support should converge at the center point.

10

To tie-in the top supports, split a round piece of wood that matches the span between the front three supports at the top. Make sure it's as long as needed. Then, using a hand drill, create two holes on each end of the split wood. Finally, carve the round pegs and hammer them through the newly drilled holes. This will securely tie in the top supports.

11

Align the piece of wood you just drilled with the top of the rightmost support. Use the hand drill to create a hole through the support. Repeat this process for the leftmost front support. Afterward, connect the wooden bracket to the support using hammered wooden pegs. Finally, trim the sharp corners to ensure the roof bracket sits flush with the supports.

12

To create the frame for the entrance, you will need an additional tree of similar thickness to the roof supports. Make sure the length of the tree reaches from the bottom of the pit to the angled roof support. It's important to cut the angle of the pillar tree so that it fits snugly against the roof support. Use a hand drill to drill through this support and into the roof support, then secure them together by driving a wooden peg through.

13

To ensure adequate support for the roof, considering the use of thick logs for the walls; an additional connection between the front angle roof supports is necessary. Begin by cutting two logs of sufficient length to span the distance between the center front support. Proceed to drill holes into each end of the support, as well as the support it will be attached to. Insert a wooden peg into each hole and firmly affix the support to the angled beams through hammering. For added security, repeat the same process applied to the top of the roof supports. Split a round piece of wood and drill holes into each side on both ends. Align it with the newly installed support and drill through. Secure the supports by inserting wooden pegs into the holes.

14

To ensure sufficient support for the roof logs, perform the same action between the central base roof support and the angled roof support. If required, consider introducing a second beam inside. The ideal location would be in the space between the front and back roof supports.

15

To build the roof covering, begin by felling a number of trees measuring approximately 12-15 inches (30-38 cm) in diameter. These trees should be of sufficient length to span the entire hole you have excavated, in this instance, around 15 feet long. They will be stacked between the roof supports on either side.

16

Begin by carefully stacking the logs on the roof support, making sure they align with the angle of the supports. To minimize gaps in the roof corners, cut the ends of the roof logs at an appropriate angle where they meet. Repeat this process for each side of the roof until it is fully sealed.

17

To seal the cracks between the logs, carefully shovel the dirt you dug from the hole onto the roof. Don't hesitate to climb onto the roof and use your hands to push the mud into the cracks. Repeat this process until the entire roof is completely sealed.

18

To create a weatherproof seal, carefully cut squares of sod using a sharp machete. Place these squares on top of the dirt, mud, and clay that you have recently used to seal the roof. Make sure to add a thick layer for maximum effectiveness.

19

To build the internal walls, you need to set up four internal supports that will be braced against the log roof. Make sure there is enough space between the support and the wall to fit the logs. Insert logs along the length of the wall into the gap between the dirt and wood supports you constructed.

20

To construct the door, begin by obtaining four logs with a diameter of approximately 5-8 inches (13-20 cm). Cut each end of the logs halfway through, reaching a length of about 5 inches (13 cm). This will allow for interlocking when assembling. Once completed, the logs will form a sturdy frame.

21

Next, take additional logs and cut them lengthwise. Place them horizontally across the door frame with the flat side facing down. To secure them, utilize a handheld drill to create holes in the top and bottom of the cut logs, aligning them with the frame. Insert wooden pegs into these holes, firmly fastening the logs to the frame.

22

To attach the door to your shelter, start by drilling a hole in the top plate and the door's bottom. Then, insert a wooden peg into both the top plate and the door, allowing it to swing open and close smoothly.

23

Creating a front window that can open and close is a process similar to crafting the front door. Begin by measuring the window frame and cutting logs that fit snugly within the designated space. Use a hand drill to create holes on each end of the horizontal supports and on the sides of the vertical frame supports. Insert wooden pegs into the holes and firmly assemble the frame using a hammer. To secure the wood to the window frame, split round logs and create a flat side. Drill corresponding holes on the top and bottom of the logs, aligning them with the frame, and then secure everything in place by hammering in wooden pegs.

24

Take a moment to inspect the window and identify any gaps that need filling. Carefully select and cut pieces of wood that will fit snugly into these gaps. It's important to angle the ends of the wood so that they can buttress against the existing supports. This will ensure a secure and seamless fit.

Maintaining a Long-Term Shelter in the Wild

Maintaining the structural integrity of your shelter is pivotal for long-term survival. Regularly check for signs of wear and tear, such as warped or rotting wood, and replace any compromised parts immediately. Ensure that your roof remains watertight, and patch up any leaks with additional layers of foliage or bark.

Repairs to the roof, especially in harsh conditions, require particular attention. It's the first line of defense against rain, snow, and wind. If the roof's integrity is compromised, start by identifying the damaged sections. In case of minor damage, such as small holes or leaks, additional layers of foliage or bark can be added to patch these areas effectively. If you have a tarp, that can be placed over the roof prior to placing the sod, allowing your shelter to be additionally protected from rain. A tarp may also be placed on top of the sod and used as a water catchment system (please see our chapter "How to Collect Rainwater in the Wild" on page 39).

For major damage, you may need to replace larger sections of the roof entirely. Always ensure to overlap the materials, starting from the bottom and working your way up, like shingles, to effectively shed water. In snowy conditions, regularly remove excess snow to prevent weight-related damage.

Pest Control

Securing your shelter against animals and pests is another crucial element of shelter maintenance. Regularly inspect the shelter for signs of infestation, making sure no small creatures have made their home in the walls or roof. If you find any, take immediate action to relocate them and seal off their entry points.

Here are some ways to deal with existing pests in your wilderness shelter:

1. **Manual Removal**: For visible pests, manual removal is possible. Wearing gloves, carefully remove any pests and relocate them away from your shelter.
2. **Natural Repellents:** Certain plants act as natural repellents for specific pests. Identify these plants in your surrounding area and incorporate them around and inside your shelter. For instance, mosquitoes dislike the scent of citronella, lemongrass, and marigold and mice hate the scent of cloves.
3. **Fire:** Use controlled fire or smoke near the infested area as many pests are repelled by smoke. However, be cautious not to ignite your shelter.
4. **Regular Cleaning:** Keeping your shelter clean can prevent many pests. Dispose of food remnants properly and avoid storing food inside your shelter.

Remember, in a survival situation, it's crucial to maintain a balance with the local ecosystem. While pests can be a nuisance, some insects and animals can be beneficial, providing food or contributing to your survival in other ways.

Moreover, consider creating a perimeter around your shelter using rocks or thorny branches, which can deter larger animals from approaching.

Building and Insulating the Shelter Bed

You already have the ground support for the bed. To build it further, lay down parallel logs or branches to serve as the main support for your bed.

Then, add logs perpendicular to the main supports, creating a grid-like structure/stable bed. Make sure they are heavy, stable logs that can support your weight. Then, use paracord or any other strong rope to lash the frame together.

There are several ways you can insulate a shelter bed for warmth; the most efficient one is adding insulation underneath you, as the ground can be a significant source of heat loss. Insulating below where you sleep creates a thermal barrier that helps prevent this heat loss, keeping you warmer. Use natural materials (debris) like leaves, grass, or pine boughs. I like to add layers daily – until I reach a thickness of ~3 feet (1m) as the weather gets colder.

These natural materials act as additional insulation and provide a cushioning effect. You can also place a space blanket underneath your sleeping pad if you have these items. This reflective material helps to reflect your body heat back towards you, preventing it from being absorbed by the ground.

Keep in mind that staying dry is essential. Moisture can sap your body heat, so make sure your sleeping bag and clothing stay dry. You can use a waterproof ground cloth or tarp to prevent ground moisture from seeping into your sleeping area.

Don't Stop Improving Your Shelter

Always be open to making improvements to your shelter. As you grow more acclimated to your environment, you may find more efficient ways to heat your shelter, better materials for insulation, or new methods to safeguard against the elements. Continuous adjustment and enhancement of your shelter is key to thriving in the wild for an extended period of time.

A smart upgrade to your wilderness shelter is the implementation of a makeshift rain collection system. In fact, your shelter's roof can serve dual purposes: protection and water collection. To do this, slope the roof slightly towards one side, ensuring the rainwater will slide in a specific direction and not stagnate. If you have a tarp, this works well for water catchment.

At the lower end of the roof, attach a hollowed-out container or any other suitable material that can act as a channel for the rainwater. This improvised gutter will direct the water to a container for storage. This system not only provides a sustainable source of drinking water, but also helps keep your shelter dry and comfortable.

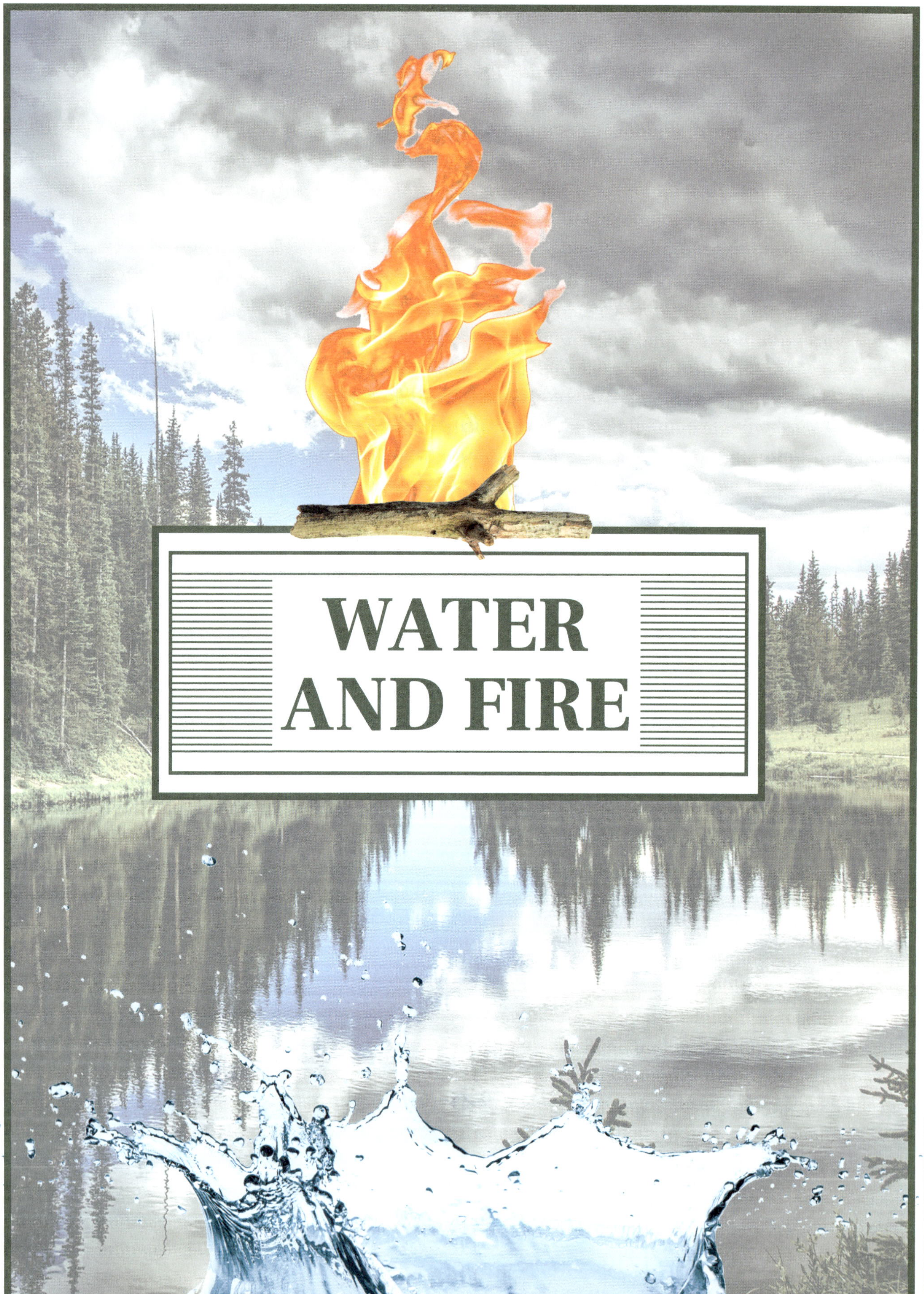

WATER AND FIRE

HOW TO COLLECT RAINWATER IN THE WILD

There are a variety of methods to collect rainwater, and many may be used together. Many people get caught in the idea that simply sticking any containers available out into the rain will suffice, but this collects a very small amount of water.

By creating a cache and installing various rain traps, dew traps, or even collecting water from plants, you can obtain enough water to survive in the wild. Keep in mind, different methods work better in certain locations, so it's always important to keep your location in mind before haphazardly setting up water traps that may or may not work.

Create a Cache

Without rain, you lose a primary source of water, making it all the more important to collect and store water for the long term. Having a water storage cache is inherent to survival because constant rain can never be fully depended upon.

There are a lot of ways to create caches in the wild when you are in a survival situation and don't have access to the plastic containers we have in the modern world. While trash is sometimes found, it cannot be relied upon. Creating a cache out of materials you find in the wild should be a skillset that comes along with you.

Many methods will work to store water and there isn't one that's better than the others. Among the various methods, you can:

- Create natural birch bowls (please see how to create a birch bowl on page 154)
- Utilize the stomach of an animal
- Utilize a tarp or any other plastic or storage container you brought with you

How to Keep Your Water Cache Clean

No matter the storage system you have, water can go bad when it isn't distilled perfectly in a sterile environment. Water provides an ideal environment for bacteria to thrive and can lead to devastating stomach bugs that will make you even more dehydrated.

Keeping your water cache clean should be a primary objective for anyone working on storing water for a long time.

Depending on the storage container, you can keep it clean through prevention and cleanliness.

Before you store any water, make sure to clean the container as thoroughly as possible. Often this can be done with boiling water and multiple rinses. If you are using natural materials like animal stomachs, always make sure to scrape away the lining and anything else you find. The same goes for any larger fruit shells, such as the hollowed-out rind of an Osage-orange. Get rid of all the fruit that provides food and a potential source for bacteria.

The best practice is to have multiple storage containers, so you can rotate through them. Use one or two of them while you clean the others. If you aren't cleaning your containers almost every other day, you're likely to experience some illness from growing bacteria. I often add Usnea (a common lichen) or chaparral (a desert plant) to my water caches as they're excellent anti-microbials.

Building Rain Traps

Once you have a spot to store your water, you can start to collect it. Now is the best time to take an inventory of the materials you have on hand. Do you have something easy-to-use like a tarp, or are you working with minimal supplies and need to get creative?

There's always a way to capture rainwater in the wild, but there are times when you'll need to figure out more complicated systems. This is why I always include a tarp in every survival kit I put together. A tarp is a multi-faceted and incredibly useful piece of equipment that will come in handy in more ways than one.

Using a Tarp to Collect Rainwater

A tarp is the most effective method of capturing rainwater because it multiplies the total surface area that the rain will hit, and then can be used to direct the water toward a collection point.

The same tarp setup to sleep under can be used to collect water. It can work for you while you sleep through a rainy night, and then you can wake up to freshwater.

Multiple different tarp setups can help to collect rainwater. We'll look at a few to determine which is the best to use for a variety of different scenarios with different amounts of equipment available.

One Storage Container

If you're out in the wild with a single storage container, whether it be a single water bottle or a handmade water storage cache, there are two ways to best set a tarp up to collect rainwater.

The first is to set the tarp up as a simple large sheet that could also potentially work as a shelter in a pinch.

- Attach two corners to a higher point, about 4 to 5 feet (1.2 to 1.5 m) above the ground.
- Using two more anchor points, either trees or "dog legs" (fixed sticks holding up the tarp with tension from the lines), fix the opposite two corners down, so they rest about 1 foot (30 cm) or 2 feet (60 cm) off the ground.
- This setup should look like a slanted roof with one side higher than the other.
- On the low side, use a weight or piece of cord to pull the center point between the two anchors down.
- This is where the water will flow, so place your storage container here.

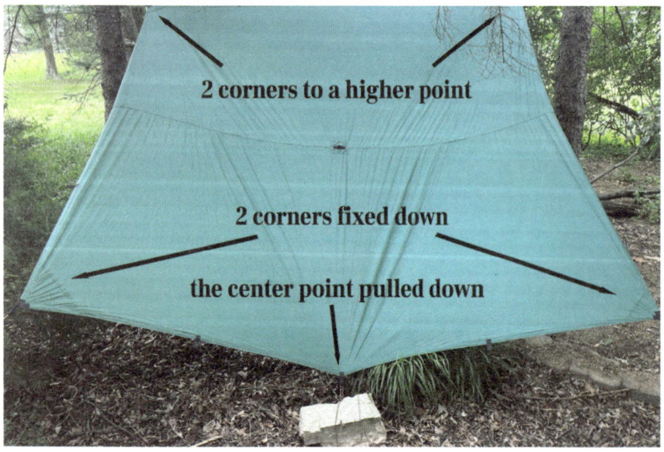

This design is great for light or heavy rain that doesn't come along with a ton of wind. Wind can grab a hold of the tarp when set up like this and turn it into a sail, rather than a nice gentle slope for collecting water.

One of the ways around this is to ensure that you pull all of the corners tight. There are a lot of recommendations out there for hanging loose tarps that are flat, but an angled tarp that is taut will stay true in winds for longer. The slope helps to guide the water without needing to pay much attention to it.

Also, at the anchor point that brings your tarp to your collection vessel, try leading a piece of string or paracord into your collection container. This helps guide the water into the container, so you don't miss any water.

This set up isn't ideal for when you need to use the tarp as a shelter as well. But, when you only have one way to store water, this is a fast way to harvest the most water possible.

Tarp as a Shelter and Rainwater Collection

Most likely, if you're carrying a tarp, you'll be using it as a shelter. In this case, setting it up to collect water is a simple variation from a normal A-frame tarp setup.

- Connect the main points of the ridgeline between two trees or high points.
- Stake out the four corners, trying to keep them 1 to 2 feet (30 to 60 cm) off the ground.
- Using a cord or weight, pull down the center of the two sides to a lower point than the corners.
- Place a collection container at each point, collecting water from both sides of the shelter.

Normal A-Frame Setup, LiAnna Davis - Own work, CC BY-SA 4.0

This is the perfect setup if you have large storage containers and want to collect overnight. If you can, have a third storage cache that is large enough to empty the two collection containers throughout the night as you wake up. This is a great system to collect a lot of water overnight while you are sleeping. If your tarp is large enough, you can also make a water cache from part of the tarp itself, using rocks, a stump, or anything else that allows you to make a cache to store water.

Collecting Rainwater with Fabric

You don't always have a tarp with you, and in that case, you need to get creative. This method is highly dependent upon your supplies and the weather. If you have extra clothing or fabric, you can use that to soak up rainwater and wring it out into a container.

In general, cotton will soak up the most water, but it's also the fabric that you don't often wear out in the wild. Denim and canvas clothing also work, but will require more attention over time. Always ensure that you are using the cleanest clothes possible to avoid creating dirty water from your dirty clothes.

Obviously, you don't want to use the clothes off your back if you are in a potentially-hypothermic scenario. Extra socks and layers can be spread out to cover more ground and collect rainwater. To harvest, simply wring out as much as possible and repeat.

You can also use fabric to wipe the moisture from various plants after it rains and collect it in one place. This can be an effective way to continue collecting water even after the rain has stopped. Strap some fabric to your ankles and walk through a field first thing in the morning, and you'll gather all of the dew from the previous night's temperature change.

How to Collect Water from Plants

If it hasn't rained for a long time, you need to find other ways of getting water. Fortunately, there are plenty of other ways to collect water without relying on rain.

One of the best methods is to harvest the water that is stored inside all the plants around you. Trees and bushes are best for this due to their size and ability to store larger amounts of water.

This process takes advantage of the process of transpiration. The leaves on trees, bushes, and all plants have stomata on the underside of their leaves that allow the plant to take in and get rid of gases. Fortunately for us, the trees give up a massive amount of water that can be easily collected by using a garbage bag/plastic, a string, and a collection container.

1. Find a branch of a tree with a high concentration of leaves.
2. Place the branch inside a garbage bag, or any other waterproof material, and tie the end as securely as possible around the branch to prevent any evaporation.
3. Tie a string from the branch to a weight or anchor in the ground to lower the collection site.
4. To collect over time, put a small hole in the bag at its lowest point and place a collection container below that point. This will collect the water as it comes out of the leaves. Alternatively, leave the bag intact and collect it when there is a significant amount of water present in the bag.

This is going to be some of the cleanest, purest water that you can get in the wild. It has gone through the entire tree after being filtered through the soil to then transpire into your collection point.

Another way to find water is to tap a tree in the springtime. Birch and maple trees provide gallons of sap each day when tapped correctly, which can be help hydrate you just as well as fresh water.

Tapping a tree involves finding the right species and carving out a small hole in the outer bark. You can insert a rounded, harder plant into the hole as a funnel (bamboo works well) and set a storage container underneath the spout. Over a day, this will produce a decent amount of water that can be put away for later. Please see our chapter on tapping trees on page 92.

However, just like with all water you find in the wild, it's always safest to treat it before drinking it. If you don't, one small mishap could be life threatening, as there are a plethora of water-borne illnesses.

Cleaning Water Before Consumption

A variety of methods are used to purify water before drinking it in the wild. For more information, please see our chapter on how to purify water in the wild on page 43. Most people have their own preferred method, but it's always important to have multiple on hand.

The most popular method is boiling your water. This is one of the easiest and doesn't require carrying extra water treatments like chemical drops or water filters. Fire will likely be around, and you can boil a lot of water at once to drink later on, assuming you can store it.

It's recommended to boil the rainwater you collect, or treat it through a natural filter if you have the materials handy. That said, I usually drink rainwater as is, as it's usually very clean. There are areas where rainwater collects more particles than usual while moving through the atmosphere and these may be dangerous to consume. You also need to be aware of what's collecting on your tarp if you are using that method to harvest water. Bird and insect poop can contaminate the water before it ever gets to your cache, so treatment is necessary.

HOW TO PURIFY WATER IN THE WILD

What Should You Look for in a Viable Water Source?

It is possible to filter water from most sources, including puddles, but it doesn't mean you should if you have other options. Stagnant water can harbor some nasty stuff that can make you sick and further dehydrate you. This applies even if the water is clear and empty of visible debris. Clear water does not necessarily mean clean water.

The first choice of a water source should always be fast flowing. This means there is a constant flush of fresh water which reduces the buildup of harmful substances. Grasses, sand, and rock act as natural filtration devices as water passes through them.

Keep an eye out for these sources for the best chance of cleaner water:

- Lakes
- Rivers
- Streams
- Creeks
- Ground springs

The cleanest sources are found at higher altitudes where there is less human activity. Additionally, stay away from farmland since the runoff from livestock can render the water undrinkable.

How Can Untreated Water Make You Sick?

At a microscopic level, water can have high levels of harmful viruses, pathogens, and bacteria. Under stress, or with a weakened immune system, we are highly susceptible to getting very sick from harmful microbes in the water.

Even worse, a lot of these things can cause vomiting and diarrhea, making you weak and dehydrated. Some common examples of harmful bacteria found in untreated water include:

- *E. coli*
- *Legionella pneumophila*
- *Salmonella*
- *Cryptosporidium*
- Hepatitis A

You mustn't assume that any water is free from impurities. There are many more harmful microbes other than those mentioned here that can cause something mild like a headache to something more severe such as intestinal distress.

Don't Forget to Pre-Filter Your Water

Filter debris out of your water before purifying it. Pieces of wood, insects, and other undesirables can be mistakenly swallowed, potentially causing you to choke.

The easiest way to filter your water is to put it through some kind of fabric cloth before it goes into a container. A handkerchief works well, but any piece of thin clothing can work in a pinch too.

Stretch the fabric over your water container. Pour the water over the fabric and it'll filter out any debris or sediment. Note this is only step one.

4 Ways to Purify Water in The Wild

Each of these methods can be made from scavenged materials. If you want to be prepared, then it's a good idea to keep some of the components handy in your emergency kit. A DIY water purification kit should include having a metal cup, a single-walled stainless steel water bottle, a steel pot, a plastic sheet, a plastic water bottle (that can be cut), and some activated charcoal stashed away in your pack.

1 Boiling

The easiest method to purify your water is to boil it over a fire or with hot rocks. For the water to be considered purified, you'll want to boil it for a minimum of 5 minutes. Ideally, keeping it at a rapid boil for 20 minutes or more will ensure the safety of your water.

A downside to this method is that the oxygen is removed from the water, causing it to have a dull taste. Cover the leftovers and keep away from direct sunlight in a cool location.

There are two methods to boil water: boiling in a container and using hot rocks.

Boiling in a container: If you have a fireproof container like a metal pot, a can, or a single-walled steel water bottle, then you can fill it with water and set it over a fire. Once it has boiled for long enough, then remove it from the fire to cool down.

Rock boiling: For this method, you can fashion your container using bark. Heat the rocks in the fire and then carefully transfer them over to the container and put them in. The water will start heating up as the rock releases its heat into it. Once the rock has cooled down, simply replace it with another rock. Keep doing this until you have achieved a rolling boil for several minutes.

2

Solar Still

Solar stills have two advantages: water collection and water purification. This makes it effective for use in areas where there aren't flowing sources of water available. To use this method, you'll need a shovel or stick to dig a hole, a container to hold water, and a plastic sheet to cover the hole.

1. Start by digging a hole 1-2 feet (30-60 cm) deep.
2. Place some green grasses, moss, or wet leaves at the bottom of the hole. If you have any unclean water, you can gently drip some over the layer of debris.
3. Place the container that will hold the water in the middle of the hole.
4. Cover the top of the hole with the plastic sheet, and place a rock in the middle of the sheet, so that it angles toward the cup.

5. Leave it alone for the day and check it as the temperature drops.

As the sun shines through the plastic sheet, it will raise the temperature in the hole. All the moisture inside will eventually evaporate and get trapped by the tarp. As it hits the tarp, it will cool down, form condensation, and then drip back down into the water container.

Since only the water evaporates, it will be purified and mostly cleaned, although it may not be crystal clear.

3
Activated Charcoal Water Filter

The most common DIY water filter is an activated charcoal filter that uses grass, sand, pebbles, and activated charcoal to purify water. The easiest way is to use a large 68-oz (2-liter) plastic bottle to build the filter. You can also use a 17-oz (500ml) single use plastic water bottle for smaller amounts.

If you don't have either of those, cutting a square section of bark from a white birch and rolling it into a cone shape will suffice. Birch bark will hold water without soaking through, which is why it is used to build canoes.

Create your own birch bark cone using the following steps:

1. Find a white birch tree that has flexible white bark hanging from it.
2. Choose a square section about 10 inches (25 cm) by 10 inches (25 cm).
3. Using your knife, press down, so the blade just cuts through the first few layers - any deeper and you can damage the tree.
4. Peel the section of bark back, starting from the cut you just made. Ensure to cut out any protruding knots, so that the sheet doesn't tear
5. Take the newly cut square sheet of papery bark and start rolling tightly from one corner to get the cone shape angle.
6. Once the cone shape is complete use paracord, long grasses, or fishing line and wrap it around the cone, so that it keeps its shape. You now have a vessel to hold your water filter components.

A layer of activated charcoal is what makes this filter effective at eliminating harmful bacteria and microbes. As the water passes through the charcoal, it absorbs all of the impurities, leaving you with fresh water.

It's important to use activated charcoal and not charcoal briquettes you buy for your barbecue. Cooking charcoal has additives to help it get hotter. These chemicals are toxic to humans and can taint the water you're trying to purify.

Activated charcoal has calcium chloride added to it and is effective in eliminating toxins for many different applications. Commonly, activated charcoal is used in city water filtration, as well as for gas absorption in gas masks. You can purchase it at grocery stores, health food shops, and bulk food locations.

3

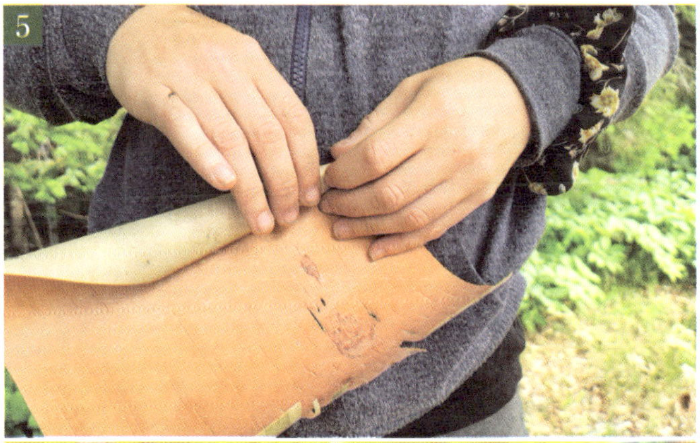
5

4

6

The process to make activated charcoal is not one you can normally apply in the wild, however, it's good to be familiar with it:

- To make your own activated charcoal, you'll need powdered charcoal from hardwood. Burn dry, seasoned hardwood for the best results. Leave the coals overnight to cool, and powder them using a rock, hammer or a large mortar and pestle. You can cheat a little by purchasing hardwood charcoal from your local store.
- Create a calcium chloride paste using a solution that is 25% calcium chloride and the rest water. For example, 100 grams (3.5 oz) of calcium chloride would be mixed with 300 ml (10 oz) of water.
- Add the solution to your powdered charcoal slowly until a thick, spreadable paste has started to form. Ensure to drain any remaining liquid.
- Let the paste dry for 24 hours and then spread it onto a clean white sheet or some cheesecloth. Whatever sheet you use should not have been washed with any sort of detergent.
- Once dried, rinse with clean water to remove any impurities from the process.
- Take your rinsed charcoal and lay it on a flat sheet, bake it at 250° F (121° C) until all of the moisture is gone. Let it cool down and then crumble it up for storage. It's best to store activated charcoal in a cool, dry area in an airtight container. There is no expiration date, but it will absorb gases and liquids from the air around it, so it's best to keep it as sealed as possible.

Constructing the Water Filter:

1. Rinse the activated charcoal with fresh water to remove any impurities. If you don't have clean water nearby, simply flush the finished filter a few times with unfiltered water before you attempt to drink from it.
2. Create the container: cut the end of a 2-liter (68-oz) plastic bottle or use a birch bark cone.
3. Collect gravel, sand, and grass which will be used as the pre-filter material.
4. Layering from bottom to top, place a piece of cloth as the first component.
5. Pour the activated charcoal in as the next layer, as it will absorb impurities.
6. Layer sand on top of that to act as a fine filter for small particulates.
7. Add small pebbles on top of the sand to filter out large pieces of debris.
8. Grass or larger stones should be the top later as they will handle the largest pieces of debris.
9. Repeat layers as needed and it's ready to use.

This filter requires only charcoal for purifying the water, but all of the added layers will get rid of algae, sediment, and surface scum.

4

Use Moss for a Quick Drink

If you're looking for a quick drink without having to build a filter or boil water, then look for some moss. Sphagnum moss in particular holds moisture really well. It also contains iodine, which is commonly used in water filtration products.

Find some clumps of sphagnum moss and squeeze it, using your thumb to direct water into your mouth. With any luck you should get a small stream of fresh water. This is a particularly good option if the area has seen recent rainfall.

5

Collect Rainwater

This is my favorite method if it's raining or dewy, as water falling from the sky is clean. Place your tarp (or any plastic) in a way to collect rainwater with a collection pot or a container made with rocks and your tarp at the bottom. This takes little effort and you can stash a large amount of clean water this way. Please see my chapter titled "How to Collect Rainwater in the Wild" on page 39 for more information.

STARTING A FIRE 101. EVEN IN THE RAIN

The Fire Triangle

Mastery of fire starts with an understanding of its creation and management. This begins with the "Fire Triangle." Fire requires three components to survive: fuel, oxygen, and heat. If you are missing any of these components, you won't be able to bring a fire to life. Take away any of these elements and you extinguish the fire.

Of the three ingredients, fuel is the most complex and we will discuss it in depth in the next section. The second side of the triangle, oxygen, is self-explanatory. Starve a fire for air and it won't grow. Working from ember to flame, too much air is as bad as not enough, as you may exhaust the ember before it catches on the tinder. With skill, you will learn to nurture your fire from coal to flame. Likewise, you'll master laying the fire to encourage enough oxygen to generate the heat you need.

The last side of the triangle is heat. While it seems obvious that you need heat for a fire, heat plays two major roles. First, heat is a key component of ignition. Without heat, you can't start a fire. We will discuss several ignition methods in the following sections. Second, heat keeps the fire going. This is critical in the early stages of starting your fire, especially in wet conditions. Building up a base of coals quickly is critical to bring new wood up to ignition temperature. If your fire doesn't have coals, then new wood may smother your young flames before they can spread to the new fuel.

Fuel Explained

Fuel for a fire can be broken into three categories: tinder, kindling, and fuelwood. Unless you are using an accelerant (e.g., gas or kerosene) or a fire starter that will catch fuelwood (e.g., road flare), then you need tinder to get things going.

Tinder is any fuel that has a great amount of surface area that easily ignites. Examples include wood shavings, fine sawdust, and dry vegetation (avoid leaves, as they often smolder and impede airflow). Most fire starters are tinder plus wax, fat, or oil, which helps the fire get established and eventually spread.

The next step up is kindling. The purpose of kindling is to catch flame from your tinder, grow it, and spread it to your fuelwood. You want branches, stems, twigs, or split wood that is smaller in diameter than your thumb. If you only have larger wood, then split it into a smaller size to expose more surface area to catch fire from your tinder.

Fuelwood is any wood that is larger than your thumb. Generally, it's large enough to burn over time. As it burns, it leaves coals that catch and burn new wood placed on your fire.

As you prepare to start your fire, gather your wood and prepare (cut and split) it first. You will need all three types in abundance if your fire-making is to be a success.

Tinder and Fire Starters

As stated above, tinder is your first piece of fuel. It must be small (e.g., have a large surface area) and flammable. While nature provides tinder in abundance, you can also purchase or make your own to improve your chance of success.

Natural tinder includes any dry wood that you can shave down to either thin chips or scrape to sawdust. A pencil sharpener and a few thin twigs can create a small mountain of tinder in a hurry. Papery tree bark, such as white birch or silver birch, is excellent. Most dry sturdy grasses also work very well.

Homemade tinder is the perfect solution to add to your camping/survival supplies. One of the most common is a cotton ball smeared with petroleum jelly. This concept can be extended to makeup removal pads (round dense cotton disks) soaked in melted wax or petroleum jelly. Tearing a disk exposes the individual fibers that easily catch sparks.

Jute or other fibrous rope, twisted, not braided, soaked in wax, is the perfect water-resistant tinder. You can cut any length you need and then tease apart the individual fibers. It catches a spark easily, and each fiber burns like a candle, as it's soaked in wax. The wax also makes it water resistant, so even soaking wet you can shake off the excess water and it will still light.

Next is char cloth. This is any sturdy cloth (like blue jeans material) that is "cooked" in a tin container to create a cloth-like charcoal. While it is not moisture resistant, it will catch a spark and smolder enough to light your tinder.

A few other options for homemade tinder include sawdust rolled up in wax paper and cotton or sawdust placed in an egg carton, then soaked with wax. Check your spare food for anything dry and greasy. If it has oil, it will most likely burn. Hand sanitizer or alcohol prep pads from a first aid kit work well. Be creative in your handmade solutions. If it's flammable, fibrous, and will soak up a little wax or Vaseline, then experiment with it. You can even use extra fine (Grade #0000) steel wool. It catches sparks from a ferro rod or ignites with a battery and creates a molten core. You can control its spread by how hard you blow on it.

Commercially, there are more fire starters than you can count. There are similar items to each homemade variant, as well as a few novel types. One of the newest multi-use tinders available online is paracord with a fire tinder central core. With these, it's easy to add 165 feet (50 m) of cord to your bag, knowing that each inch/centimeter can help start a fire.

Create a tinder bundle by layering tinder from the finest (your fire starter) to increasingly more substantial tinder. You can also create a roll or cone of course tinder around a core of fine material. Remember that the tinder bundle is the foundation of your fire and must be compatible with your method. The more primitive your method, the more you need to perfect the tinder bundle. Using a lighter? You can start small twigs. A coal from a bow drill or fire plow requires the driest and finest tinder materials. Prepare according to your method and skills.

Kindling

Kindling grows your fire from the flames in the tinder bundle to those substantial enough to catch your fuelwood. The first rule about kindling is it must be dry. Too damp and it won't catch. For small twigs, they must snap. If they bend, then they are too green and won't catch quickly.

The second rule is you want it no larger than your thumb. If necessary, split up larger pieces to reduce their size. Large shavings off a log work well. Splitting increases the surface area and exposes fibers that catch easily. Pine needles and pine twigs are perfect as they contain flammable pitch, burn hot, and are small enough to catch quickly. Near the base of the tree, they usually stay dry even after heavy rain. If you are lucky enough to find a recently downed white pine, harvest the wood at the base. This is commercially sold as fatwood and is loaded with pine pitch.

As with tinder, gather kindling along the trail while you are out. Add high-quality kindling to your pack as you find it. Always gather more than you think you will need. It goes quickly and if it's damp, you'll need it.

Fuelwood

Any wood larger than kindling is your fuelwood. Start small and gradually increase size as your fire will support it. When possible, break or cut pieces to length to avoid the fire spreading beyond your prepared fire ring.

As with kindling, splitting wood will help it to catch faster and burn quicker. In the woods, you may be limited to a knife, hatchet, and possibly a small saw. Use the most efficient method to cut and split your wood to save calories. If you are limited to a knife, carry a sturdy one

that you can baton (split) wood with. To baton a short stick, lay the blade of the knife on the end of the log, then pound on the spine of the knife with another log to drive the knife like a wedge through the stick.

While dry and split wood works best, you don't need perfectly dry wood. It takes a very long time for wood to become so wet it's unusable. Often you can split wood to expose its dry center. You can also set damp logs around the edge of your fire pit to dry them.

Ignition Sources

Fire starts with ignition. You need to generate that first ember, spark, or flame. The method you choose will be guided by your skills and the immediacy of your need.

Manual methods are good to use in perfect conditions. When you have the time and can find the right materials, a fire plow, hand drill, or bow drill is a great skill to have (learn how to make a bow drill in the wild on page 152). Having the skill to start a fire with these methods will help you perfect your use of selecting tinder and kindling as nurturing a coal has little room for error.

The next option for ignition is a Ferrocerium (ferro) rod. When scraped with steel (e.g., the back of your knife) a ferro rod throws an impressive number of sparks. You need a fine tender to catch the spark such as char cloth, cotton and petroleum jelly, and most commercially prepared fire starters. When using a ferro rod, place the rod into your tinder bundle and the knife at the edge of the bundle on the rod. Then, move the rod and not the knife. By drawing the rod back and not moving the knife, you minimize the chance you will disturb the tinder bundle. If you move the knife along the rod, you will inevitably push on the bundle and disturb it. Ferro rods work even when wet, making them a valuable addition to your pack.

Every wilderness survival bag should have a lighter and every hiker should have a lighter in their pocket. A Bic lighter (keep with the known brands as the cheap brands do not always work as well) is the perfect ignition source, especially in rainy conditions. Other lighter options include torch lighters, great in windy conditions, or a Zippo. If using a Zippo top off its fuel before you head out the door, as they are prone to evaporate and dry out.

The next recommendation is a small flare. If you absolutely need to get a fire going, there is no better option. You can use the entire flare or cut off a piece and use that as your fire starter. Even in a downpour, a 15-minute flare adds only ounces to your pack and will get any pile of firewood burning.

There are other options to get your fire going, including pocket lenses, water lenses, and fire pistons that can be carried or improvised. Regardless of your chosen method, you must practice and develop proficiency sufficient to start a fire under most conditions.

Location and Structure

When building your fire, first consider location and preparation. It's important to protect yourself and your immediate environment from accidental fire spread. First, look up. Fire can spread to overhead branches just as easily as it can jump to neighboring grasses. Likewise, a warm fire can melt overhead snow and unexpectedly extinguish your fire.

Once you have identified the ideal location away from hazards, clear away any debris down to the soil. Clear away any roots as well. They can quickly catch and smolder, then travel outside of your cleared circle. If you are building a substantial fire (e.g., more than a few small sticks to cook a quick meal), consider forming a circle of rocks. The rocks will contain the fire and prevent dangerous spread.

Next, prepare the structure that will become your fire. The goal is to contain the tinder, kindling, and small fuelwood to direct heat and flame from the tinder through the kindling and to the fuelwood. This requires height and you have a few options:

One is to build a teepee structure. Build a tall pile of kindling layering from smallest to largest, leaving room for your tinder bundle at the bottom. Then, lean small split logs against each other to form a teepee or pyramid over the kindling.

The next structure option is a log cabin. Again, start with layers of kindling and stacking logs, cabin style, around the kindling. A modification of this method is a lean-to structure. Here your log stack is three-sided, making it easier to add kindling and small fuelwood to the fire without disturbing the structure.

In all three cases, the shape directs the heat upward to and through the fuelwood. Secondarily, the structure can either direct any wind or protect your young fire from the wind. Build it according to your situation. If starting a fire in the rain, a teepee structure is best as it protects the kindling and tinder. Also, keep the tinder bundle dry until you are ready to start your fire.

Always have extra tinder and kindling on hand. You may need it to restart the process or to build up coals.

Starting Small and Building

The key to starting and nurturing your fire through its first few precious moments is patience and discipline. Overfeed it and you may extinguish it. Rush your tinder bundle and it won't hold flame long enough to catch the kindling. Take it slow and steady and you'll be rewarded with flame.

If you are using a primitive method, you will need to start your fire in your tinder bundle outside of the kindling pile. Insert the coal into the bundle and blow gently to kindle a flame. Once the tinder flame is growing on its own move the bundle to the kindling.

If you are using a ferro rod, lighter, or other more robust means, you can afford to start the tinder in your structure. Get the tinder bundle lit, nurture the flame with gentle blowing, and position it within the structure for best contact with kindling and the fuelwood.

As your fire grows, add oxygen either by blowing or fanning. A long steady blow is better than short gusts. The same goes for fanning. Consistent gentle fanning may be required until the kindling takes.

Remember that fire is sustained by its coals. One of the mistakes of a novice is underestimating the amount of kindling and small fuel that is needed to get a true fire going. As your kindling catches and burns, continue to add more kindling and smaller fuelwood to the center of your structure until you have a good base of coals and embers. It is at this stage that most novices miss with a flame that isn't sustained enough to catch the fuelwood. Always have enough small wood prepared to get you through this stage.

Gradually introduce larger fuelwood and migrate from small sticks to split logs. As the initial logs burn through, position them so that they add to the sustaining coals. For example, as the logs at the top of your log cabin burn through, add them to the center of the structure rather than move them to the outside.

Sustaining Your Fire

Your job doesn't end here. Once you get the fire going, you need to keep it going. How you proceed depends on your goals.

If your fire is meant to be short-lived (e.g., heating or cooking a single meal) then feeding your fire with small pieces of fuel is ok. You only need enough coals and flame to complete your task. In fact, too big of a fire may be a liability when it is time to put it out. Keep it small, feed it often, and put it out when your task is done.

If you want a sustained fire for cooking or heat, choose your fuel appropriately. Large dry pieces and an established coal base will meet your needs best. Lay damp logs near the fire to dry before you feed them. This will cut down on the smoke. If using your fire for signaling, then applying damp or green wood with a measured approach will generate the smoke you need without smothering your fire.

Finally, if you need to preserve your fire for several

hours while you are away from camp it's often best to lay a large dry log over the coals. Over the hours the large log will burn slowly, merely smoldering without much oxygen. When you return, you'll have live coals under the log to start a new fire.

Special Considerations If It's Raining

Perfect your skills for preparing and lighting a fire while the sun shines, so that you can start a fire quickly and effectively when it's raining. During bad weather, you will need to go in prepared to be successful.

Fire starts with tinder. It is important that you have lots of it and that it's all dry. Form a habit of gathering tinder along the trail. Stuff a bag or your pockets with tinder and keep it there to keep it dry. If you have room in your backpack, gather dry kindling as well.

Focus on pine if it grows in your area. The sap is flammable and virtually waterproof. Dry, brown pine needles catch and flame up rapidly, albeit quickly, even when damp. Again, avoid deciduous tree leaves.

In a survival situation, don't be afraid to get aggressive. A road flare in your pack can get a fire going even in the most severe weather. Stack kindling and fuelwood and place a lit flare in it. You'll have heat in just a few minutes.

Wood takes a long time to get wet. When it's raining, you can split off the outer layer, often just the bark, to get to the dry portions. If you can find straight-grained wood, you can split it or baton it easily to kindling size. I often "feather" my wood when it's raining, making feather sticks. This process involves shaving the edge of a stick of wood with a sharp knife so that you get a mass of curls (much like ribbon curls on a present) – this increases the surface area allowing the piece of wood to catch.

Next, have much more tinder and kindling than you think you will ever need. When it's raining, you may fail more than once and you'll need backup supplies. The same goes for your fuelwood. Prep it before you need it and keep it dry. You'll need to quickly advance your fire past the kindling stage and build a substantial layer of coals. Have a significant quantity of small fuelwood available to build your coal base.

Elevate your fire-building surface to keep the logs off the wet ground. Split a few small logs and build your fire on those. They will keep your tinder and kindling dry while the fire gets going and will eventually contribute to your coal base.

Finally, start your tinder bundle where it's dry. Use a tarp, shelter under a tree, or huddle under your jacket. Tinder will take a few seconds to get going and, in that time, you can move to the prepared fire ring. This takes practice, but you'll be surprised how long a good tinder bundle will last.

ADVANCED FIRE TECHNIQUES

Basic fire-making gets you from point A (no fire) to point B (fire) under the best conditions, with the best materials, usually with the easiest methods. While it takes skill and patience to do it quickly and efficiently, add in a single challenge (e.g., wet weather) and what was easy becomes difficult at best, and impossible at worst.

Mastery begins with confidence born out of practice. Do not expect your mastery of fire to happen overnight. Skills take time to build, and they are often built over many years. Master one element at a time. Start with perfecting your tinder bundle, then learn about how long char-cloth or a coal made from polypore shavings will last. Pick a technique, material, or fire use, and practice it until you have mastered it under all conditions. Then move on to a new technique.

What Makes a Technique Advanced

Fire is easy to make under perfect conditions. The weather is dry; the fuel is dry, kindling and tinder are plentiful, and your ignition source is foolproof. Degrade one of these and they may stress your beginner skills to failure. Advanced techniques allow you to broaden every aspect of fire making. Your ability to find and utilize materials extends beyond synthetic (store-bought or prepared at home) to those you can gather on the trail regardless of the season. Your ability to start a fire spans every month of the year and you can improvise an ignition source. There is tremendous ground to cover when improving your talents.

First, advanced fire-making techniques work with sub-optimal materials. This includes damp or green woods. Ideally, you want dry tinder, kindling, and fuelwood. However, these aren't always a reality.

The next advanced technique is using a friction fire method. The Bic lighter and ferro rod move aside for the bow drill (you can find out how to make a bow drill in the wild on page 152), hand drill, and fire plow. Half of mastering a friction method is technique and half is selection of the proper materials. To be successful, you need to identify the best wood for your fireboard and spindle, then be able to generate, catch, and preserve the coal.

Finally, advanced techniques apply to each season. Spring, summer, fall, and winter all present unique challenges. Summer may have ideally dry materials but a dry environment requires safe preparation of your fire location. Fall has an abundance of dry tinder (cattails, milkweed, dead grasses, etc.), however, much of your environment may be wet. Winter and spring are particularly challenging, as wet and usable tinder may be difficult to find.

Your mastery of each of these elements will lead to confidence in being able to make a fire any time you step out your front door.

Advanced Materials

Tinder is the base of all fire-making. Failure to prepare a proper tinder bundle often means your kindling won't catch, or you will exhaust the tinder before you can work your kindling.

When perfecting tinder preparation, you want to maximize its surface area. When using a lighter, the flame can catch anything given enough time. When nurturing a friction fire coal or char cloth, you need very fine material to catch it. Grasses, cedar bark, and dry milkweed stalk can be rubbed between your hands to fray and expose their fibers. Thistle, milkweed pods, and dried bracken ferns are all naturally fine and will easily catch a spark if you prepare enough of them.

Don't neglect the world of mushrooms. Several tree-growing polypore mushrooms are excellent for use in forming a coal or holding a coal for transferring fire. The easily recognizable horse hoof mushroom (*Fomes fomentarius*), as well as the medicinal mushroom chaga (*Inonotus obliquus*), are both excellent for immediate use or to stash in your pack. Powdering either with a rock or harvesting the dust from sawing provides a perfect medium for catching a spark and growing a coal.

Horse Hoof (*Fomes Fomentarius*)

Inonotus obliquus f. sterilis, Christine Young - INaturalist, CC BY 4.0

Even a green branch can be used for tinder if properly prepared. Shave the outer and inner bark with the spine of your knife into a pile. Placing the pile in the sun for 15-30 minutes will be sufficient to dry it enough for use as tinder.

Finally, if you can find a felled pine tree, then harvest part of the stump or exposed roots. These parts store sap, and once they are dry, they are filled with resin and are highly flammable. This "Fat Wood" is highly prized, as it's very flammable and almost waterproof. Scrape or shave off a pile of sawdust into your tinder bundle to catch a spark or flare up a coal.

Shaved Bark into a Pile

Know what plants are available year-round. For example, cattail fluff is only available in the fall and winter, while milkweed pods pop in the late summer, and pine needles are available year-round. Selecting the right materials is one of the first steps toward fire-building success. Under stressful conditions, the knowledge to assess your environment and select the proper materials for your situation is the first key to mastering fire making.

Advanced Tinder Bundles

We've already covered basic tinder bundles, however, as your ignition methods get more primitive, and the environment gets more antagonistic, it's even more important to perfect your tinder bundle.

Your tinder bundle should start with dry, fibrous material. Both physical factors enhance the chance for the coal or a young flame to catch quickly. With practice, you will learn the density of the material that balances flame growth (dense) with airflow (loose).

Next is layering. You need to have the finest material with the most surface area at the center where the coal or sparks will be placed. As you move out from the center, layer in larger, slightly thicker, more dense material. For example, start your nest with cattail fluff, and wrap it with dry grasses. Wrap this with fibrous bark (e.g., well-rubbed cedar bark), then with small twigs. This layering encourages the nurturing of the coal or flame to larger and larger fuel sources.

The shape of the bundle is up to you and the preferences you develop through practice. Some like a simple bird's nest, others a cone, and still others prefer to form a large ball. Regardless, use a shape that you can hold in your hand. With a handheld bundle, you will learn a lot about how flames grow and spread. This is much harder to learn with a bundle on the ground within a log cabin fire structure. Second, you will learn how long a fire will

Nest with Cattail Fluff

persist in a bundle. One of the most common beginner mistakes is rushing a fire. When you do things right there is no need to rush the steps.

Advanced Fire Starting

The chapter "Starting a Fire 101. Even in the Rain" (page 48) discusses various methods for ignition methods including a lighter, ferro rod, and hazard flare, as well as primitive methods such as the bow drill, hand drill, and fire plow.

Primitive methods allow you to dive deeper into advanced techniques. All three are challenging and will take many, many practice sessions to master. Most of your learning will be dedicated to material selection and perfecting your technique (e.g., maintaining the proper angle between your body, drill or plow, and the fire board). This is the nature of perfecting primitive methods and entire books have been dedicated to the subject.

Another advanced fire technique that deserves practice is the ability to persevere through injury. Orthopedic injuries are some of the most common on the trail and often involve hands, arms, feet, and ankles. Therefore, make a practice of immobilizing a limb while building your practice fires once you have learned them with all limbs intact (please see our "Firewood Safety" chapter on page 59).

Hand and arm injuries are the most impactful on your fire efforts and you should practice the two most critical skills: preparing kindling and ignition, one-handed.

Preparing tinder and kindling can be challenging with one hand. The key is to isolate and secure your knife. One technique is to pound your knife into a log and then pull branches against it to shave off tinder-sized pieces. Alternatively, to split larger pieces, lay them end first against your knife blade and tap with another larger branch (known as batoning) to split it into smaller pieces.

Next is one-handed ignition. A bow drill (please see our chapter "How to Craft Tools and Weapons in the Wild" on page 152) and hand drill require two hands (I have seen people do a bow drill one-handed, but they were very skilled and practiced). However, a fire plow can be pulled off one-handed. This technique will take a lot of practice and no shortage of blisters.

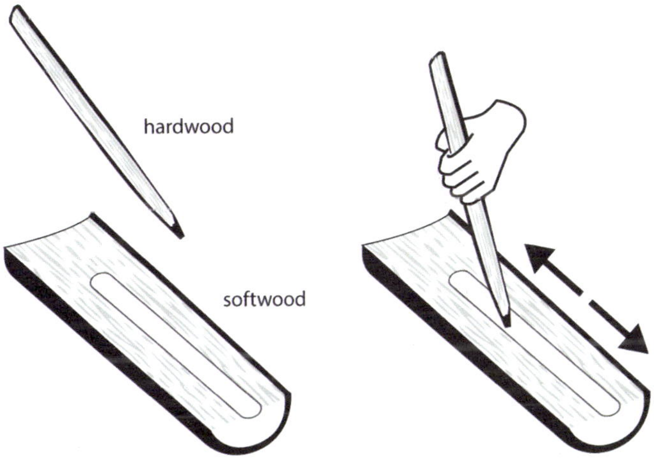

On the other end of the ignition spectrum is a lighter. A Bic is easy to use and requires little to no practice. Carry one.

A ferro rod can be easily used one-handed with the right technique. First, place your knife on a log or rock. Second, place the tinder bundle, or char cloth, under the base of the blade (on the spine side). Finally, draw the ferro rod against the spine of the knife, throwing sparks into the tinder bundle.

Injury in the woods can be serious. Minimize your risk with a master skill set that includes fire.

Advanced Fire Structures

Fire isn't a single-use tool. It heats, cooks, signals, provides company, and performs a host of other duties for us. Your basic camping fire (teepee or log cabin) will satisfy most of your needs and you can do a lot with it. However, there are several options to fit specific needs, including signaling, being covert, long duration, cooking, and smoking.

Signaling Fires

A signaling fire must be large, bright, or smoky to gain attention. For a large signaling fire, lay several logs, radiating out from the central fire, like a star. As the logs burn, the larger radius will be more noticeable from the air, while the odd shape will stand out against the natural background.

The second option is to make a bright fire. Bright means flame. A visible fire must be bright and tall. For a bright fire use the driest wood you can find. Dry wood is more apt to burn rather than smolder. Ideally, you'll be able to find dry pine branches or even a small dead pine tree. Add it to your base fire and you're guaranteed a large, bright fire (albeit quick). Next, make the fire tall. The height increases the draft and upward airflow. The stronger the airflow, the more intense the flames. The height will also increase visibility.

Another option is to make a smoky fire. To generate smoke, you need a solid base fire that is hard to smother. When you need smoke, add green wood, or even better add fresh pine boughs. The sap will flare up and keep the fire going. Another option is to use scavenged plastic or rubber. These generate a thick black smoke that is highly visible.

Covert Fires

Your next advanced fire set is a covert fire. Fire makes smoke and to become smokeless, you need efficient ignition. An excellent option for a covert fire is a Dakota Fire Hole. Start with digging a hole in the ground approximately 1 foot (30 cm) deep and 8 inches (20 cm) in diameter.

Next, dig at least one hole at an angle from the surface (6 to 8 inches/ 15 to 20 cm away from the edge of the hole) down to the base of the fire hole. This can be done by pounding in a thick branch. You want the hole to be at least 2 inches (5 cm) in diameter. This hole (or holes) will provide the air intake for your fire. The air holes and the depth create a strong updraft, which aids in complete combustion. The design is similar to that of a Rocket stove. Once the fire is going, add small dry branches for fuel. The result is a fire that nearly smokeless.

Air Hole - Dakota Fire Hole

You can also build a primitive rocket stove if you can find an abundance of stackable rocks. Stack the rocks in the shape of a box or chimney with a small opening at the bottom to feed in wood. If you are near a source of mud or clay, you can improve its performance with a layer around the outside of the stones. Leave the bottom few inches mud free to provide oxygen and a strong draft.

Primitive Rocket Stove

Long Duration Fires

A long-duration fire has several uses including freeing you from time and effort maintaining it throughout the day and night. The free time allows you to sleep, forage, or hunt.

The first, and easiest, long-duration fire is the upside-down fire. Modeled after the traditional log cabin, the upside-down fire differs in two important ways. First, the tinder and kindling are laid on the top instead of on the bottom. Second, instead of a hollow structure, you will stack up a solid structure. With the tinder bundle and kindling set on top of the fuelwood, the fire burns down from the top into and through the fuelwood.

Upside-Down Fire

Unlike a traditional fire where the coals on the bottom feed the fuel on the top causing the fuel to burn through quickly, with an upside-down fire, the coals burn down through the fuel. The result is a slow-burning and long-lasting fire. You will need to nurture the initial fire long enough to catch the logs underneath it. The advantage is that you can leave this fire unattended for hours at a time.

A variation on this concept is the Self-Feeding V Fire. Here, you create one or two ramps that roll logs into the fire as the earlier logs burn out. This design can be single-sided or double-sided based on your time and materials. Create the ramps out of green saplings lashed together. Each pair should be set apart about ¾ the length of your logs so that the logs don't fall through. Experiment with the angle. Too steep and the logs may fall off, too shallow and they won't roll into the fire. As in the upside-down fire, you can get hours of cooking or heat without giving it attention.

Self-Feeding Fire

Cooking Fires

Next, there are cooking and smoking fires. The fire lay for these fires can be your traditional log cabin or teepee (please see our chapter "Starting a Fire 101. Even in the Rain" on page 48). The main goal is a bed of coals. Coals cook at a more even rate without burning your food. You may also wish to make a multi-level fire. By raking the coals out, you can create areas of different intensities. This allows you to cook multiple items at the same time without over-managing your meal.

To smoke your food, you simply need to manage two items: heat and smoke. Heat is simple as you can raise the food above the fire. Smoking for preservation can take hours so you will have to build a support structure (e.g., a lashed tripod) to hang your meat and fish. Secondly, you may want to construct a large teepee over the fire (out of green wood and leaves) to contain the smoke and maintain the heat.

Managing smoke is an easier matter. Fires naturally smoke. If you want to add a little more you can add damp or green wood chunks or maintain a coal bed without adding too much new wood to avoid flare-ups. Next, choose your wood wisely. Hickory (wood and bark), cherry, mesquite, and most fruitwoods add the best flavor. Avoid most pines as they may produce off flavors.

Swedish Torch

One final specialty fire is the Swedish Torch. A Swedish Torch is made by splitting a log four ways or burning several logs close together. The log(s) are stood up on end and like the upside-down fire, the kindling is started on the top of the log(s). Over time the fire burns down through the center of the log creating a torch/rocket stove combination.

To prepare a single log, select a straight-grained log 8 or more inches (20 cm or more) in diameter. Split the log into quarters, then set the quarters back together with a small air gap between them. If using multiple logs, select three of the same diameter. Split 1 inch (2.5 cm) off the side of each log. Place them together with split sides toward the center (split sides should form a triangle). Stuff the gap with kindling and start your fire. The Swedish Torch is perfect for cooking and can even be moved if not burnt too long. Your torch will act as a self-consuming rocket stove and you should get at least an hour burn-time out of it.

Swedish Torch (using one log)

Swedish Torch (using multiple logs)

Training and Patience

Fire making is a perishable skill and you must practice it to maintain your abilities. Take time out of your schedule to maintain and build your skills. Luckily, there's no need to make your training boring and tedious. Mix it up.

Practice in all forms of weather. The best way to do this is to set a repetitive date (e.g., every other Wednesday, or the first Saturday of the month) to practice your skills. This forces you to make a fire no matter the weather. It doesn't need to be a massive fire, just enough to catch your largest kindling. The goal is practice and perseverance regardless of the season and conditions.

Next, schedule dedicated practice times where you work on a particular skill. It may be experimenting with various forms of tinder or working to perfect a primitive ignition technique.

For added difficulty, add cold. Do a few barehanded push-ups in the snow, or hold a bag of ice for a few minutes. The goal is to experience making a fire with a significant loss of dexterity. Losing your dexterity is a high probability and a serious issue in a real survival situation. Be prepared for it.

Last of all, have patience. Many fires are ruined by rushing. Get to know your components and skills. Did you know that char cloth can burn for a minute or two and a polypore coal can burn for 3-5 minutes? There's no need to rush.

Learning new skills takes patience, especially primitive methods. Expect challenges. Expect failure. Setbacks are a part of the process. Learn from them. Keep going despite any obstacles.

FIREWOOD SAFETY

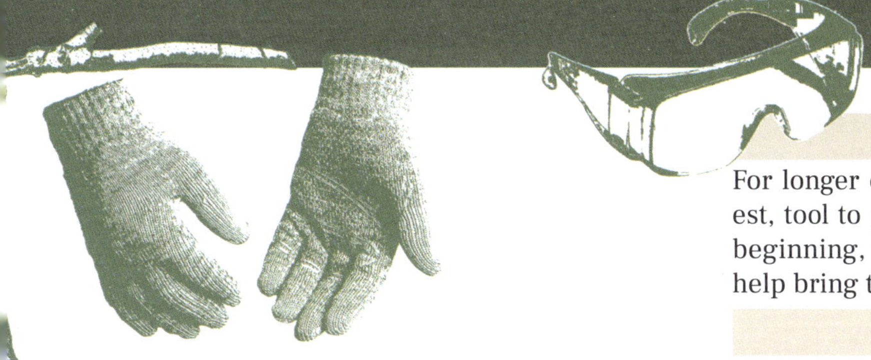

Different techniques and strategies have been developed over the ages to ensure cutting wood is safer and less injury-prone. From the beginning of the job to the very end, care and precision are extremely important.

In this chapter, we will primarily talk about how to safely chop wood for kindling. That's because chopping smaller sizes can often lead to more injuries due to the smaller working surface on the log. There are a few different ways that you can practice to efficiently, quickly, and safely chop firewood to get ready for the next cold snap.

Necessary Tools for Chopping Wood

Before starting, get all of the necessary tools ready. The process is one that requires close attention and focus; preparation will help keep you on task.

Axe or Hatchet

An axe is your primary tool for splitting logs down to size. Many people will choose a splitting axe over a maul for its multi-faceted uses and its lighter weight that can be easier to handle. You can find out how to make a primitive axe in the wild on page 142.

Hatchets are typically anything that ranges shorter than an axe handle and are used for more precise chopping of smaller wood. This is the perfect tool for chopping kindling, as you can be more accurate with your strike and not need to worry about swinging an axe all the way.

All-in-all, hatchets are a great tool for when you have logs that are smaller in diameter and you are wanting to create kindling.

Work Gloves

Wearing gloves is an easy way to protect you from any splintering wood, which often happens while chopping. A pair of thick leather or canvas gloves will also work as light protection from the blade of the hatchet when handling it.

Saw

For longer chunks of wood, a saw is the best, and safest, tool to get everything down to size. From the very beginning, unless you are using a felling axe, a saw will help bring the tree down and size it properly.

Eye Protection

While using a saw and chopping wood with a hatchet, sawdust and splinters will be flying around. Getting a stray bit of wood in your eye can be one of the more dangerous parts of chopping wood, and it's also an easy thing to avoid by wearing glasses, if available, or wearing a low hat to provide as much protection as possible.

Before Starting

Start off by assessing the area and yourself. Look around and make sure that no one will be in the way, there are no obstacles to swinging an axe, and you won't have any serious distractions pop up in the middle of chopping wood.

For yourself, make sure you have all the proper safety gear on and are in the right headspace to be handling large tools. Sometimes, if you are too physically or mentally tired, doing a hard chore like chopping firewood can easily become more dangerous when you don't have as much control.

Only start after you've made sure you have all the necessary gear on hand and you are clear of any distractions.

Cut Firewood to Length

Splitting kindling requires cutting firewood down to the right length. This can be any range of length, depending on where you'll be using the wood. If your stone oven (please see our chapter on how to build a stone oven on page 160) has a certain length, you will want to cut the kindling much shorter than the space available, so you can build a small fire easily to get everything started.

Cutting logs that are around 4 to 5 inches (10 to 12 cm) in diameter to about 10 or 12 inches (25 or 30 cm) in length will set you up for splitting a large amount of kindling.

Having a lot of logs ready to be split is a great way to make the process both safer and more efficient. You can get a large pile of logs ready to split before ever grabbing a hatchet. This helps to keep you on one task at a time, as the transitions are often when accidents happen and time is lost.

Seasoning the Logs

Some species of wood are nearly impossible to split when green, while others will split just as easily and toughen as they dry out. Since we're talking about splitting logs by hand, it will often be easier to split the wood after letting the logs dry out for almost a year. You want to make sure the wood is in a sheltered space protected from rain, and where there is enough air circulation to take the evaporating water away.

After the wood is seasoned, you can work on splitting the logs. This is one reason why chopping your own firewood can be such a long chore, you have to do it every year to make sure you're ready for the next.

Where to Split Wood

Before you split your wood, find a flat and hard surface to do it on. This can be a flat bit of ground, hard dirt, or a large cut log round. It's good practice to use a splitting log to help hold your wood higher up and save your blade from hitting the hard ground and chipping.

Always avoid soft ground as the impact of your axe or hatchet will drive the log into the ground and bury it deep, making it difficult to split, and can damage both the ground and your blade. Also, to ensure safety, choose a spot that is calm and quiet to avoid any distractions.

Split into Kindling

Kindling is one of the most important pieces of wood in the entire process of building a fire. With the perfect kindling, you can get a fire started with little hassle. If your kindling is too large or too small, you may quickly find that you are having trouble getting the kindling to light from tinder, or getting larger logs to light off the kindling.

Splitting a large amount of high-quality kindling is one of the most important parts of chopping firewood. Splitting kindling can also be one of the more dangerous, as you need more precision and are working with a smaller surface area. Aiming and swinging an axe or hatchet can be much more difficult when the target gets smaller, but there are a few great tips and tricks to chopping firewood safely.

This chapter reviews three techniques that can be used to safely chop kindling using a hatchet, axe, or a large bushcraft knife. Depending on the tools you have on hand, you can try out each technique. A hatchet is often the perfect tool to use for all three techniques.

Safe Techniques for Splitting Wood

Safely splitting wood, especially when splitting kindling, is primarily about avoiding the risk of fingers and toes being in the danger zone and protecting yourself from wood that can fly around when splitting.

That means that the goal is to provide support for the wood that will help it stand on its own, rather than relying on your hands to hold it vertically. Each of these techniques removes your hands from below the hatchet, knife, or axe blade.

Smart Stick aka "Chicken Stick"

A smart stick, aka a "chicken stick", is a simple concept. This is used for smaller chunks of wood and you are supporting the log with another stick, the smart stick, while chopping with the other hand.

Because this method requires using one hand for the smart stick, it is best performed with a hatchet. You have much better control over the hatchet with one hand, whereas with an axe, you may lose control with the heavier weight and longer handle.

To use a smart stick, all you need to do is:

- Find a flat surface, preferably a log used as a chopping block.
- Position the log you are chopping vertically while sitting next to it on a chair or log of a similar height.
- Find a smart stick that's about 1 foot (30 cm) in length. This gives you enough stability to hold the log still while providing enough distance to avoid cutting your fingers.
- Apply pressure with the end of the smart stick on the top of the log you will be splitting.
- Split the log with the hatchet.

If you miss your target, the only thing that gets cut will be the smart stick, rather than your finger!

Ropes, Bungees, or a Tire

This method is the best for cutting a lot of kindling, or larger logs, all at once. It uses the stability of all the logs being cut in order to stand up straight, all supported by an exterior barrier holding the group together.

This barrier is often either a rope tied around the bunch, multiple bungee cords, or an old tire.

Tires can be a great solution to use in this scenario, but in a survival situation, you are far more likely to have a bundle of rope on hand and ready to use. The rope will work just as well, but you may want to be more careful to not cut the rope if you need it for other purposes.

- Gather as many logs as you are planning on splitting and stand them up, right next to each other, in a circle, making sure they are touching and as tightly packed as possible.
- Use a rope or bungee cord to tie all of the wood together and hold it all upright (with the tire method, you can simply stand the logs inside of the tire from the beginning).
- Now, using a hatchet or an ax, start chopping wood.
- The support from the surrounding logs will help everything stand up, even after being split. You can move from one log to another quickly and split everything before untying the rope and collecting the wood to stack it.

Batoning

Batoning is the term for using a knife or hatchet as a sharp blade to split wood while hitting it with a large, strong stick. This method helps you chop firewood safely because you avoid swinging a blade and needing to aim it perfectly. Instead, you swing a small log and hammer the blade into the log until it splits.

This method is very useful for splitting kindling, especially if you only have a strong bushcraft knife available. The preference is a hatchet, as the wedge shape of the blade works to push the wood outwards while the blade drives down and splits the wood.

This is a very simple and straightforward process.

- Place the log to be split into kindling on a flat surface, preferably a chopping block.
- Position yourself so you have close control of the wood and your hatchet or knife.
- Find a sturdy, 2-3 inch (5-8 cm) thick log that is at least a foot long to use as your baton.
- Align the blade of your hatchet or knife with where you are wanting to split the wood and hold it steady on the surface.
- Using the baton, hit the butt of the hatchet or knife with enough power to drive the blade down into the wood. Continue hitting with the baton until the wood splits.
- If the hatchet or knife becomes buried, you can baton the handle as close to the log as possible to drive it deeper.

FOOD

HOW TO AND WHERE TO SET UP TRAPS FOR SMALL GAME

Rabbits, squirrels, groundhogs, moles, mice, grouse, and other small animals are located across the world in various environments, making them a great target for anyone needing to find food.

The difficulty comes when attempting to set up traps for the first time. It can look simple, a small noose on a well-trodden game trail, but in reality, it involves much more thought and experience. There are many different styles of small game traps, and each animal species requires much thought about how to catch them.

With the right know-how, small game can be trapped and brought back to camp for a meal that can potentially save your life in a survival scenario.

Tools for Building Traps

Part of any survival gear setup should be a kit for building a wide variety of traps. There are a lot of ways to go about building traps, so your tool kit will vary depending on what you want to catch, your location, and your methods.

Simple traps that can be set easily are available to buy, but aren't always affordable or portable. In a smaller survival kit, you can't haul around dozens of metal foothold traps that weigh multiple pounds each. But you can bring hundreds of feet of wire or line to build traps that can work just as well.

The simplest trapping tool kit includes:

- 50-100 ft. (15-30 m) of snare wire
- Cordage or strong fishing line
- A sharp and durable bushcraft knife
- A multi-tool

With two or three of these tools and materials, you can build a wide array of small game traps that can lead to a successful hunt.

Traps for Small Game

There are several categories of traps commonly used for trapping small game. The style you choose will depend on the species you are after, what tools you have available, and the environment in which you are building the trap.

Once you know the area and the animals that you can potentially trap there, you'll be able to choose and set up the right style of trap. This is an important first step in setting up any trap, as these are specific for each species. There's no trap that is a "one size fits all," and setting up the wrong trap may come at the cost of going to sleep hungry.

Traps have been developed over thousands of years, leading to a large number of different methods that are used around the world. This is a list of the most common traps. Try practicing each type of trap to find which ones suit your skills, region, and prey the best.

Snares

Snares are a simple concept. A wire or rope is set up as a noose to grab ahold of any part of an animal, typically the neck. Once the animal has entered the snare, the wire or rope cinches down tightly to either hold the animal in place, tightening it until the animal is strangled, or efficiently killing the animal by breaking its neck.

Game trails and dens are the best places to set up snare traps, as these are where animals most frequently travel. There are some exceptions to this, like squirrel snares that are set up along branches, which are akin to larger animals' game trails.

The various types of snares function off of the same basic premise, a noose that will kill an animal quickly. The snares below are different ways to set these up; pick the one that seems most appropriate for the species you are trying to trap.

• Tying a Noose for a Snare Trap

The knot used for a noose is called a poacher's knot and is incredibly simple. Take about a foot (30 cm) of cordage, depending on the size of the animal you are going to trap, and cut it from the spool.

1. Create a bight with the rope near the tail end and wrap the tail around both pieces of rope two times.
2. Pass the tail through the gap formed between the loops and the rope.
3. Pull this tight.
4. Adjust the size of the loop to the appropriate sizing for the animal you are trapping.

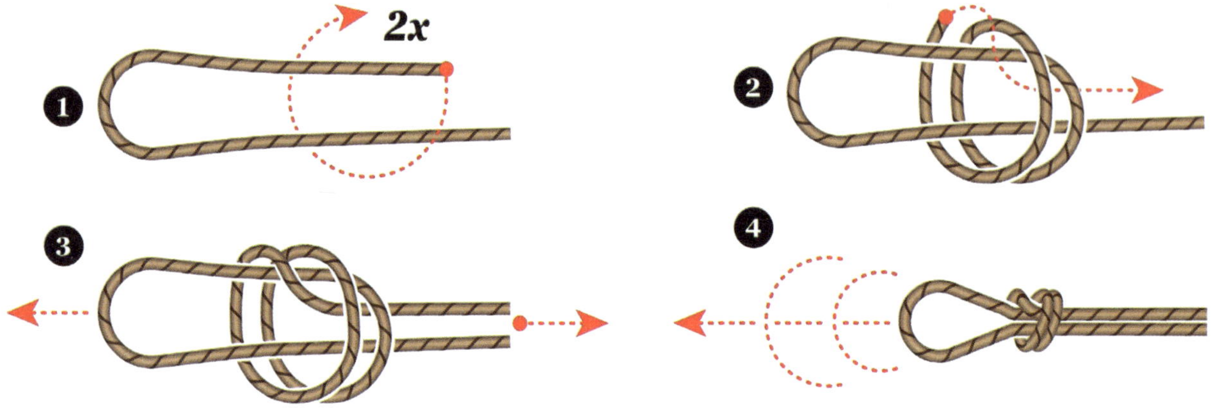

If you are using wire, your noose is even easier to make – simply make a small loop with one end of the wire, twisting the bottom of the wire to hold it in place. Then take the opposite end of the wire and put it through your loop, creating a snare loop/circle. Then tie off the end you put through the small loop, adjusting the circle to the size of the animal's head you are trying to trap.

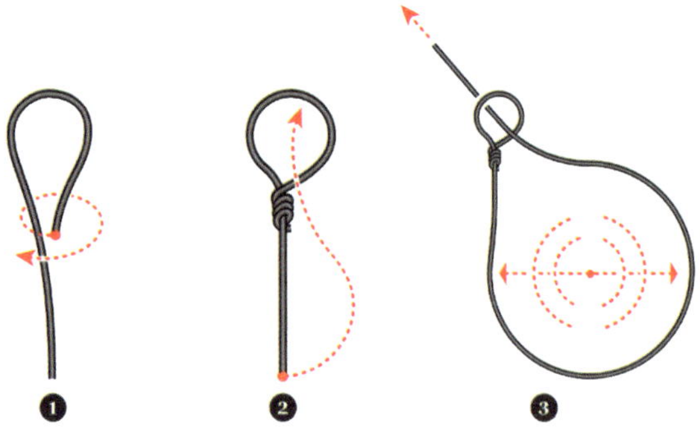

Setting Up the Wire Snare

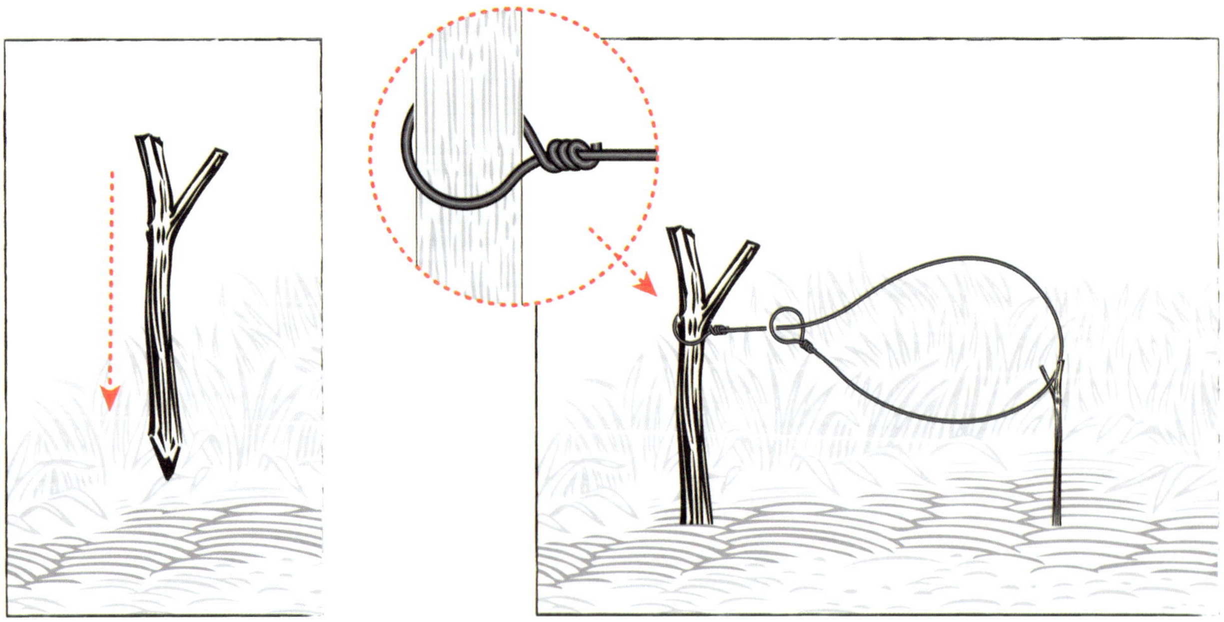

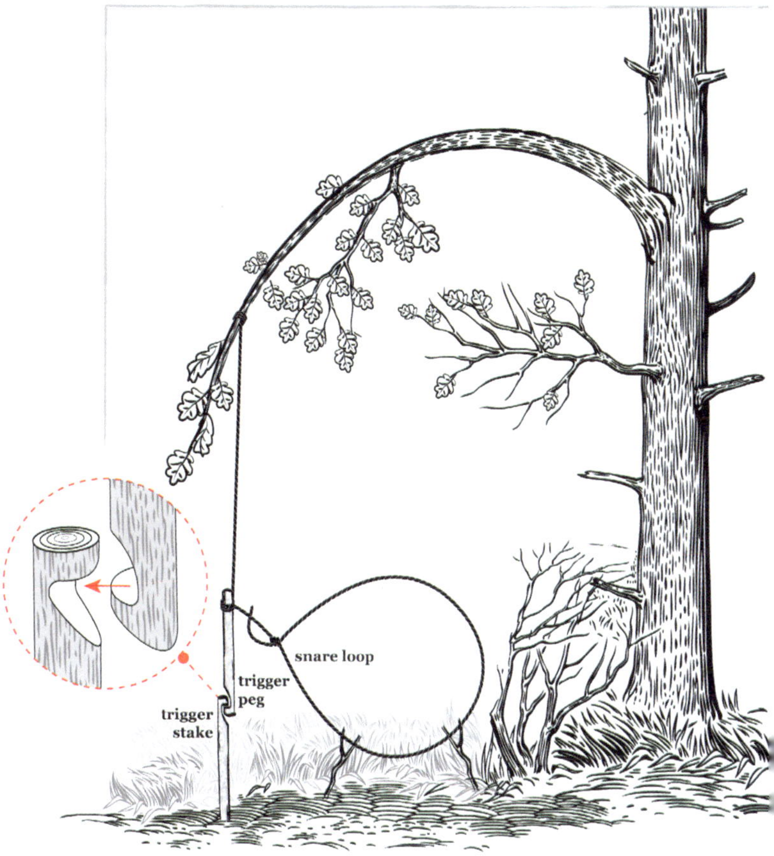

• Slip Noose Snare

The most basic snaring method is the slip noose. This is a wire or cord that is formed into a snare and positioned in the path of your target species. When the animal passes through the loop, the noose tightens down on the animal, trapping it in place, sometimes strangling it as the animal fights to break free.

One of the most important aspects of building a proper slip noose snare is getting the sizing right. This can make the difference between successfully trapping an animal and watching them just walk right through it or pushing the snare aside. A well-made snare will be big enough for the head of an animal to pass through it, but small enough to stop the torso from passing through. This creates just enough tension to tighten and trap the noose around the neck.

- If you're using rope, tie a poacher's knot and adjust the size of the loop for the animal's head. If you're using wire, follow the instructions in the last section.
- Use a stick to hang the noose from.
- Set the snare at the proper height for the animal's head.

If not using wire, use smaller pieces of fishing line to help maintain the shape of the snare if necessary.

• Trigger and Spring Snares

A simple snare with a trigger is like the slip noose, but with the addition of a trigger that greatly increases the likelihood of trapping an animal. The trigger will hold the snare in place until the animal passes through it and disturbs it. A bent sapling or a small stick works to then move the snare, encouraging it to take hold of the animal rather than letting it pass through.

Spring snares utilize a trigger and, usually, a bent sapling that acts as a spring to pull the noose tightly around the prey's neck and off of the ground. Bringing the animal up off the ground helps keep other predators from taking what you have caught before you check your traps, and often kills the animal more quickly.

- Make your snare and adjust the size of the loop for the animal's head.
- Find a branch or tree along the trail to act as the spring.
- Create a trigger stake and peg from a branch. Carve a down-facing notch in the stake and a notch facing up on the peg that will interlock under tension.
- Position the trigger stake firmly in the ground underneath the spring.
- Attach the snare to the spring pole and pull the pole down to put it under tension
- Tie the trigger peg to the line and connect the peg to the stake in the ground with the notches.
- Position the snare loop in the trail.

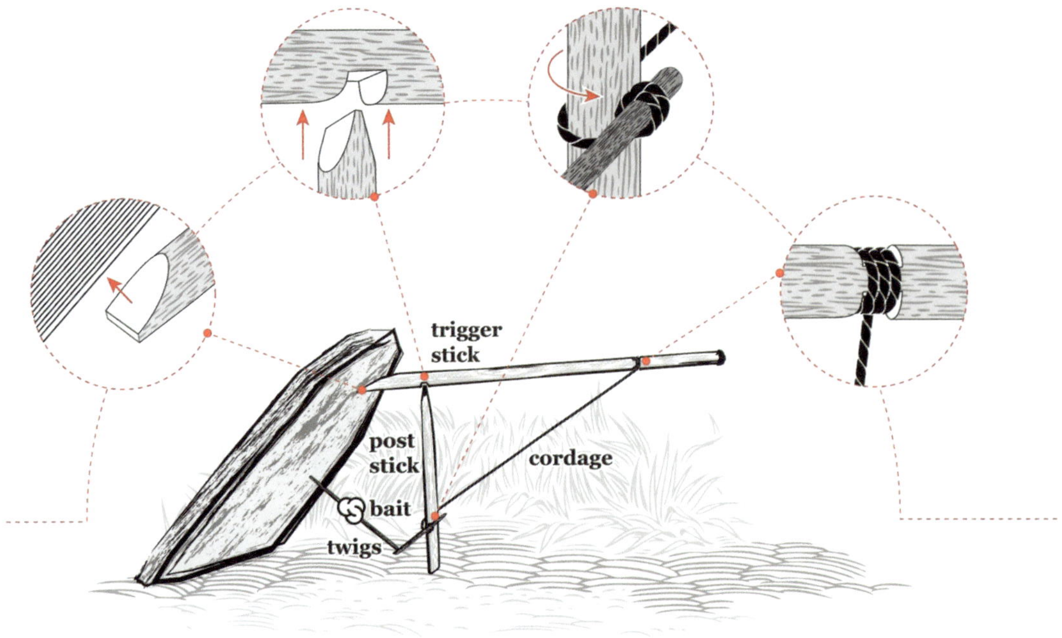

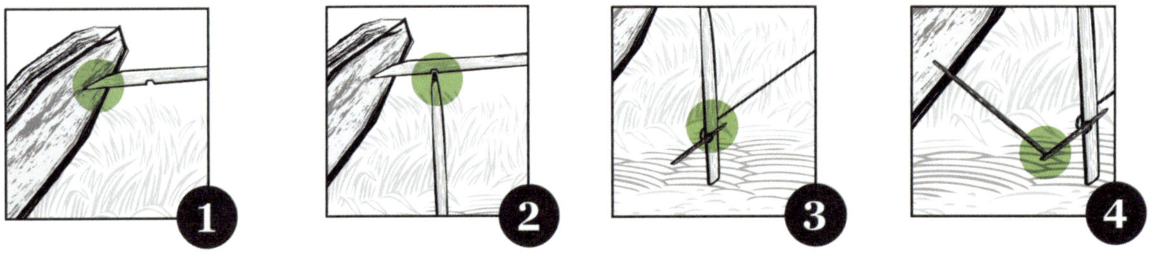

Deadfalls

There are two primary deadfall traps that work well for small game; the Paiute deadfall trap and the Figure Four trap. Both of these traps use sticks to balance heavier rocks or logs at an angle. The sticks have a baited trigger point that, when moved by an animal, will cause the rock to fall down on top of them.

Paiute Deadfall

The Paiute deadfall trap uses two main sticks that balance the rock in place and a string that provides the appropriate leverage that, when removed, will drop the rock.

To create a Paiute deadfall trap:

- Find two sticks that are about as thick as your index finger (thicker for larger traps).
- Cut the longer trigger stick between 8 and 10 inches (20 and 25 cm).
- On the trigger stick, rasp down one end of the stick with a gentle angle where the rock will balance. The goal is to make this part of the stick lie flat against a rock.
- At the beginning of this angled point, carve a notch on the opposite side of the trigger stick.
- On the other end of the trigger stick, carve a shallow ring around the end, where the cordage will sit.
- Cut the post stick to the length between the ring and the notch.
- Carve one end of the post to a point that will fit in the notch of the trigger stick.
- Tie a piece of cordage to the trigger stick the length of the distance from the ring to the end of the trigger stick.
- Attach a small twig to the end of that string.
- To set the Paiute deadfall:
- Set the trigger stick on top of the post, with the post resting in the notch.
- Holding the end of the trigger stick, balance a rock that leans onto the angled end of the trigger.
- Bring the twig on the cordage and wrap it once around the post, about one-third of the way up the post.
- Choose a small twig to be your bait stick that reaches from the cordage to the rock and carefully position it horizontally between the post and the rock to hold the cordage in position.

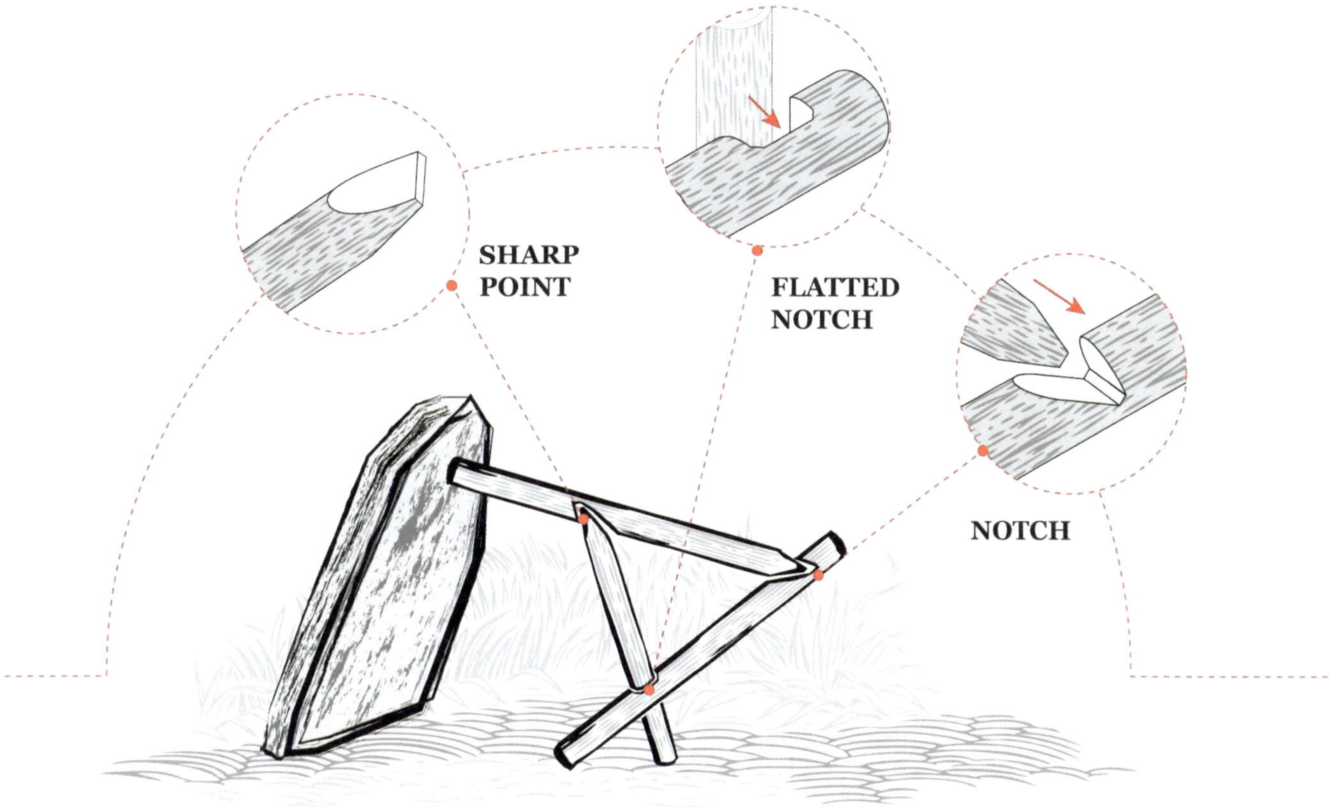

Figure Four Deadfall

A figure four trap is named after the shape it takes when fully constructed. There are three main sticks that use different notches to hold each stick in position, propping up a larger rock that will fall when triggered.

Building a figure four trap can be a bit more of an art than the Paiute deadfall, but the design can be used repeatedly. There are three main pieces, the vertical, diagonal, and horizontal sticks that are used for the construction.

- Carve the vertical stick by bringing one end to a sharp point and square off the sides. The vertical stick can be any size, depending on the size of your rock, but generally somewhere between 8 inches (20 cm) and 1 foot (30 cm) works well.
- Carve the diagonal stick by carving one end to a blunt rounded end that will fit up flush against the rock.
- Create a notch in the diagonal stick about 2 inches (5 cm) down from the rounded end. Use a hooked shape to help hold the vertical stick in place.
- Carve the other end of the diagonal stick to a flat point that will sit in the notch on the horizontal stick.
- Create the horizontal stick by carving a rounded point on one end. On the other end, carve a notch on the side it will be facing up, where the sharp end of the diagonal stick will be connected.
- On the "left" side of the horizontal stick, the side that will be up against the vertical stick, carve a flattened notch that holds the vertical stick in place with the backward pressure from the weight of the rock. This should be just big deep to hold the vertical stick, but not so deep it will hold it on its own.

Setting the figure four up involves putting the sticks together in the way they were designed and leaning a large rock onto the end of the diagonal stick. The pressure of the rock pushes down and back on the diagonal stick, holding everything in place. The horizontal stick is often baited where it sits right underneath the large rock.

Pitfalls

Pitfall traps are a simple system in which a hole is dug deep enough that an animal will be unable to crawl out of it. The depth of the hole may also act to wound the animal as it falls in, making it more difficult to escape. All pitfall traps should have completely horizontal sides, sometimes lined with wooden planks.

There are two main types of pitfall traps, wet and dry. The main difference is that wet traps use water at the bottom of the trap to drown thev animal once they land in the trap. This can be a highly effective method of ensuring that your prey doesn't escape.

This form of trapping small game can be effective, but can also be incredibly energy-consuming. There is a lot of energy that goes into digging a hole deep enough that animals cannot escape.

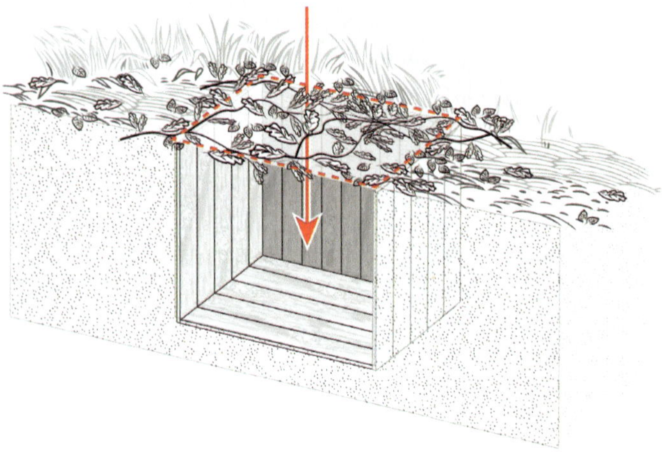

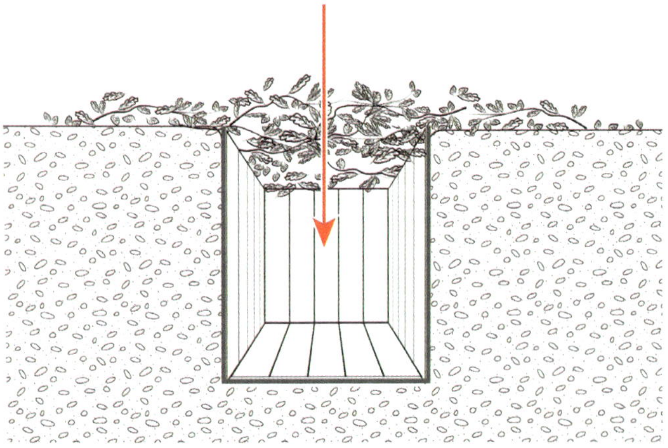

Funneling Traps

Most funnel traps are used for catching fish. These take the form of building a fish basket where a fish can enter, but will struggle to exit once it has been funneled into a smaller area. Another method is to build a shore trap that will funnel fish into a walled-off area when the tide rises, leaving them trapped as the tide wanes. Please see our chapter on fishing techniques on page 86.

Often, funnels are used alongside other types of traps. By using sticks and other branches to build a fence, the animal is forced towards the direction you want it to go. This can lead an animal towards a snare trap, deadfall, pitfall, or any method of trapping that you are utilizing.

The key to using funnels is to try and make them look as natural as possible. Branches with leaves may not force an animal in a certain direction, but it will encourage them to take the path of least resistance. This method is incredibly effective, unless the animal becomes suspicious of something that is new and different from the rest of their habitat.

Positioning Traps

One of the most important aspects of catching small game with traps is positioning them correctly.

There are two primary places where a trap is most successful; on a game trail, and outside of a den. These are the two places that animals travel frequently, increasing the odds of catching one.

To identify game trails, look for well-traveled paths that show signs of recent use. This can be signs of scat, tracks, browsing, or you may witness the animal using this path. This signs help tell you what is using that path and how long it's been since they were around. An old game trail that shows little sign of recent use is much less likely to provide.

Next, look for natural funneling points that use features like bushes or rock formations. If there are few natural funnels, you can build one that will gently guide the animal in the right direction.

Another thing to look for is a natural food source. If there are berries on a nearby bush, the animal you are after may be visiting that area more frequently and you can set a trap up on their trail nearby the berries.

When you have found the perfect location, setting the trap correctly includes positioning it at the right height. If there are no natural anchor points, you can drive a pole into the ground securely enough to act as an anchor or a spring for your trap.

Finally, when the trap is set, work on concealing it. This will help ensure that the animal doesn't sense anything is off and will still visit the area, rather than finding a new way around it. Animals can be highly intelligent, meaning you need to be even smarter.

Building Alarms

Since most traps won't be very close to your camp, building alarm systems to alert you when something is in the trap can help you get to the animal before any other predators do.

This can be a simple system where you tie fishing line to a bunch of old cans that hit against each other when the trap is triggered.

Fishing line can be run a long distance into camp where you can be waiting, out of view of the animal. With a good alarm system, you'll get fresh meat without having to check your traps every moment of the day.

Baiting Traps

Baiting traps can greatly increase the odds that you attract something to your trap.

The most important aspect in baiting traps is being familiar with the species you are targeting. This will tell you what they eat, what they are currently used to eating, and how to lure them in. If you use the right food during the right season, the animal will be likely to come for it.

Place the bait in a manner so that the animal will get caught in your trap. For a Paiute deadfall, it will be on the bait stick.

For snares, place bait near the snare so that the animal has to lean through the snare in order to reach the bait.

While artificial bait can be appealing, natural bait is often the most successful. This is what the animal is most accustomed to eating, so they will believe it to be safe. To bring the animal closer to your trap, you can create food scent trails to lure them in.

Above all else, be patient and learn to adapt. Baiting traps can be a bit of a science and it takes practice to learn your area as well as local animal habits. Be patient, try different baits in different locations, and set as many traps as you can. Trapping is a numbers game - you want as many traps working for you while you sleep as you can. Once you learn these trapping techniques, it will be an invaluable resource.

EDIBLE PLANTS, MUSHROOMS, AND POISONOUS LOOK-ALIKES

In this section, you will find 20 edible plants and mushrooms found in Europe. These plants include Fennel (*Foeniculum vulgare*), Borage (*Borago officinalis*), Plantain (*Plantago major*), Burdock (*Arctium lappa*), Old Man's Beard (*Clematis vitalba*), Butcher's Broom (*Ruscus aculeatus*), Stinging Nettle (*Urtica dioica*), Common Purslane (*Portulaca oleracea*), Elmleaf Blackberry (*Rubus ulmifolius*), White Goosefoot (*Chenopodium album*), Ramsons (*Allium ursinum*), Hops (*Humulus lupulus*), Elderberry (*Sambucus nigra*), Dandelion (*Taraxacum officinale*), Rough-stemmed Bolete (*Leccinum scabrum*), The Prince (*Agaricus augustus*), Cep (*Boletus edulis*), Honey Fungus (*Armillaria mellea*), Oyster Mushroom (*Pleurotus ostreatus*), and Chanterelle (*Cantharellus* spp.).

1. Fennel

Foeniculum vulgare, H. Zell - Own work, CC BY-SA 3.0

Description: Fennel (*Foeniculum vulgare*) is also known as sweet anise and common fennel. It is native to southern Europe in the region surrounding the Mediterranean Sea; however, it grows wild in most parts of temperate Europe.

Identification: This plant grows upright, up to 8 ft. (2.5 m) tall, although it does not usually reach that height. It has feathery, yellow-green leaves that are somewhat similar in appearance to those of carrots or dill. Its stems are hollow and its leaves grow up to 15 inches (40 cm) long. Fennel has a sweet, aromatic, licorice-like scent. It flowers in mid- to late-Summer. Its flowers are small and bright yellow, and attract bees and other insects. The flowers cluster together forming umbels, each umbel containing 20-50 flowers. Fennel seeds are 0.1-0.4 inch (4-10 mm) in length; they appear after the flowers.

Edible Parts: The leaves, seeds, and root are edible.

How to Eat: Fennel can be eaten raw or cooked. Its flavor is similar to that of anise (licorice-flavor), but not as strong.

Fennel flowers

Poisonous Look-Alike: Hemlock (*Conium maculatum*) is the most notable Fennel look-alike. It is a relative of Fennel, and when it is dried (dead), it looks very similar to Fennel. Hemlock, however, is highly poisonous. The easiest way to tell live Fennel and Hemlock plants apart is to look at their flowers. Fennel flowers are yellow, while Hemlock flowers are white. Although they do have some similarities, Hemlock seeds differ from Fennel seeds in that Hemlock seeds do not have the licorice-like smell that Fennel seeds have. To be safe, you should avoid collecting Fennel seeds from dried Fennel plants in the wild. When dried, the two plants look very similar, so you may actually be collecting poisonous Hemlock seeds.

Hemlock (*Conium maculatum*)

2. Borage

Bracken - *Pteridium aquilinum*, Björn S, CC BY-SA 2.0

Description: Borage (*Borago officinalis*) is also known as Cool Tankard, Cover Crop, Starflower, Tailwort, and Talewort. It is native to Syria, but now grows wild throughout most of Europe.

Identification: Borage grows upright, usually 2-3 ft. (~1 m) tall. Its stems and leaves have whitish hair-like bristles on them, and the leaves typically grow 2-6 inches (5-15 cm) long. Borage flowers are small, and can be blue or pink. Each flower has five triangular pointed petals, which makes the flowers appear star-like in configuration.

Borago officinalis, Giancarlo Dessi, CC BY-SA 3.0

Edible Parts: The stems, leaves, and flowers are all edible.

How to Eat: Borage can be eaten raw or cooked. The stems and leaves are frequently eaten in salads and soups. The taste is crisp and briny, like a salty cucumber. The flowers taste like honey, and are commonly used to decorate desserts. The seeds contain high amounts of the omega-6 fatty acid gamma-linoleic acid; their seeds are pressed to make borage seed oil.

Poisonous Look-Alike: The most important Borage look-alike is Foxglove. Foxglove is a fairly common plant that contains digitalis and other cardiac glycosides, which have very potent effects on cardiac function. The drug digoxin is extracted from the leaves of the foxglove plant. Just as taking too much digoxin can be lethal, consuming the foxglove plant can have toxic and even lethal effects. You can tell the difference between Borage and Foxglove by their flowers (obvious) or by looking at the hairs on the leaves. Borage has whitish hairs that are rough and similar to bristles, while the hairs on the Foxglove leaves are soft and similar to velvet. Foxglove leaves radiate outward from the center in a rosette configuration, and their underside has a grayish tint.

Foxglove

3. Plantain

Plantain *(Plantago major)*

Description: Plantain (*Plantago major*) is also known as Greater Plantain, Broadleaf Plantain, and Common Plantain. It is native to most of Europe and northern and central Asia.

Identification: This plant typically grows from 4 to 16 inches (10 and 40 cm) in height. The leaves of the Plantain plant radiate from a central point forming a rosette-like configuration. The leaves are rounded on one end and tapered to a point on the opposite end. Each leaf has 5 to 9 veins and averages 2 to 8 inches (5 to 20 cm) long and 1.5 to 3.5 inches (4 to 9 cm) wide. The flowers are small and greenish-brown. They grow upright on a long stem and have purple stamens.

Plantain (*Plantago major*)

Edible Parts: The leaves and seeds are edible.

How to Eat: The leaves can be eaten raw or cooked. The mature leaves are somewhat tough, but the young leaves are frequently eaten in salads. The seeds may be eaten raw or dried and used like a grain.

Notable Look-Alike: There are few plants that truly resemble plantain. Fortunately, they are all non-toxic. The most notable plantain look-alike is the Plantain Lily. The leaves of the Plantain Lily are larger than those of the Plantain plant, and Plantain Lily flowers are large and of various colors, whereas Plantain flowers are small and greenish-brown. Both plants are edible. The unopened shoots or the open leaves of the Plantain Lily can be eaten raw, cooked in a stir-fry, or used as a substitute for spinach. They are slightly crunchy, similar to Iceberg Lettuce, and their taste is described as a cross between a scallion and asparagus.

Plantain Lily

4. Burdock

Description: Burdock (*Arctium lappa*) is also known as Greater Burdock and Gobo. It is native to Europe and Northern Asia.

Identification: Burdock can grow as tall as 10 ft. (3 m) tall. Its leaves are dark green and can grow as long as 18 inches (45 cm). Most of the leaves are large and oval-shaped, but the leaves that grow toward the bottom of the plant are heart-shaped. The leaves are green and rough, and have hairs on the underside. Burdock contains burs that easily stick to animals or clothing and are difficult to remove. It blooms between July and October. The flowers are pink to purple, and there are spiky, green bracts at the bases of the flowerheads, similar to the flowers of Milk Thistle and other thistles.

Edible Parts: The roots, young leaves, and immature stalks of the plant are all edible.

How to Eat: Burdock root can be peeled, sliced, and eaten raw or cooked in a stir-fry or soup. It has a crunchy texture and sweet flavor, similar to that of Lotus Root. The young leaves and immature flower stalks can be harvested before the flowers appear, cooked, and eaten. The taste is somewhat bitter.

Deadly Nightshade (*Atropa belladonna*)

Poisonous Look-Alike: The most important Burdock look-alike is Deadly Nightshade (*Atropa belladonna*). Deadly Nightshade is highly toxic. It is sometimes confused with Burdock because their roots have similar appearances and they both can have purple flowers; however, Deadly Nightshade flowers do not have the thistle-like bracts that characterize Burdock, and Burdock does not have the shiny, black, poisonous berries that are typical of the Deadly Nightshade plant. Because of the risk of harvesting Deadly Nightshade instead of Burdock, it is important to only harvest Burdock from the wild when you have identified it with 100% certainty.

Notable Look-Alike: Burdock can also be confused with Rhubarb (*Rheum rhabarbarum*), which has triangular leaves and smooth, glossy, bright red stems, and it can be confused with Yellow Dock (*Rumex* spp.), which has darker green and smooth leaves. Fortunately, both Rhubarb (cooked) and Yellow Dock are edible.

Rhubarb (*Rheum rhabarbarum*)

5. Old Man's Beard Plant

Old Man's Beard (*Clematis vitalba*)

Description: Old Man's Beard (*Clematis vitalba*) is also known as Traveler's Joy. This woody vine is native to Europe and western Asia.

Identification: This vine typically grows up to 30 ft. (9 m) long, although it can grow as long as 100 ft. (30 m). It is commonly found in forests and woodlands, and can completely cover trees and other plants. It has branched stems, and its leaves are rounded on one end and tapered on the other. Each leaf has a partner on the opposite side of the stem, with the exception being the leaf at the very end of the stem. The vine blooms in summer. Its flowers are yellowish-white to greenish-white and they grow in clusters all over the vine. The flowers have a vanilla-like scent. In early autumn, fluffy seed heads that look similar to an old man's beard appear. While this vine loses its leaves in fall and winter, the seed heads remain.

Old Man's Beard (*Clematis vitalba*)

Edible Parts: The young shoots are the edible portion.

How to Eat: This plant must be cooked; it is harmful to humans when eaten raw. Heat causes the toxic constituents to break down and dissipate. The young shoots can be harvested, cooked, and eaten like the shoots of the Hops plant.

Poisonous Look-Alike: English Ivy (*Hedera helix*) is a toxic plant commonly confused with Old Man's Beard. English Ivy is also a woody vine that can cover the surrounding trees and ground, and it also has greenish-white to greenish-yellow flowers. You can tell the difference between the two by looking at the plants in winter. English Ivy is an evergreen, so it does not lose its leaves, whereas Old Man's Beard is a deciduous vine and loses its leaves in winter.

English Ivy (*Hedera helix*)

6. Butcher's Broom

Butcher's Broom (*Ruscus aculeatus*)

Description: Butcher's Broom (*Ruscus aculeatus*) is also known as Knee Holly and Piaranthus. It is native to Europe, the Black Sea area, Northern Africa, and the Azores.

Identification: The plant typically grows up to 3 ft. (1 m) in height. Interestingly, the leaves of this plant are technically microscopic. The leaf-like structures that we see are actually flattened shoots called cladophylls. Each leaf-like shoot is typically 1.5 inches (4 cm) long, dark green, oval-shaped, thick, and glossy. The plant is evergreen, so it does not lose its leaves in winter. Butcher's Broom blooms in late winter to spring. Each flower has 6 petals arranged in a star-like configuration. The flowers are greenish-white, and are followed by sphere-shaped, red berries that mature from late summer to winter.

Edible Parts: The young shoots and the seeds of the Butcher's Broom plant are edible.

How to Eat: The young shoots are typically harvested in spring. Cook and use as an asparagus substitute. The taste is pungent and bitter. The seed, which is within the fruit, may be roasted and used as a coffee substitute.

Poisonous Look-Alike: The most notable Butcher's Broom look-alike is Alexandria Laurel (*Danae racemosa*), which is also known as Poet Laurel. Alexandria Laurel is classified as toxic to humans. Like Butcher's Broom, it is an evergreen with berries and glossy green leaves. You can tell the difference between the two by looking at the flowers and berries. The flowers and berries of Alexandria Laurel are attached to stems or stalks, whereas the flowers and berries of the Butcher's Broom plant are not attached to terminal stems; instead, they appear to come directly out of the center of the "leaf."

Alexandria Laurel (*Danae racemosa*)

7. Stinging Nettle

Stinging Nettle (*Urtica dioica*)

Description: Stinging Nettle (*Urtica dioica*) is also known as Common Nettle, Burn Nettle, and Nettle Leaf. Stinging Nettle is native to Europe, temperate Asia and western North Africa; however, it is now found worldwide.

Identification: Stinging Nettle usually grows near water, and can grow 6 to 8 ft. (1.8 to 2.4 m) tall, though it's often shorter. Its leaves are thin, dark green, and covered in hair-like needles. The stinging needles can break off into your skin when you touch the plant, releasing chemicals like formic acid, serotonin, and histamine, causing an inflammatory reaction. Each leaf is 2 to 4 inches (5 to 10 cm) long, and is rounded at one end and tapered at the other. The leaves are partnered and situated opposite each other. Stinging Nettle blooms in summer to late autumn. It produces flowers that are small, green, and arranged in clusters on strands that are about 3 inches (7.5 cm) in length.

Stinging Nettle (*Urtica dioica*)

Edible Parts: The roots, stems, seeds, and young, tender leaves of the Stinging Nettle plant are all edible.

How to Eat: Stinging Nettle must be blanched or cooked to remove the stinging needles. The taste of Stinging Nettle is similar to that of spinach, but more potent. It is also highly medicinal, especially for allergies, RA, and inflammation.

Poisonous Look-Alike: Hemp Nettle (*Galeopsis tetrahit*) is the most notable poisonous Stinging Nettle look-alike. These plants can be mistaken for each other because they tend to grow in similar locations; however, you can tell the difference between the two plants as Hemp Nettle does not typically have the stinging hairs that characterize Stinging Nettle.

Hemp Nettle (*Galeopsis tetrahit*)

8. Common Purslane

Common Purslane (*Portulaca oleracea*)

Description: Common Purslane (*Portulaca oleracea*) is also known as Verdolaga, Little Hogweed, and Pusley. It is native to southern Europe and Asia; however, it now grows worldwide.

Common Purslane (*Portulaca oleracea*)

Identification: This plant grows more outward than upright. It typically grows about 8 inches (20 cm) tall, but spreads 1 to 2 ft. (0.3 to 0.7 meters) in an outward direction, forming a dense mat. In areas of high moisture, it can grow up to 16 inches (40 cm) tall. The stems have a red tint and are highly branched. The leaves are oval-shaped. Common Purslane blooms from late spring through late summer. Its flowers are small and yellow. Each flower contains 5 two-lobed petals.

Edible Parts: The entire plant is edible, but the leaves and stems are most commonly eaten.

How to Eat: Common Purslane can be eaten raw or cooked. It can be cooked in soups, sautéed, steamed, or pickled. The leaves are commonly added to salads. The flavor of Common Purslane is slightly sour or salty, and similar to that of watercress.

Poisonous Look-Alike: The most notable Common Purslane look-alike is the potentially toxic Prostrate Spurge (*Euphorbia humistrata*). Prostrate Spurge secretes a milky latex that can be toxic and cause blindness if it comes into contact with the eyes. You can tell the difference between Common Purslane and Prostrate Spurge by looking at their leaves. Prostrate Spurge has smaller leaves and stems than Common Purslane. Also, Common Purslane does not secrete a poisonous milky latex when cut, while Prostrate Spurge does. Also, Purslane has a yellow flower that is seldom seen and, after it is pollinated, its seed pods can hold many seeds.

Prostrate Spurge (*Euphorbia humistrata*)

9. Elmleaf Blackberry

Elmleaf Blackberry (*Rubus ulmifolius*)

Description: Elmleaf Blackberry (*Rubus ulmifolius*) is also known as Thornless Blackberry and Zarzamora. It is native to Europe and North Africa, but it has also been naturalized in parts of the United States, Australia, and South America.

Identification: This deciduous tree can grow up to 8 ft. (2.5 m) in height. Its leaves alternate up the stem, and each leaf is 1 to 3 inches (2.5 and 8 cm) in length. It blooms in late spring to summer. Its flowers can be pale pink or white. Each flower has 5 circular to oval-shaped petals, ranging 0.3 to 0.6 inch (8 to 15 mm) in length. The fruit is mostly round. Each berry is about 0.6 inch (15 mm) in diameter. It is green when young, turns red as it ripens, and is black when fully mature.

Edible Parts: The fruit is the edible portion of the Elmleaf Blackberry.

How to Eat: The fruit can be eaten raw or cooked. Its taste is slightly acidic, and it can be enjoyed alone or in desserts and other dishes.

Notable Look-Alike: Dewberries are the most notable Elmleaf Blackberry look-alike. They grow on a trailing bramble (rather than an upright bush or tree), and they rarely grow to be taller than 2 ft. (2/3 m). Their fruit is slightly larger than Elmleaf Blackberries. In addition to Dewberries, there are many other species of wild fruit that resemble blackberries, most of which are edible.

Dewberries

10. White Goosefoot/Lamb's Quarters

White Goosefoot (*Chenopodium album*)

Description: White Goosefoot (*Chenopodium album*) is also known as Lamb's Quarters, Baconweed, and Frost-blite. It is mostly native to Europe although some subspecies are believed to be native to North America.

Identification: It is an upright plant and can grow up to 6.5 ft. (2 m) in height, but is often much shorter. Its leaves are waxy, toothed, and diamond-shaped. Each leaf is approximately 1 to 3 inches (3 to 7 cm) long and 1 to 2 1/3 inches (3 to 6 cm) wide. It blooms from July to September. Its flowers are grouped into dense balls. They are small, green, and directly attached to the stem. The flowers form small seeds that are similar to quinoa or other cereal grains.

White Goosefoot (*Chenopodium album*)

Edible Parts: The seed, leaves, and young stalks are the edible portions of the plant.

How to Eat: Prior to preparing, the seeds should be soaked in water overnight and thoroughly rinsed to remove their saponins. They can then be cooked like a cereal grain. The leaves and young stalks can be eaten raw in salads, smoothies, and juices. They can also be steamed, sautéed, curried, and added to soups. The flavor is mild, and tastes like spinach when cooked.

Poisonous Look-Alike: Black Nightshade (*Solanum nigrum*) is a notable White Goosefoot look-alike that can be toxic under certain circumstances (use with care). For example, unripe Black Nightshade berries are toxic due to their solanine content. The leaves are considered to be toxic but young leaves may be eaten cooked. You can tell the difference between White Goosefoot and Black Nightshade by their flowers. Black Nightshade flowers are much larger than those of White Goosefoot. They are also white or violet and have five petals, compared to White Goosefoot's green flowers. Furthermore, Black Nightshade has round berries that are green when young and turn black when they mature, but White Goosefoot does not have such berries.

Solanum nigrum, Vinayaraj - Own work, CC BY-SA 3.0

11. Ramsons

Description: Ramsons (*Allium ursinum*) is also known as Wild Garlic, Cowleekes, Buckrams, and Eurasian Wild Garlic. It is native to the damp, shaded woods of Europe and northern Asia.

Identification: The Ramsons plant typically grows 6 to 12 inches (15 to 30 cm) tall. Its leaves are elliptical and grow up to 10 inches (25 cm) long and 2.8 inches (7 cm) wide. Ramsons bloom in mid-spring to early summer. Each flower consists of 6 white petals arranged in a star-like configuration and attached to leafless stems that rise above the leaves. The flowers are clustered together in groups of up to twenty. The root is white, bulb-like, and cylindrical.

Ramsons (*Allium ursinum*)

Edible Parts: The entire plant is edible, including the flowers and bulbs.

How to Eat: Ramsons can be eaten raw or cooked. The stems and leaves are typically added to salads for a subtle garlicky flavor. The bulb can be used as an equal-part replacement for garlic cloves in cooking. The flowers are typically used to garnish salads.

Poisonous Look-Alike: The most notable garlic look-alike is Lily of the Valley (*Convallaria majalis*). This medicinal plant contains potent active constituents that work on the heart muscle and can lead to death if unintentionally consumed. The leaves of Lily of the Valley and Ramsons are very similar; however, Lily of the Valley has white or pink bell-shaped flowers that are grouped together in clusters of 6 to 12 and confined to one side of the stem. Ramsons, on the other hand, has white star-shaped, six-petaled flowers that are grouped together on a sphere-shaped head. Furthermore, Lily of the Valley produces berries that eventually turn red, while Ramsons do not.

Lily of the Valley (*Convallaria majalis*)

12. Hops

Description: Hops (*Humulus lupulus*) is also known as Hop and Common Hop. It is native to Europe, Western Asia, and North America.

Identification: Hops can grow 25 ft. (7.5 m) tall. Its leaves are mostly divided or sharply toothed. Each leaf has 3 to 7 lobes and is 1 to 6 inches (2.5 to 15 cm) in length. Hops blooms from mid-summer to autumn. Its flowers are creamy yellow and clustered together. It has green strobiles that are similar in appearance to closed pine cones. The green strobiles grow up to 3 inches (7.5 cm) in length. They change to a straw-like color as they ripen, then turn brown and remain on the vine throughout the winter.

Edible Parts: The young leaves and shoots are edible.

How to Eat: The young leaves and shoots of the Hops vine can be eaten raw in salads or cooked. When cooked, their flavor is similar to that of asparagus or fiddleheads.

Notable Look-Alike: The most notable Hops look-alike is American Hophornbeam (*Ostrya virginiana*), also known as Hop Hornbeam, Ironwood, Leverwood, and Deerwood. You can tell the two apart as the Hornbeam catkin is easily opened to reveal almond-sized edible seeds that can be eaten raw or dry-roasted. Hops strobiles, on the other hand, are not as easily opened and do not contain an edible seed.

13. Elderberry

Description: Elderberry (*Sambucus nigra*) is also known as European Black Elderberry, Elder, and Black Elder. It is native to Europe, southwestern Asia, and northern Africa.

Identification: This tree grows 8 to 20 ft. (2.5 to 6 m) tall. Its leaves are rounded at one end and tapered at the opposite end. The leaves are paired, with the exception of the leaf at the very end of the stem. The leaves and stems have an unpleasant smell when they are crushed or cut. Elderberry trees bloom around June or July. Their flowers are white, very small, and clustered together. In autumn, the tree begins to produce its fruit. The fruit is glossy and dark purple to black. Each berry is 0.1-0.2 inch (3-5 mm) in diameter, and berries are clustered together.

Elderberry (*Sambucus nigra*)

Edible Parts: Both the flowers and the fruit are edible.

How to Eat: The flower clusters can be dipped in batter and fried. They have a sweetish taste. The petals can be eaten raw or steeped to make a tea. The berries should be cooked; their flavor is fairly bland, but they can be used to make jam, syrup, or desserts. They are also highly medicinal and commonly used as an antiviral.

Poisonous Look-Alike: The most notable Elderberry look-alike is Pokeweed (*Phytolacca americana*). It can be found in parts of southern and western Europe, including France, Italy, Spain, and Germany. Pokeweed has an unpleasant taste and the plant is highly toxic. It has reddish purple stems and its toxic berries change from green to dark purple when they are ripe. You can tell the difference between Elderberry and Pokeweed by looking at their berries. Pokeweed's berries are much larger than those of the Elderberry tree, and Pokeweed berries tend to hang in a cylindrical fashion. Pokeweed berries are typically 0.2 to 0.4 inch (6 to 11 mm) in diameter, with 6 to 12 seeds in each berry.

Pokeweed (*Phytolacca americana*)

14. Dandelion

Description: Dandelion (*Taraxacum officinale*) is native to Europe and Asia, although it has been naturalized throughout southern Africa, South America, Australia, New Zealand, North America, and India.

Identification: Its leaves are long, narrow, and irregularly lobed. They grow outward in a radial pattern. The leaves grow up to 10 inches (25 cm) long and up to 2.5 inches (6.3 cm) wide. Dandelions bloom in both spring and autumn. Their flowers are bright yellow with a light green stem that secretes a milky sap. The flowers eventually turn into a silvery-white, feathery mass of seeds.

Dandelion (*Taraxacum officinale*)

Edible Parts: The majority of the plant is edible. The only exception is the stem, which is hollow and contains a very bitter, milky sap.

How to Eat: Dandelion can be eaten raw or cooked. The leaves are frequently added to salads, although they do have a sharp and slightly bitter taste when mature. The roots have a turnip-like flavor and can be cooked and eaten like a vegetable. I like to batter the flowers and eat them like a fritter.

Notable Look-Alike: The most notable Dandelion look-alike is the edible Cat's Ear (*Hypochaeris radicata*). Cat's Ear has a flower that looks very similar to that of Dandelion; however, Cat's Ear does not have a hollow stem like Dandelion, and its stem branches, while Dandelion's stem does not branch. Cat's Ear also has hairy leaves, while Dandelion leaves are fairly smooth. Both are edible but Cat's Ear isn't as palatable due to its slightly hairy leaves.

Cat's Ear (*Hypochaeris radicata*)

15. Rough-Stemmed Bolete

Rough-stemmed Bolete (*Leccinum scabrum*)

Description: Rough-stemmed Bolete (*Leccinum scabrum*) is also known as Birch Bolete and Scaber Stalk. Thought to be native to the United Kingdom, it is now commonly found throughout mainland Europe as well as in North America.

Identification: This mushroom grows up to 8 inches (20 cm) high. It typically appears under Birch trees in summer and autumn. This mushroom can be various shades of brown, sometimes with a gray or red tint. There is also a rare unpigmented form that is all white. The cap of this mushroom is usually misshapen. When it is young, the surface of the mushroom cap is similar to that of velvet, but as the mushroom matures, it becomes smoother. The stem of the mature mushroom is typically regular in diameter, and it tapers slightly towards the cap. The flesh of the stem is white, and it can sometimes turn slightly pink when it is cut or broken. The flesh of this mushroom's stem will never turn blue when broken, which helps differentiate it from other mushrooms.

Rough-stemmed Bolete (*Leccinum scabrum*)

Edible Parts: The fruiting body (mushroom) is the edible portion.

How to Eat: This mushroom must be thoroughly cooked.

Notable Look-Alike: Greyshank Bolete Mushroom (*Leccinum cyaneobasileucum*) is a notable edible Rough-stemmed Bolete look-alike. You can tell these two apart by looking at their stems. The flesh of the stems of both the Greyshank Bolete and the Rough-stemmed Bolete are white, and both can turn pink when the mushrooms are cut. However, the Greyshank Bolete will always have a blue tinge where the mushroom has been damaged at the base, while the Rough-stemmed Bolete will never turn blue.

Greyshank Bolete Mushroom (*Leccinum cyaneobasileucum*)

16. The Prince

The prince (*Agaricus augustus*)

Description: Named and famed for its rich flavor, the prince (*Agaricus augustus*) is a close relative of the common button or cremini mushroom (*A. bisporus*). Common in Northern Europe and the British Isles, it is also found in the western United States, especially California and the Pacific Northwest.

Identification: Woodland margins and edges are the prince's preferred habitat, including hedges and thickets. In North America it is most common under conifers, but in Europe it is just as often associated with deciduous trees, particularly Holm oaks (*Quercus ilex*). Appearing from early summer to autumn (Jun-Oct), it grows in clumps rather than the "fairy rings" typical of other species in the genus. The ringed stalk is white, about 10 to 20 cm long, and scaly below the ring, a distinctive trait. The cap is white and covered with flat brown scales, which turn yellow with age. The gills are free, white in younger specimens but turning brown over time. The flesh is white, bruising yellow, and has a distinctive aroma often compared to almonds. The spore print is dark brown or purple.

The prince (*Agaricus augustus*)

Edible Parts: All parts of the fruiting body are edible. Older specimens are to be avoided, as the flesh is often mealy and infested with insects.

How to Eat: Delicious alone, especially sautéed in butter, or use in any recipe calling for button or portabella mushrooms.

Notable Look-Alike: The prince's combination of scaly stalk, flat brown scales, and almond-scented flesh are sufficient to distinguish it from most lookalikes. A number of amanitas are superficially similar to the prince, but have warty rather than scaly caps, and often have an unpleasant smell. Additionally, the flesh of amanitas turns yellow when bruised or broken. The inky mushroom (*Agaricus moelleri*) is similar in appearance, and is commonly found growing with the prince. It has yellow-staining flesh like the amanitas, and has a strong smell often compared to iodine or ink.

Inky mushroom (*Agaricus moelleri*)

17. Cep

Cep (*Boletus edulis*)

Description: The cep or penny bun (*Boletus edulis*) is one of the most popular and widely used wild mushrooms. It has a cosmopolitan distribution in the Northern Hemisphere, occurring throughout Europe and Asia as well as North America. It is also recorded in Australia and New Zealand, presumably as an introduced species.

Identification: Woodlands are the preferred habitat of ceps, which form symbiotic associations with forest trees. It is frequently associated with conifers, but can be found in mixed and deciduous forests as well. The fruiting bodies appear singly or in small clusters from mid-summer to late autumn (July-Nov), usually after a rain. They are quite variable in size, anywhere from less than 10 cm to 30 cm or more in diameter; smaller individuals are generally to be preferred, as they have a superior flavor and texture. The cap is dome-shaped and smooth, chestnut brown in color and with a velvety texture that becomes slightly tacky when wet. The underside of the cap is covered in small tubes, which are white when new and turn yellowish as they age. The stem ranges from 3 to 25 cm high and up to 8 cm in diameter, widening near the base; it is white in color and covered in a reticulate (net-like) pattern, which is most distinct at the top of the stem. The flesh is dense and white, unchanging when bruised or cut, and has a mildly sweet "mushroomy" smell.

Cep (*Boletus edulis*)

Edible Parts: All parts of the mushroom are edible, and the stem is as flavorful as the cap.

How to Eat: Ceps are edible and delicious in raw, cooked, or dried form. Raw, they are excellent in salads, and both fresh and dried ceps are commonly used in pasta, soups, and stews. They are also among the few mushrooms commonly eaten pickled.

Notable Look-Alikes: Ceps have few true lookalikes, and none of them dangerous — though some are unpalatable or mildly toxic. Most can be ruled out by their flesh, which will turn blue when bruised or cut. The devil's bolete (*Rubroboletus satanas*) has a similar shape to the cep, and can cause severe poisoning if ingested. However, it is unlikely to be confused with the cep, due to its vibrant red stem and unpleasant odor.

Devil's bolete (*Rubroboletus satanas*)

The bitter bolete (*Tylopilus felleus*) (has a similar appearance, including a reticulate stem like the cep's; it is not dangerous, but has an intensely bitter flavor that will spoil any dish to which it is added. It can be distinguished by its pore surface, which is pink rather than white, and by the dark reticulation on its stem (the stem of the cep is entirely white).

Bitter bolete (*Tylopilus felleus*)

18. Honey Fungus

Honey fungus (*Armillaria mellea*)

Description: The parasitic honey fungus (*Armillaria mellea*), sometimes called the stump mushroom or pinky, is easily recognized by its growth habit, emerging in large clusters from the base of infected trees. Native to Europe and eastern North America, it is widely reviled by foresters for the damage it does to forest plantations; it is also a choice edible, though only with proper preparation.

Identification: Honey mushrooms are parasites of trees: hardwoods, oaks in particular, are their preferred hosts, but they are occasionally found on conifers. Large clusters of mushrooms generally grow at the bases of infected trees, but may also grow on buried roots and dead wood, appearing to emerge directly from the soil. They emerge between summer and late autumn, most often after rain; in warmer climates they may appear well into winter. Individual mushrooms are quite variable in size and appearance: the golden-brown caps, 3 to 15 cm in diameter, are convex in younger specimens but flatten with age, often developing a depression in the center. The gills, which are attached and sometimes extend down the stem, are white initially but turn yellowish or brown as the spores develop, and leave a white spore print. The stems are 5-15 cm long and tough to the point of inedibility. Stems are golden-brown or dark brown at the base, fading to nearly white just below the cap, and often have a thin yellow ring. The flesh is white and not strongly scented, but is exceptionally bitter and astringent when raw.

Edible Parts: Generally only the caps of young specimens are eaten, as older specimens become unpalatably tough, even when cooked.

How to Eat: Honey mushrooms must be cooked thoroughly before eating, as they are not only unpalatable but mildly toxic raw. Some authors recommend blanching the mushrooms in boiling water (which is then discarded) before using them, to avoid undercooking and spoiling the flavor. In some individuals, honey mushrooms can cause stomach upset even when cooked, so eat them in moderation when trying them for the first time.

Notable Look-Alikes: Ceps have few true lookalikes, and none of them dangerous — though some are unpalatable or mildly toxic. Most can be ruled out by their flesh, which will turn blue when bruised or cut. The devil's bolete (*Rubroboletus satanas*) has a similar shape to the cep, and can cause severe poisoning if ingested. However, it is unlikely to be confused with the cep, due to its vibrant red stem and unpleasant odor.

Funeral bell (*Galerina marginata*)

Sulphur tuft (*Hypholoma fasciculare*)

19. Oyster Mushroom

Oyster mushroom (*Pleurotus ostreatus*)

Description: The oyster mushroom (*Pleurotus ostreatus*), as well as numerous other species in the genus) is a choice edible, not only for its flavor and texture but its reliability, emerging from the same tree year after year. It is also one of the best mushrooms for beginning foragers, as its distinctive appearance makes it relatively easy to identify. Oyster mushrooms have an extremely broad geographic distribution, with *P. ostreatus* occurring throughout the Northern Hemisphere and closely related species found nearly worldwide.

Identification: Oyster mushrooms grow on dead wood of deciduous trees, particularly beeches (*Fagus* spp.), appearing most abundantly in autumn. Mushrooms appear in overlapping, shelf-like clusters of asymmetrical, seashell- or kidney-shaped caps 6-14 cm in diameter and gray-brown in color. The caps of younger specimens have a distinctive silvery or metallic sheen and often curl strongly downward at the edges, flattening and often splitting as the mushroom grows. The gills are white but turn yellow with age, and like chanterelles are somewhat decurrent, extending down the stem. The stem itself is often rudimentary or absent, but may grow up to 7 cm long in some individuals. When present it often has an s-shaped curve, and is almost always attached asymmetrically to the cap. The flesh of both cap and stem is dense and white, with a mild, sweet smell that is difficult to describe but easy to recognize and quite distinctive.

Oyster mushroom (*Pleurotus ostreatus*)

Edible Parts: The entire mushroom is edible, though the stem (when present) is often too tough to be worth eating. Oyster mushrooms are frequently infested with insects, even when young, so inspect your harvest carefully before eating.

How to Eat: Oyster mushrooms should be cooked, as their meaty texture is almost unpleasantly rubbery when raw. They tend to absorb flavor from other ingredients, which combined with their firm flesh makes them quite versatile: they can be stir-fried, deep-fried, grilled and even pickled.

Notable Look-Alikes: Oyster mushrooms have few lookalikes outside of their genus, nearly all of them easy to distinguish with careful observation. The mock oysters (*Phyllotopsis nidulans*) resemble yellow or orange oysters and have a strongly unpleasant smell.

Mock oysters (*Phyllotopsis nidulans*)

Jack-o'-lantern mushrooms (*Omphalotus olearius*) have a similar growth form, emerging in shelf-like clusters from rotting wood, but are orange inside and out (and glow in the dark). The ivory funnel (*Clitocybe dealbata*) is common and highly poisonous, with an appearance sometimes strongly reminiscent of oysters. However, it grows from soil rather than dead wood, and never emerges in large clusters like oysters.

Jack-o'-lantern mushrooms (*Omphalotus olearius*)

20. Chanterelle

Chanterelle (*Cantharellus* spp.)

Description: The distinctive saffron color and complex, peppery flavor of the chanterelle (*Cantharellus* spp.) has made it one of the most iconic wild mushrooms, though in fact the name "chanterelle" refers to over a dozen species with a similar appearance and flavor. Widespread throughout Eurasia and North America, they are easily distinguished from lookalikes by their thick forked 'gills', which are actually folds on the underside of the cap.

Identification: Chanterelles grow in woodlands and forests, particularly beneath conifers and beeches. They are found from mid-summer to late autumn and even into the winter in mild climates. The striking golden-yellow caps, 3-10 cm in diameter, are asymmetrical and somewhat irregular in shape: flattish when young, becoming strongly concave or funnel-shaped as they grow. The primitive "gills" of true chanterelles are really no more than blunt folds in the cap and share its distinctive coloring. They are strongly decurrent (extending down the stem) and distinctively forked — a key trait in ruling out lookalikes. The stems are similar in color, though often paler, and taper towards the base. The flesh is white or pale yellow and has a faint, sweet scent often described as reminiscent of apricots.

Clitocybe dealbata, Dick Culbert, CC BY 2.0

Edible Parts: All parts of the mushroom are edible.

How to Eat: Chanterelles have a rich, complex flavor, ranging from fruity to slightly spicy, and are quite versatile: they can be eaten alone, sauteed in butter or olive oil, or added to sauces for both flavor and color. They do not freeze well but are excellent candidates for drying as they lose none of their flavor. Freshly harvested chanterelles are often quite dirty and absorb water when rinsed, so clean with a dry brush before using or storing.

Notable Look-Alikes:

The false chanterelle (*Hygrophoropsis aurantiaca*) has a similar shape and color to true chanterelles, and though it has true gills, these may be forked and/or decurrent, giving it a similar appearance overall. It is deep orange rather than yellow, and its gills are more densely packed than the false gills of chanterelles. It is also relatively soft and flimsy, where true chanterelles are quite sturdy.

False chanterelle, *Hygrophoropsis aurantiaca*

Jack-o'-lantern mushrooms (*Omphalotus olearius*) are similar in color and have decurrent gills like true chanterelles, and though they grow on decaying wood, they may appear to grow from the ground if growing on roots or buried logs. Unlike chanterelles their gills do not fork, and their flesh is orange rather than white. Neither the false chanterelle nor the jack-o'-lantern mushroom has the distinctive apricot aroma of true chanterelles.

Jack-o'-lantern mushrooms, *Omphalotus olearius*

FISHING TECHNIQUES

Fishing is one of the best ways to secure a high-protein meal with a minimal expenditure of calories. Remember, you can only carry so much in your pack and thousands of calories of meat probably aren't in your weight budget. Therefore, you need to be prepared for, and practiced at, fishing. This includes items you bring with you and tools you can improvise in the field. Here we'll look at various fishing techniques, including traditional fishing methods.

Fishing With Line and Hooks

It will never be easier to fish than with modern equipment. When and where possible, pack a small amount of line, hooks, weights, and bobbers. There is a lot of flexibility in modern fishing tools. Here are several traditional methods and a few improvised survival counterparts.

Hooks

Nothing will beat a modern barbed hook. Their shape, size, and strength have been perfected for landing that trophy trout or bass. You can approximate it, but you will be hard-pressed to create the equivalent of a modern fishing hook. Much like making a fire, the knowledge that comes with improvising a fire is great, but when you need to get warm, a Bic lighter is always easiest. Make some room in your pack or EDC (every day carry) kit for a few hooks and a few lengths of fishing line. It'll make catching a meal much easier.

If you find yourself in need of a hook, you can still improvise one. Start with metal options, as they will be the easiest and strongest.

You can convert a pull tab from a can into a hook with a pair of tin snips, or with the careful use of a knife. Cut the tab in such a way that it forms a 'J' or a hook shape. Nipping off one side at an angle and then a little more at the top (e.g., remove from 7 o'clock to 11 o'clock) and you will have shaped a simple hook.

Hook from a pull tab

Similarly, if you have a safety pin, you can shorten the free side and make a hook. The stronger the pin, the better your chances that it will survive the struggle with a fish. The same can be done with a paper clip. Simply bend the paperclip into a fishing hook shape, making sure to include an eye to attach the string to, and you will have a passable hook.

You can store a few pins and paperclips in your kit or pocket (or, even better – hooks). Likewise, if you pass a discarded can, pull off the tab and add it to your pack.

The next option for a hook is to make one out of bone or wood. In both cases, you will want to leverage natural shapes that resemble hooks for strength. When using bones, the wishbone of a bird is the perfect shape for fashioning a hook. Simply cut one end shorter than the other. Do this at an angle to create a hook. For carving your own from a branch, use the crotch of two branches. This is where the strength lies. Cut a point on one end and carve a groove on the other end to hold the string. If you're careful with both, you can even carve in a little barb to hold the fish fast to the hook.

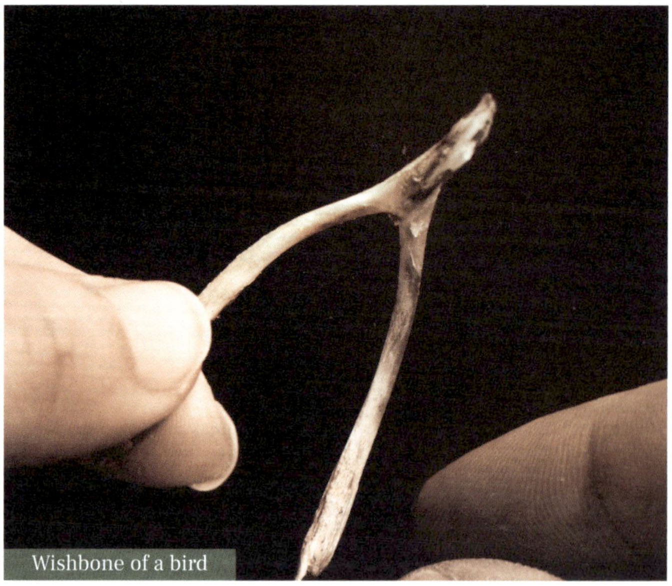
Wishbone of a bird

If you can't find an appropriately shaped stick, you can create a gorge hook. A gorge hook is simply a small stick sharpened on both ends. Fashion one from a branch, a long thorn, or even a splinter of bone. The goal is to attach the line to the center of the hook and bury ¾ of it in your bait. Leave the free end parallel to the line pointing back along the line. The goal of a gorge hook is to allow the fish to swallow it and then set the hook not in the mouth but in the throat or stomach.

Gorge hook

Traditional Fishing

Now that you have your selection of hooks, commercial or improvised, it's time to go fishing. The first method is to attempt traditional casting. Attach your line to an improvised pole and toss the line into the river or pond and wait. If you get a nibble, then set the hook and bring the fish to land.

You won't be able to cast as far and reel as smoothly, but with practice it is possible. If you're using an improvised hook, be ready to lose a few fish. Just don't give up.

Trot Line and Jug Line

A better approach is to let your equipment do all the work. In a survival situation, it's best to conserve calories when and where possible. If you can set a line out for hours at a time, then do it. The best way to accomplish this is with a trot line.

A trot line is a main line that has multiple hooks attached to it with a land anchor at one end and a water anchor at the other. You can also attach a float or jug to create a jug line. As the jug floats, it keeps the hooks off the bottom or at a specific depth.

Regardless of your layout, the goal is to string several hooked lines onto the main line and then set it in a river, lake, or ocean and let it sit. After a few hours or overnight, pull in the line with the hope that some of the hooks have caught fish. Just like setting snares or a trap line, a trot line does all the work while you are free to tend to your fire, gather and process wood, forage for other edibles, or sleep.

Limb Fishing

Limb fishing keeps your line offshore and off the bottom of the river or pond and is as simple as tying the line to a long limb and hanging it over the water. You will need to anchor your improvised fishing pole and tether it to the shore. A few rocks over the shore end of the pole will keep it in place but I prefer to tie the pole to an additional anchor. It does you no use if you see your pole being dragged away by a sizeable fish.

You can also tie your line to the limb of an overhanging branch of a tree. If you choose this method, do so carefully. Adding injury to starvation will not help your success.

Net Methods

Netting fish improves your chance of success given a few factors. First, you will need a net. The manufacture of a net in the field works but they're lightweight and easy to bring with you. Creating a useful net requires a great deal of practice. You need to know the knots and need to know your target species. Tie a net with holes that are too large and you'll let many meals through to freedom. Making a net with small holes may be a waste of time and materials.

You will need a lot of rope to make a net of a useful size. One of your best options is to disassemble a length of paracord and separate the internal strands. Using these you can string together a net. For example, a 4-foot (1.2 m) square net with 1-inch (2.5 cm) holes will require approximately 96 4-foot lengths of line or nearly 400 feet of rope.

If net-making is beyond your time and skill level, then pack a small net. This is especially true if your travels take you along streams, rivers, ponds, lakes, and coastal regions.

With this in mind, let's look at fishing options for your commercially manufactured or expediently made net.

Dip Net

Dip netting is simply scooping fish out of the water. Maybe it's not this easy, but the process is simple. Dip netting requires a hoop to keep the net open while you scoop for your quarry. Often, the hoop is attached to a stick or handle, providing you with additional reach.

A dip net is also useful if you catch a fish on a line. Many people lose their fish when they are bringing it to shore; a dip net increases your chances of keeping the fish you catch.

Virginia State Parks staff - Jr rangers with dip nets
Uploaded by AlbertHerring, CC BY 2.0

To be successful at dip netting you need to know where the fish are. You can cast your success to chance, but it's more expedient to know where the fish are first. There are several ways to increase your chances. First, lure them in. This is particularly useful when catching bait fish (smaller fish that are fed upon by larger fish). Baiting is also useful when fishing for crabs. Any bit of food will bring them over in numbers.

You can openly bait the water (e.g., cut and cast bait near you like chum). You can also anchor the bait and run the dip net in the area, scooping up anything that comes by. Finally, you can bait the net. As fish enter the net to get to the food, scoop them up. Once you have caught one fish, you can use their entrails to bait for additional meals.

Cast Net

Esin Üstün from Istanbul, Turkey - Cast Net Thrower, CC BY 2.0

Out of all the netting techniques, cast netting requires the most skill. It also requires a correctly shaped and weighted net. A cast net is usually a large circle that has weights around the perimeter. When thrown, a cast net spreads out to its full diameter. When it is pulled in, it traps the fish within it.

You can't cast a square net and expect the same results as a proper cast net. Likewise, casting even the proper net requires practice and perfection of form. That being said, for open water such as lakes and coastal regions, it can be very effective in collecting many meals in one successful cast.

Gill Net

Gill net fishing, PoojaRathod - Own work, CC BY-SA 4.0

Keeping with the idea of letting your equipment do the work for you, a gill net is an ideal solution. A gill net is shaped and sized for a specific size or species of fish. They are designed to tangle and bind the fish as they swim through the net. With holes too big, the fish swim straight through. If the holes are too small, the fish won't get tied up in the net. Target the species of fish in your area.

For survival use, spread a gill net across flowing water, anchored at each end. This will either be across a stream or river or across the tidal flow of an ocean or a large lake. As the fish follow the flow of water, they pass through and get caught up in the net. Once you have it strung, your work is over; let the net do its work. After a few hours or overnight (or at low tide), the net is retrieved and any fish in it are harvested.

When placing the net, make sure that you anchor it properly. Ideally, you want it upright, with the bottom anchored to the bottom of the stream, if possible. This keeps fish from swimming under it. Note that gillnetting is illegal in most places for the majority of people - it is usually only used in a true survival situation or with a special license.

Trap Methods

A modification of the concept of a net is a trap. A trap uses a porous design that allows water to flow through while catching any fish that enter it. Most fish traps use a funnel shape just large enough that the fish can make their way into the trap. The funnel is small enough at the bottom that the fish can't find their way out. There are several variations to this design.

Basket Trap

Basket traps are used around the world. A basket is woven in a shape that includes a funnel and a holding chamber. The basket is then anchored in a water body and left to soak for several hours or days. The basket is woven in two halves: the funnel and the holding chamber. This design allows easy access to the fish after the soak. Simply pull the trap out of the water, separate the halves, and pour the fish into your holding vessel.

To make a basket, you need two materials. First, you'll need thin and pliable sticks. Green wood ½" in diameter or less will form the sides of your trap. Often, people would cut a tree down and then, after a year or two, harvest the shoots growing from the stump. This process is called coppicing (please see our chapter "Tending the Land: How to Cultivate the Land and Food" on page 106). The root system of the tree has enough energy to send up shoots from on and around the stump. These are perfect for basket making.

If you can't find a coppiced tree, work with any pliable saplings or branches. If you can find a willow tree, harvest all the thin branches within reach. These will be your spokes.

Next, you will need a material to weave between the spokes. Again, thin branches will work, but if you can find vines, they will work better. If you have a surplus, then paracord or the inner strands from paracord will also work. You may also use bark stripped from larger branches, though this requires long branches without smaller branches off the main branch. Each hole in the bark will be a weak point that will break as you try to weave it.

Start by binding several spokes together. Select an odd number of spokes and then tie one end together with your vines, bark, or rope. Now start weaving, over under style, spreading the basket apart. The goal is to make a wide vase. It needs to hold several fish comfortably. Continue weaving, over and under, tucking in the end of each vine as you use up its length. At the end, you should have a wide cone.

Basket trap - main cone

Now repeat the process, however, use spokes that are ½ to ⅓ the length of your main basket. Make a similar cone to your first basket with the base the same size as the top of the first basket. Weave it down so the top diameter is 3 inch (7.5 cm) or smaller. Weave the funnel over and under just as you did the main basket.

Basket trap - second cone

Basket trap - both cones

Basket trap - complete

An easier variation on the basket trap can be made with a plastic 1-liter or 2-liter soda bottle. Cut off the top where the shape changes from a slope to the straight sides. Next, punch several small holes in the bottom of the bottle to allow water to flow. Finally, invert the top (without the cap) and put it into the body of the bottle. The result will be a bottle with a funnel. This works surprisingly well, especially for catching bait fish or many small fish to make a meal.

Bottle trap

Bottle trap setup

To use your trap, add bait to the bottom of the main basket (e.g., fish entrails or worms) then place the funnel in the main basket. Tie the two together so they don't separate in the water, weight it down (rocks work well), and place it in an area with good flow and let it soak. Even with the soda bottle trap, you can catch bait fish to use for other fishing options (e.g., hook and line) or simply boil the fish and eat them whole.

Weir

A fish weir is a trap that you can build within a stream, river, or tidal zone. Just like a basket trap has a funnel and holding area, a weir has the same.

Weir using rocks - underwater image

Weir illustration using sticks

Start with building a funnel-shaped damn out of sticks, logs, or rocks. The funnel will direct fish into the holding chamber that you will build next. Simply extend the sides of the funnels in a circle creating a holding area. The result will be a trap that the fish can swim in but can't find their way out. It should look like the cross-section of your basket trap. Stop by the weir daily and net out or pull out any fish within it.

Natural Chemicals

One way to capture the fish in your weir, or in any enclosed or pooled area, is with chemicals that stun fish. Mullein, black walnuts, pokeberries, and several other plants contain natural toxins that will stun fish.

Each of these plants can be safely used to stun fish, making them easier to catch and gather. For example, if you have built a weir, you can crush mullein seeds and add a small handful to the weir. The fish in the trap will soon be stunned and easy to collect. After gutting them, make sure to wash them off in fresh water to remove any of the toxins. Beyond foraging, there are many uses for plants that are worth learning. Knowing plants that can be used for fishing can increase your chance of success.

Bludgeon and Spears

Fishing can be finessed with line and hook or can be accomplished via a wait-and-see technique with traps. The last method for gathering protein is with brute force.

Bludgeon

For fish near the surface, try smacking one with a stick. Green wood works best as it has a little spring to it and is less likely to break when it hits the water.

Start with selecting a sapling the same length as your height. You can go shorter, however, you will want some reach. Next, trim off any branches to leave your staff smooth and easy to grab. Finally, when you see a fish near the surface, quickly swing the bludgeon down onto the fish.

Spears and Gigs

A little more finessed than smacking a fish with a stick is using a spear or gig. A spear can be as simple as a sharpened stick or it can be a spearhead made from found materials (knife or shard of glass), or with a flint-knapped spear point. If you choose to sharpen a stick, dried wood will hold a point better and you can further harden the wood, especially green wood, by fire hardening. To do this, sharpen a green stick to a blunt point, then roast it over an open fire to drive out the water and harden the tip. Once it cools, continue sharpening it to a point.

A gig is like a spear. However, a gig will have more than one point. Once you have selected your staff, split the end into two- or four-pieces, either through splitting it with a hatchet, or batoning it with your knife. To keep the sections separate, place a thin stick in between the two halves. Lash the one or two spreaders into place with vines or cord. Next, sharpen each split section to a point.

For both spears and gigs, you may want to add a barb to the point(s). This may weaken the points so it will take a little trial and error.

When using both spears and gigs, remember that refraction fools the eye. When spearfishing, the fish appears higher in the water than it actually is. You will need to aim lower in order to hit the fish. The deeper in the water, the lower you will have to aim.

Spear

Gig

HOW TO TAP TREES

How to Tap Trees

Trees can be a rich source of clean water and nutrients that can provide much-needed hydration and energy. This comes in the form of tree sap - the water and nutrients that the tree is bringing in and turning into its own food.

The problem is how to access the hundreds of gallons of flowing sap that moves through the tree throughout the season. The sap flows through the cambium layer of the tree, often protected by a thick bark that can make the sap difficult to obtain, especially in a survival scenario.

With the right methods, accessing the sap and consuming the nutrients and minerals inside of it is simple, leading to a magnificent source of hydration and nutrition.

What is Tree Sap?

Well-known for being a sticky substance that gets all over your clothes when you accidentally brush against a tree, tree sap is much more than this thick sticky residue.

Tree sap is made up of both the xylem and phloem of the tree's cambium layer. The xylem transports nutrient- and mineral-rich water up the tree to the limbs and leaves to help provide energy for photosynthesis. Xylem dies off each year, leaving behind rings, which may be counted to ascertain the tree's age. This is why tree rings are good indicators of drought years, as the xylem cannot grow as much when it lacks sufficient water.

Phloem, on the other hand, holds the sugars that are made during the photosynthetic process and are used during the tree's growing season. Phloem is much more nutrient-dense, but note that neither xylem nor phloem are as nutrient-rich as the fruits and nuts that trees produce.

When certain creatures feed on sap (many birds, bats, squirrels, and even porcupines), they need to ingest a large amount in order to get the sustenance they need. The same goes for humans, as most of the sap we take out of trees for syrup production is made up of water. We boil this down, evaporate the water, and are left with a thick sugary substance that we drizzle over our favorite breakfast foods.

The tree sap that we take from trees and use is from the xylem of the tree; when we tap trees, usually late winter/early spring, there is stored sugar flowing through the tree's xylem. This is a watery, semi-sweet substance that can be consumed just like you would drink water. In a survival situation, you can use this for both hydration and to get a few calories. A fully-grown maple tree can produce around 15-20 gallons (57-76 liters) of sap each year.

What Trees Provide Edible Sap

Maple trees are well-known for their sap and the syrup we make out of it, but they aren't the only trees that we can tap. Birch trees are a popular tree that we make syrup from, but their sap is significantly lower in sugar content when compared to maples. Birches do, however, have a large number of minerals and antioxidants in their sap.

White walnuts, black walnuts, heartnuts, and English walnuts produce a sap that is both delicious and nutritious. Even sycamore trees are well-suited to be tapped if you are merely looking for a source of hydration, and not to make syrup.

The largest difference between the sap of these tree species is the sugar content. Sugar maples are the most popular for syrup producers because they produce one gallon (3.8 liters) of syrup for every forty gallons (151 liters) of sap collected.

For comparison, a birch tree will produce a gallon (3.8 liters) of syrup for every 150-200 gallons (567-757 liters) of sap collected. For those in survival scenarios, or those living in the wild long term, sugar content is important for surviving off of sap as one of your main sources of caloric uptake. Maples are going to have more calories per ounce because of the higher sugar content than birches will provide.

When to Collect Sap

Unfortunately, the sap isn't flowing all year long. It starts to move around in the springtime for most maple trees, and birch trees don't start flowing until right around when the maples stop.

The best time to collect sap is when the nighttime temperatures are dropping below freezing and the daytime temperatures are reaching upwards of 40 degrees Fahrenheit (4 degrees Celsius).

For maple trees, this tends to happen between mid-February and mid-March. Birch trees can be tapped around the second week of March, right before the leaves come back, and need the water and nutrients that the sap provides.

How to Tap Trees for Sap

In this section, we will go over the way in which trees are typically tapped outside of a survival situation. In the wild, you'll be lacking the same tools, but using similar methods to achieve the same result.

Selecting the Trees to Tap

The first step is choosing the right trees to tap. This starts with species identification and finding the right maple, birch, walnut, or sycamore tree.

Since tapping trees happens in the winter, tree identification can be more difficult without leaves to look at. The bark will be the most distinguishing feature for most of these species. Maples and birches grow in abundance, so once you find one, you're likely to find several.

Adult sugar maple trees characteristically have grayish brown bark with rough vertical plates or ridges running along it. The older the tree, the more ridges present. A silver maple has longer strips of bark that flake and can grow more erratically than their cousins. Red maples are smoother, but will become darker and furrowed with age. Younger maples will all have smooth gray bark.

Any species of birch will work to tap, but the yellow birch is popular for its higher level of antioxidants. The bark of birch trees has light-colored white, yellow, or gray bark that often separates into thin strips and peels away from the trunk. They are also marked by lenticels (long horizontal dark and raised lines).

After you find the right species, you need to find the right size. Try to choose trees that are healthy and more mature, as tapping them will be less harmful to the tree and will produce a higher sap yield. Choose trees that are 12 inches (30 cm) or more in diameter.

If you have the ability to be picky about which trees to choose, the trees that get the most sunlight will produce the most sap due to the heat and the higher level of photosynthesis happening in the leaves.

Each mature tree can be tapped two or three times, but it's best to keep it to one tap per tree each season.

Tapping Trees with a Drill and Spile

A power drill and a spile are two tools that make tapping trees easier when you have these tools with you. The spile is a spout that sits inside of the hole you drill, also featuring a small hook to hang a bucket on.

Tapping with the drill and spile is a simple process.

Choose a spot on the tree that's easy to access, as you'll have to haul a heavy bucket up to that point and off of it later, that is preferably on the southern-facing side of the tree (as it tends to flow more with the sun). With a 7/16 or 5/16-inch (1 or 0.8 cm) drill bit (depending on the size of the spile you have), drill a 2 to 2 ½ inch (5 to 6 cm) deep hole in the bark.

The shavings that come out of the hole you drill should be light brown, an indication of healthy wood. If you drill in and get dark brown wood, the tree isn't healthy and no sap will be running through that spot in the trunk.

Next, insert the spile and place a collection bucket or any other container underneath. The spile can be hammered in lightly, just enough to keep it in place and sturdy enough to hold a bucket as it fills up. Once the spile is in, you'll likely see sap flowing immediately if the environment is right.

Hang the bucket from the spile and move on to the next tree. It's smart to use a lid to cover the bucket and a rubber tube connecting the spile to a hole in the bucket, as the sap will collect a large number of insects if left open.

Tapping Trees without a Drill

There are a couple of ways to tap a tree if you're attempting to do so without a drill and a spile. Both methods require a knife, which should be on your list of survival supplies.

The first method is to simply carve out a hole with a knife, similarly to how you would with a drill. This might be a bit messy, but you can do a good job of it if you're careful, especially if you have a multi-tool with a smaller penknife on it.

In place of a spile, you can use a piece of bamboo, a reed, or a hollowed-out piece of wood. Anything that resembles a straw and can fit inside the hole you created.

Finally, use some string and whatever bowl you have available to hang from the improvised spile to collect the flowing sap.

While this method is simple, it can be much more destructive to the tree than is sustainable. The second method is much more sustainable for the tree, and can yield a respectable amount of sap for anyone looking for hydration in a survival situation. It won't yield enough sap to make syrup, but most survival scenarios don't call for that.

The second method involves finding a tree with new, live branches lower down on the trunk. These smaller branches are still moving sap through them to the leaves that will start to grow. Look for fresh branches that don't break easily when bent and have healthy bark all along them. These don't need to be any thicker than a normal pencil to work.

Next, since the sap we're trying to get flows upwards, you may want to tie the branch down so it functions almost like a faucet. If you have the right branch, you may be able to hang your collection container from the branch while it still is pointing upright.

Cut the branch diagonally with your knife. It should look almost like a spout or a spear shaved off to one side. If sap is currently flowing, you'll be able to see it almost immediately. If it's slower to come, test for moisture. If there is none, you may want to look for another branch or reassess the time of day, temperature, or tree you've found.

This sliced branch will act like a spout from the tree to your collection container. Find a way to connect your container or bend the branch downwards to the ground where it can sit. It's best to have both up in the air to avoid insects from making their way inside your container and eating the sap before you can.

You can use this method on the same tree year after year, as long as you keep finding new branches. You can also easily tap multiple trees with this method as it's quick, easy, and doesn't harm the tree much at all.

Uses for Pine Tree Sap

Pine sap has been utilized by cultures across the globe for thousands of years for both medicinal and practical purposes. In times of survival, pine sap served as a valuable resource due to its antiseptic, anti-inflammatory, and waterproofing properties.

The properties of pine sap are remarkable. This resinous substance contains terpenes that are known to repel insects and heal wounds. Moreover, its waterproof and adhesive nature makes it an excellent sealant. Whether it's for wound healing, crafting tools, or starting fires, the versatile nature of pine sap continues to be valued in modern times.

Identifying and Collecting Pine Sap

When identifying pine trees, look for certain characteristics. Pine trees are evergreen, with clusters of long needle-shaped leaves. They typically bear cones, and the bark of a pine tree usually has a reddish-brown color and a scaly texture.

Not all pines are equal when it comes to sap collection. Species such as the Ponderosa Pine and the Eastern White Pine are known for their abundant sap production.

Timing is critical for sap collection. The best time to gather pine sap is in the late winter or early spring when the tree's sap production is at its peak. To collect the sap, look for damaged parts of the tree and use your knife to scrape away the sticky substance.

Medicinal Uses of Pine Sap

- **Pine Sap as a Natural Antiseptic:** Pine sap is rich in antibacterial properties, making it an effective natural antiseptic. To use, apply a small amount of the sap directly to the cut or scrape. Let it dry and form a protective 'bandage' over the wound.
- **Using Pine Sap for Wound Dressing:** Apart from being antiseptic, pine sap also acts as a barrier, keeping dirt and debris out of wounds. To use pine sap for wound dressing, first clean the wound with water. Then, apply a layer of pine sap over the wound and cover it with a bandage if you have one.

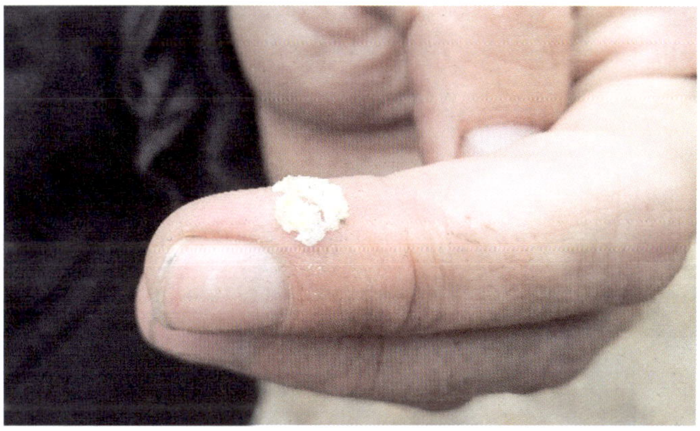

- **Treating Skin Conditions with Pine Sap:** Pine sap is known for its anti-inflammatory and soothing properties, making it an effective treatment for skin conditions like eczema and psoriasis. To use, gently rub a small amount of pine sap onto the affected area daily. Ensure the skin is clean before application.

Pine Sap in Survival Situations

- **Using Pine Sap as a Fire Starter:** Pine sap, with its high flammability, is an excellent fire starter. Gather dry pine sap and tinder. Ignite the sap with a spark or flame, and it will help ignite even damp wood due to its high heat and long burn time.

- **Crafting Waterproofing Agents:** Pine sap can create a natural waterproofing agent. Heat the collected sap until it turns into liquid. Apply this warm sap to the material (like boots or a canvas tent) you wish to waterproof. Let it dry for a durable waterproof coating.

- **Creating Glue:** Pine sap can be used to create strong adhesives, ideal for survival situations. Heat the sap to a liquid state and mix with ash or charcoal to create a sticky adhesive, using a stick to stir. This can be used to secure tools or in place of cordage. Remember to let it dry thoroughly for maximum strength.

HOW TO PRESERVE FOOD IN THE WILD

Modern society has become reliant on electricity and refrigeration to preserve their food and as such, would not be able to store their food long-term without it. Preserving food in the wild takes effort and a lot more time to prepare.

The main types of food that you would be preserving in a wilderness setting are meat, root vegetables, berries, and foraged mushrooms. Fortunately, traditional methods provide accessible ways to preserve your food.

A. MEAT

Preserving meat is essential if you plan on storing it for more than a day or two. In a short time (usually after day 2), meat will become rancid, especially in warmer temperatures.

Luckily, there are primitive methods that can help you preserve meat past that limited shelf life, with some processes keeping meat fresh for up to a month.

What Causes Meat to Go Bad?

Meat spoils quickly as it decays and bacteria start to eat away at it; the excrement from these bacteria is toxic to us. The process is expedited or delayed based on environmental conditions.

For example, a hot day can cause a steak to become inedible within a matter of hours. However, on a cool fall day, you might be able to get a day or two out of it before you start to notice anything wrong.

The main culprits are light, heat, and moisture. A balance of these three can create the perfect storm that rapidly breaks down the cells in the meat. Bacteria and fungi take advantage of the easy food source and decomposition accelerates.

Bacteria and other microorganisms flourish in certain conditions, including:

- High humidity (above 50%)
- Little to no airflow
- Temperatures above 40°F (4°C)
- Oxygen exposure
- Large surface areas
- Acidic PH (between 5.0-8.0)

If you can control the climate, or at least make it so microorganisms cannot grow, then you can preserve your meat for the long term. The best ways to accomplish this are to reduce humidity and temperature, eliminate any moisture from the meat, and protect it with some kind of covering.

5 Ways to Preserve Meat in the Wild

Now that you know the key mechanisms for bacterial and fungal growth, you can understand how preserving meat is about controlling heat, light, and moisture. These methods have been used for centuries and only need the natural resources around you.

1 Sun-Drying

Using the sun to dry out meat is the oldest method of preservation. It is used all across the world. It involves cutting your meat into thin strips that sit out in the sun to dry.

Depending on the tradition, you can either lay the meat strips on pre-warmed rocks and place them in the sun or have them hanging from trees that are facing the sun. Both of these methods require constant tending to keep away flies that will lay eggs in your meat.

You'll know the meat is done when you bend it and it snaps. If there is still play in the meat, it means there is still moisture. Jerky (thin strips of meat that have been dried or smoked) have a surprisingly long shelf life if you keep moisture away from it.

Sun-Drying Step-by-Step

Step 1

Cut your meat into thin strips (as thin as you can get it).

Step 2

Option 1: Pre-heat a rock in a fire and then move it to a sunny spot.

Option 2: Find a tree in a sunny location with easily accessible branches (or build a drying rack in the sun using branches).

Step 3

Option 1: Lay the meat strips on the rock. Regularly flip and rotate.

Option 2: Drape over branches and flip regularly.

Sun-drying using branches

You may have a smoky fire nearby to help keep the insects away. If some of the smoke blows by the meat that's okay, it'll simply help speed the process along.

2 Smoking

Smoking creates a dry, arid environment that bacteria can't live in. It has an added bonus in that it can provide amazing flavor to your meat. This method was mainly used as an alternative to salting, in times when getting salt was difficult.

Smoking meat breaks down the connective tissue within the meat, creating a tender final product. It eliminates moisture and creates a coating that prevents flies from laying their eggs in the meat.

The type of wood you use affects the final taste. Using a strong wood, such as mesquite, will give a great smoky flavor. Birch or Oak has a milder flavor that won't be as perceptible.

Please refer to the chapter "How to Build a Smokehouse in the Wild" on page 164, to learn how to build and use a smokehouse.

3 Burying

If you've been in a basement, then you know it stays cool. It's the main reason people put their cold cellars down there. This is because the ground temperature is generally colder than the ambient temperature above.

Burying your meat underground is a great way to eliminate light and heat from getting to it. It may not be the most hygienic method unless you have a covering over the meat. However, it will keep the temperature cool enough to delay microorganism growth. Keep in mind that this is only a temporary solution and doesn't extend the shelf life as much as drying or smoking.

This method should only be used if you're keeping the meat for no more than 3-4 days before consuming it. While it does provide protection against heat and light, if the ambient temperature is above 77°F (25°C), then it will spoil quicker. Burying is a technique best used in the spring and fall seasons when the ground is soft.

Burying Your Meat Step-by-Step

Step 1

Pick a spot that is not in direct sunlight.

Step 2

Dig hole that is 2-3 feet (60-90 cm) deep for easy retrieval.

Step 3

Wrap your fresh meat in a plastic bag (if you have it). Sheets of birch bark, butterbur leaves, and/or skunk cabbage work well if you have access to these. Place it at the bottom of the hole.

Step 4

Backfill the hole to cover it completely. You don't want any air or light to get at it. Mark the hole so you can find it again easily.

The meat is ready to consume; all you'll have to do is dig it up. Remove the covering and inspect the meat for spoilage before eating.

Step 1

Step 3

tied handles so the inside of the bag doesn't flood. Tie it off if needed so it doesn't float away.

Step 3

Check on the meat throughout the day to make sure predators haven't eaten it.

4

Submerging

Much like being underground, underwater is generally cooler than the ambient air temperature. Flowing rivers are a great refrigeration alternative that can help you squeeze a little more shelf life out of your meat.

In the spring and fall, when the water temperature doesn't go below 39°F (4°C), it is perfect for delaying bacterial growth. In the summertime, river temperatures can fluctuate depending on how hot the climate is. Generally, the water temperature will stay around 49°F (9°C), which is cooler than the ambient air. It may not get you more than 2-3 days of shelf life, but it's better than the meat spoiling within hours from the summer heat.

Submerging Step-by-Step

Step 1

Ensure your meat is in an airtight container or a plastic bag that is securely tied shut. Find a shady spot by a river or flowing creek.

Step 2

Submerge the meat into the water. If you are using a plastic bag, ensure that the water doesn't go over the

5

Pemmican

Pemmican is largely considered the ultimate survival food and is a great way to preserve meat even longer than jerky. Pemmican uses dried meat that is pulverized and mixed with dried berries and tallow (rendered fat). The result is a brick of nutritious, shelf-stable ingredients for a quick high-calorie snack.

Pemmican is a way to preserve meat for years. It is filled with fat and protein with a 2-ounce (57 g) serving providing around 300 calories.

Pemmican Ingredients:

- Beef, moose, venison, deer, or bear jerky
- Dried berries
- Rendered animal fat (preferably of the animal the meat came from)

Pemmican Step-by-Step

Step 1

Using a mortar and pestle (or a rock) pulverize your dried meat until it becomes a powder.

Step 2

Grind the dried berries until they become a powder.

Step 3

Mix the berries and meat.

Step 4

Heat the rendered fat until it becomes liquid and pour it over the meat/berry mix. You want about a 1:1 ratio of fat to meat and at least twice as much meat as berries.

Step 5

Cool it completely and then form it into balls or bars.

Step 6

Ensure to wrap the finished product so that no flies or animals get to it.

B. ROOT VEGETABLES

Root vegetables are packed with dense nutrition but can spoil quickly in the wrong conditions. Root vegetables like carrots, onions, potatoes, sweet potatoes, and ginger can have their shelf life extended with proper preparation and storage.

The Basics of Storing Root Vegetables

Root vegetables have traditionally been stored in root cellars where the environment is dark, dry, and cool. Proper storing of your root vegetables ensures that they don't start to rot quickly. Additionally, with the right conditions your root vegetables may sprout and start to grow into a new plant!

It's important to keep root vegetables in a dark place so as not to encourage bacterial growth. Insects are also attracted to light which will inevitably bring them to your root vegetables for their next meal.

Try to keep the environment cool to help slow down the decomposition process. If your root vegetables get too hot, it often encourages root growth, changing the vegetable into a seedling.

Moisture is the enemy of preservation, and as such, should be kept away from your root vegetables during storage. Bacteria and fungi love moisture and can quickly proliferate if kept unchecked. It's the primary reason why you shouldn't store your root vegetables in plastic bags for long periods.

The concept is simple, yet the execution can be tricky, depending on where you live. As long as the climate isn't scorching hot or always raining you should be able to store these relatively easily.

3 Ways to Preserve Your Root Vegetables

Before storing, you may want to snip the green end off of the root vegetables to help stop growth.

1

Preserving Root Vegetables by Drying

As with most types of food, drying root vegetables out will also improve their shelf life. The best way to accomplish this is with some cheesecloth (or other thin cloth material) and a nice sunny spot.

Simply slice your root vegetable into paper-thin slices and place it on a rock that is sitting out in the sun. Cover your root vegetable slices with the cloth to keep the insects off. It also helps to deflect a lot of the heat of whatever it is you're drying.

The reason you don't want intense heat is that it'll end up cooking the vegetables instead of just drying them out. This process is quite long, extending over a few days. If you notice the root vegetables getting too hot, move them to a less exposed area.

You should wait until the slices are fully dehydrated - you will notice that they will have shrunk in size substantially. Storing it at this stage will give you the longest storage life.

2

Store Root Vegetables in Sand

Storing root vegetables in dry sand is an effective way to squeeze a little more shelf life out of them. Dry sand absorbs excess moisture, preventing it from getting to the vegetables and thus speeding up the decomposition process. Keeping the humidity low also helps stop the vegetables from sprouting.

Before storing your vegetables in the sand, remove the leafy tops and let the roots sit in the air for a couple of days to let the skins toughen up and cure.

The best way to store your root vegetables in sand is to have a dedicated container. Fill the container about 1-2 inches (2.5-5 cm) full of dry sand and then place the root vegetables onto it.

Don't wash root vegetables before storing them as that will cause them to rot quickly. It's best if the vegetables have dirt on them as it'll keep moisture away. Keep the vegetables separate as you want to ensure optimal airflow.

Fill the container with sand until the vegetables are covered. Then move the container to a dark location. Keep the container away from rain and direct sunlight and periodically check for freshness.

3 Build a Root Clamp

A root clamp is a traditional method of storing root vegetables in the event of a frost. It's also an effective way to protect your root vegetables throughout the winter. It requires only natural materials to create.

1. Select an area that does not retain water, and look for soil that has excellent drainage. Avoid low-lying spots as that's where water tends to pool during storms.
2. Place a layer of straw or dried grasses on the ground in a circular area. Ensure that it is at least 5 feet (1.5 m) wide and 8 inches (20 cm) thick.
3. Check for damaged or rotting root vegetables and toss them away since they will just continue to rot in the root clamp. Cut the green tops off of the good vegetables before placing them on the straw.
4. Create a mound of root vegetables no more than 3 feet (1 m) high. Cover this mound with another layer of straw roughly 8 inches (20 cm) in depth.
5. Afterward, pile 8 inches (20 cm) of fresh soil on top of the straw layer. Keep one small area of straw poking out to act as a chimney. This will allow any heat to escape from inside the mound.
6. Pat the soil down so that any rainwater will run off of the mound. If you need to access the root vegetables you can take material off of the top or excavate the sides. Just be sure to seal it up properly afterwards to prevent anything from getting inside.

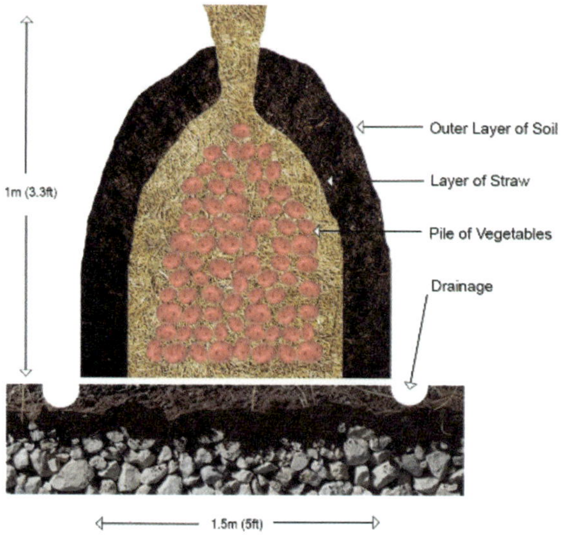

C. MUSHROOMS

Wild mushrooms have a short shelf life both in the wild and when harvested. One day you may walk through a location and see nothing, but the next day you'll see tasty mushrooms popping up all over the forest floor.

As a disclaimer, be sure to properly identify what mushrooms you're attempting to eat. There are lookalike species that can be deadly if consumed. If you're unsure about consuming a specific mushroom, it is best if you don't use it.

Mushrooms can effectively be treated much like meat, in terms of preservation. Although burying your mushrooms in sand or soil won't keep them fresh, there are a few alternative ways to extend their shelf life.

3 Ways to Preserve Mushrooms

Full of potassium, fiber, and other antioxidants, some mushroom species have incredible properties for healing and their potent medicinal qualities are often used for remedies. For example, Lion's Mane and Reishi are commonly used in tinctures and teas to promote immune balance and provide anti-viral support. This makes mushrooms a prime candidate for more than just munching, you can also preserve them for healing purposes.

Mushrooms are full of moisture. If you've ever sauteed mushrooms in a pan, you may have noticed that they can reduce up to ¾ of their original mass. If you want to preserve your freshly foraged mushrooms, start the process as soon as they are harvested.

Here are the three best methods that you can use to keep your mushrooms from spoiling quickly. Both sun-drying and dehydration also work well for preserving berries.

❶ Sun-Drying

Much like meat, using the sun to dry mushrooms is an effective technique. There aren't many predators that you need to worry about while they're drying. Flies and other insects are also a small risk, but you can keep a smoky fire nearby to help keep them away.

1. Depending on the size of the mushrooms you can slice them thinly or keep them whole; the drying time is changed accordingly. Choose an area that is sunny and has a slight breeze.
2. Lay out your mushrooms on a warm rock. If you have a metal screen, you can lay them on it for even air circulation. Otherwise, just rotate them several times a day.
3. Allow for 7-10 days to completely dry whole mushrooms and about 3 days if you have them thinly sliced. You'll know they're ready when you squeeze them and they have no give in them. This means the moisture has been successfully removed.

❷ Smoking

Using a smokehouse to preserve mushrooms is a great way to impart a smoky flavor and evaporate all of the moisture from within. Use a smokehouse if you can't dehydrate your mushrooms or if you want a smoky flavor imparted into them.

The general idea is to create an enclosure that sits over a smoldering fire. You want the enclosure to be relatively sealed for capturing as much smoke as possible. The more smoke exposure you provide, the faster the mushrooms will dry out.

Sitting them on a small grate inside the smokehouse works well as long as you rotate them throughout the smoking period. If you notice the mushrooms getting smoked unevenly, then rotate them.

They'll start to change color and shrivel up slightly as an indicator that they are drying. The longer you leave them in the smokehouse, the more moisture will evaporate; the smoky flavor will become stronger as well.

Please check out our chapter on building a smokehouse for full details and instructions on creating your own.

❸ Dehydrating

Dehydrating mushrooms is perfect if you have an indoor fire or a wood stove, as it'll use the dry heat to passively sap the moisture from the mushrooms. It works in the same way as using a commercial dehydrator.

For this method to be successful, ensure there is ample airflow around each of the mushrooms. You can do this process with whole or sliced mushrooms, depending on the thickness.

1. Choose a spot that is close to a heat source. If it's a fire, then lay the mushrooms on some rocks close by. If you're doing it inside near a wood stove, then you'll want to lay them on some form of grate that is 2-3 feet (60-90 cm) away from the stove. You want the heat to reach the mushrooms, but not necessarily cook them.

2. Rotate the mushrooms as needed for even drying. Just like with the other methods they will begin to take on a deeper color and shrivel. As the process progresses, the mushrooms will become difficult to squeeze and you'll know they're done when you can't squeeze them anymore.

Making Salt from Plants

Obtaining salt from plants is an ancient practice that dates back to prehistoric times. Halophytes, plants that thrive in salty conditions, accumulate salt in their tissues, and we learned to extract this valuable mineral from the ashes of these burned plants. Such a practice was not only essential for the survival of communities with no access to sea or rock salt, but it also held cultural and economic significance, as salt was often used as currency.

In environmentally sensitive areas where mining or sea salt production might be damaging, deriving salt from plants offers a more sustainable solution. Moreover, plant-based salts are perceived as healthier alternatives to traditional table salt. They contain a mix of essential minerals and trace elements, offering a diverse mineral profile.

Understanding Plant-Based Salts

Plants like Hickory, Walnut, Pecan, and Coltsfoot are known to accumulate salts in their tissues, a trait that allows them to thrive even in soil with high salinity.

They belong to a group of plants known as halophytes, which have developed a unique mechanism for absorbing, managing, and storing salt in a way that does not harm their growth. They take in salt-laden water from the soil, filter out the salt in specialized cells, and store it within their leaves or bark.

The nutritional value of plant-based salts varies by the type of plant but generally provides a wealth of essential minerals and trace elements, often in lower sodium concentrations compared to regular table salt. This varied mineral profile not only imparts a unique taste but also contributes to improved health in the wild.

For instance, potassium, calcium, and magnesium found in these salts are vital for various bodily functions, including nerve transmission, fluid balance, and muscle contraction. Transitioning from table salt to plant-based salts can be a beneficial move for those seeking a healthier and more sustainable lifestyle.

Identifying Salt-Rich Plants

Knowing how to identify salt-rich plants such as Hickory, Walnut, Pecan, and Coltsfoot is crucial to leverage their health benefits. These plants have distinct characteristics that make them easy to identify.

Hickory trees have large, compound leaves and shaggy bark. Walnut trees bear round, green fruits enclosed in a thick husk, and Pecan trees have long, compound leaves and bear elongated, smooth nuts. Coltsfoot, on the other hand, is a low-growing plant with bright yellow flowers and hoof-shaped leaves.

If you live near coastal waters then you have access to an abundance of seagrasses, which are also high in salts.

Harvesting the Plants

The process of harvesting these salt-rich plants involves careful extraction of roots and gathering of leaves, ensuring the plant's sustainability.

For Hickory, Walnut, and Pecan trees, the extraction process begins with careful removal of the soil around the base of the tree to expose the roots. Using a sharp, clean tool, cut a section of the root while ensuring not to cause excessive damage to the tree. The roots can then be washed, dried, and used for extraction.

When harvesting Coltsfoot, pick the leaves. Coltsfoot leaves are best harvested in the early to mid-summer when the plant is in full bloom.

To harvest, simply pick the leaves directly from the plant, ensuring to leave enough foliage for the plant to continue its growth cycle. Remember, sustainable harvesting is key to preserving these plants for future generations.

Extracting Salt from Plants

After harvesting, the next step is to extract salt from the roots and leaves. There are two main methods: boiling and ash-leaching.

For the boiling method, chop your harvested roots or leaves into small pieces and place them in a pot filled with water. Bring the water to a boil and allow it to simmer until the water has evaporated, leaving behind salt crystals. The higher the temperature, the faster the water will evaporate, but be cautious not to burn the salts that are left behind.

Ash-leaching involves burning the plant material until it turns into ash. The ash is then leached with water to dissolve the salt, which can be separated through decantation or filtration. The remaining liquid is then evaporated to crystallize the salt. You can use the ash itself in a pinch, but the unburned carbon doesn't have a nice taste.

You can also purify your extracted salt. This is achieved by dissolving the salt in a small amount of clean water, filtering the solution to remove any impurities, and then evaporating the water once again to leave purified salt crystals. It may take several hours for the water to fully evaporate and the salt to crystallize.

Storing and Using Plant-Based Salt

Storing plant-based salt correctly is crucial to maintaining its unique flavors and nutritional value. Keep your salt in an airtight container and store it in a cool, dry place. Avoid placing it near heat sources or in direct sunlight, as these conditions can cause the salt to lose its flavor and mineral content.

As for using plant-based salt, the possibilities are virtually limitless. Use it as a finishing touch on a fresh salad or incorporate it into your baking to add a subtle, earthy flavor. You can also use it in marinades and rubs for meat, where it will not only add flavor but also help to tenderize the meat.

TENDING THE LAND: How to Cultivate the Land and Food

The land around you has the potential to provide sustenance for a lifetime. Its capacity to produce a vast abundance has supported human life for thousands of years.

Since the inception of industrialized agriculture, there are issues that are diminishing the land's potential, leading to a possible collapse in nutrient levels of the soil. One of the largest movements today is towards rewilding the land. Rewilding is a term for moving the land back toward restoring sustainable and biodiverse swaths of land. When applied to food production, rewilding, reforesting, and sustainable land use is termed 'regenerative farming'.

Regenerative farming helps put nutrients back into the soil while still producing nutritional foods that are sustainable over the long run. It provides more food over a longer period of time, as well as more usable plants for other traditional uses. On a small-scale basis, this idea can be transferred to starting a garden in the wild and having it provide enough food to sustain you in a wild living scenario.

Tending the Land

Humans have tended to the land for thousands of years. Over time, new and innovative practices have allowed us to manipulate our crops in ways that allow for better growth and higher food yields. Below are ways you can implement land tending to increase your wild food sources.

Certain wild species are favored over others when tending the land in the wild, as some will provide medicinal benefits while others are better for food or for material goods.

Wild Species

Depending on where you are, there are likely hundreds of edible species that can be used in a wild garden. Once you know your needs, you can find the right plants for those purposes.

For example, Aspirin, one of the most common over-the-counter drugs, was historically derived from meadowsweet, willow tree bark, and other plants that have high levels of salicin. You can harvest certain plants to turn into pain-relieving medication.

Several other tree species have helpful medicinal uses. Betulinic acid in birch trees is an anti-inflammatory and pain reliever, pine trees have high levels of antioxidants, the elder tree's berries are used for immune boosts and as an antiviral, tea tree oils are used for their antiseptic properties, etc.

In addition to these tree species, wild mushrooms, onions, garlic, berries, greens, and more can be found and used in wild gardens.

With the right methods of land tending, you can create an abundant area of forest space that provides for most of your needs. The practice of wild-tending has grown significantly. These methods are widely used in survival scenarios and long-term living in the wild.

Pruning

One of the most basic techniques for tending and maintaining wild plants is pruning. Pruning simply involves the removal of certain sections of a plant in order to make space for more growth. This tends to be used when plants are diseased, overgrown, or simply damaged. If you are creating a wild garden, pruning is necessary to help balance out natural competition for light and other resources.

Removing branches from a tree or shrub can be incredibly beneficial for the plant. Many trees even self-prune as they grow taller and the lower branches are no longer as productive with the lower levels of light they receive. Doing this for a tree or shrub speeds up the natural process and can encourage faster growth in one direction over another.

When pruning, make sure not to over-prune and remove too many branches, leaving the plant without enough nutrition-producing leaves. Start by looking for dead or damaged branches and removing those before moving on to the crowded sections. You can also use pruning to shape the plant in order to make space for the others around it, increasing the efficiency of the space you're using.

Coppicing

Coppicing is the practice of cutting a tree, shrub, or plant all the way down to its base, while leaving the roots intact, and encouraging rapid new growth. This is a method often used in sustainable production of materials, like arrow shafts or basket-making materials. You harvest the material, but leave the plant alive enough to continue producing, to then be harvested years later.

It's important to coppice in the winter or early spring while the plant is dormant. This allows for all of the spring growth to be put into its recovery and quick growth from the small leftover stump.

One of the most important aspects of coppicing is to continue managing the regrowth in the next season. This includes pruning and shaping the plant as it grows back vigorously, making any attempt it can to survive. You may need to encourage growth by pruning back the new shoots as they attempt to grow back.

Propagating

The propagation of plants is simply encouraging more growth of new individuals. This can be done to increase the number of plants you have in one area, but can also bring new species into an area they weren't naturally in before.

Propagation techniques vary from seed propagation, stem and root cuttings, to layering and division. Seed propagation tends to be the most common as it's the most widely available and most natural system in place. Other techniques can be more involved.

Propagation by taking a stem or root cutting is done by taking a piece of the stem or root and replanting it in the soil or a pot. If you keep the soil warm and moist enough, the stem will eventually take root, or the root will eventually flourish and put-up stems.

Some plants are better equipped for taking cuttings than others. If you have a lot of houseplants, you may have seen how easily a spider plant can be propagated with a stem cutting. In the wild, many plants can be propagated through stem cuttings:

- Wild mint
- Elderberry trees
- Willow trees
- Blackberries
- Wild rose
- Spicebush
- Cottonwood trees

Wild plants that are propagated through root cuttings:

- Wild ginger
- Wild carrots
- Sarsaparilla
- Echinacea
- Jerusalem artichoke

Candidates for propagation through layering:

- Black raspberry
- Wild honeysuckle
- Wild grape
- Wild roses

Propagating wild plants through division can be done with:

- Beebalm
- Wild bergamot
- Wild onion
- Wild garlic
- Wild leek
- Strawberry
- Raspberry

Propagation through stem cutting

Splicing

Splicing, or grafting, is encouraging the growth and joining of two different parts of a plant to grow as a singular individual. There are wild plants that can be spliced together in order to produce more fruit or to create a plant that produces different types of fruit that can be disease resistant or designed to taste a certain way.

Fruit trees are one of the most common candidates for splicing. It can increase fruit yield, but has been historically used for producing fruits that are disease-resistant. This can be an incredibly useful technique in the wild as you can drastically increase your production of a food supply.

Splicing can be a difficult process, as it involves carefully cutting certain parts of each plant and joining the two together. A popular method of splicing is called cleft grafting.

With this method, you want to start by finding a good piece of wood or stalk that was grown the previous year, as this is the best to use in the splicing process.

This piece of stalk will be inserted into a cut trunk or thicker branch that has been split vertically, just deep enough to take the new pieces of plant.

With a fine razor, shave both sides of the wood into a wedge and insert them into the split trunk. You can do this with two different scions (new pieces of growth) on the same trunk. Once the scions are in place, tie some cordage tightly to hold the split trunk or branch tightly around the scions.

Finally, you can utilize wax to pour over the various open cuts, wrap the entire area with insulating tape, or use well-packed clay in the wild, and seal it off for the plant to start splicing together and growing as one.

With all of these different techniques, you can bring together a wide variety of edible and medicinal plants to start a garden in the wild that provides for your basic needs.

Starting a Garden in the Wild

Taking these practices and putting them into place is a whole different story. A wild garden, or a survival garden, takes work and dedication to ensure that enough food is produced to help keep you fed.

Choosing Your Crop

One of the first steps in starting a wild garden is to choose suitable crops to be planted. This will affect the amount of land you need, how much sun you should account for, and basically, everything you should do in preparation.

Most small gardens will include resilient and common vegetables that can survive in more difficult conditions while still providing a lot of nutrition.

Popular crops include zucchinis/courgettes, potatoes, beans, radishes, spinach, tomatoes, cucumbers, kale, and carrots. There are also many medicinal plants that will grow well in difficult conditions such as chamomile, echinacea, peppermint, St. John's wort, yarrow, plantain, and sage.

While all of these crops are fairly resilient and easy to care for, you still need to choose crops that are going to do well in the climate you're growing in. Also, it's well worth growing crops that you like eating. Just because it's a survival garden, it doesn't have to taste bad.

In order to know how much you need to grow, you'll need to calculate the required calories of whoever is going to be relying on this garden for food. This will help you figure out the space you'll require and how many of each crop is needed for your nutritional needs.

Getting the Garden Going

Once you've decided what to plant, it's time to get your hands dirty. This can be one of the most exciting parts of the entire process, aside from actually eating your first harvest, so be sure to put the time into it that it deserves.

- **Materials**

The shopping list of materials will likely change often as you encounter different issues, but for the start of the garden, you don't need much. This basic shopping list should help you be ready to get a garden started:

- Metal rake
- Scythe
- Shovel
- Organic fertilizer
- Seeds
- Fencing and posts
- Poles for training certain plants

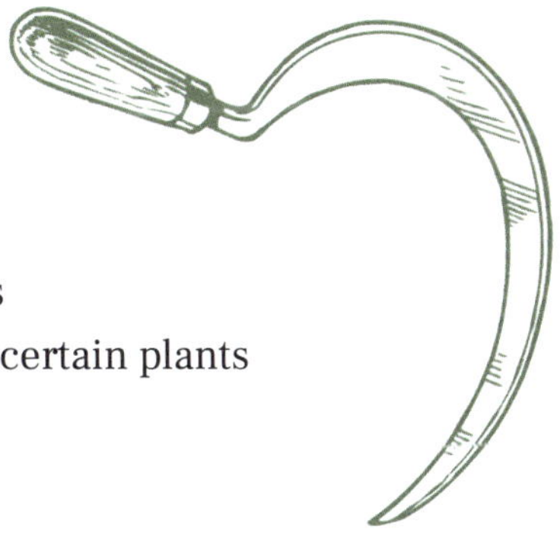

When starting a garden in the wild, you may need to improvise with these tools. It can be done by hand, without any tools, but tools do make the process much easier. Obviously, you'll have to harvest seeds and can likely go without fertilizer if you pick an area of forest with a thick duff layer that's already rich in nutrients.

Harvesting seeds will greatly depend on the plants you are hoping to cultivate. With any fruit or nut plants, you can use the entire fruit or the nut itself to grow from the very beginning. This can be an effective method, but you may need to collect a large number in order to have success. Note that these may take many years to bear fruit.

- **Location**

Head out and try to find the best spot for your garden. There are a lot of different factors for choosing the best location. You might not get all the best features, but shoot for as many as possible.

1.Sunlight

One of the most important factors is the amount of sunlight the area gets. With a high level of sunlight, vegetables will flourish, but in hot arid areas they may be damaged by too much sun. In that case, it's often easier to build sunshades than to avoid the sun entirely. More sun is the best choice.

2.Accessibility

If your garden is miles away, it will be difficult to tend to and to defend from critters. Choose a plot of land that you can visit frequently.

3.Water

Access to water is incredibly important. With little access, you'll find yourself hauling buckets of water from far off, which can get tiresome quickly. You also need to be aware of plots that are prone to flooding as you can lose your entire crop this way, so it's best to find a balance between an arid and a riparian system.

4.Fertile and Well-Drained Soil

Finding fertile and well-drained soil plays a large part in the success of your garden. Small plots can have a lot of fertile soil if there is already a lot of plant life that has been dying and decomposing on site. If you are stuck with no other option, you can fertilize heavily, preferably with organic compost.

Prepare the Land

With the best spot in mind, it's time to bring the tools out to the field and start clearing the space. This process starts by simply getting rid of what's already growing there with a scythe to cut everything down, and a metal rake to remove as much material as possible.

The goal is to get rid of all the natural plant material that was in the way and have easy access to the soil. You want nothing remaining, especially roots. The better you do this job, the better the garden will grow. Leftover plants and roots will compete with your vegetables and will need to be pulled later on.

Get as much brush away as you can with your rake, use a shovel if you are having difficulty with certain roots, and start a compost pile in a spot that's nearby. It will be a great source for future fertilizer.

Separate into Plots and Organize the Garden

Now you can look back on the cleared plot and be proud of yourself. This is when the garden starts coming into view much more clearly. This step involves taking the entire plot and subdividing it into small areas for each kind of plant you're going to grow.

Mark out the different plots so you don't get confused later on. You can arrange these in any way you want, but it can be good to have a flow of different planting and harvest times so you don't have to jump across the garden multiple times in one working session.

For example, you can create a garden in a circular pattern, where the harvest time moves clockwise throughout the year.

Fertilize and Plant

Once everything is separated out, continue setting the garden in the manner that you prefer. Many use a raised row method that incorporates fertilizer, such as organic compost, into the soil and brings the crops up off the ground. This is a common method in areas that are farmed often to add more nutrients to the soil.

If you are just starting the garden and have fertile soil, making distinguishable rows may help with organization. Either way, now is the time to start planting.

There is a lot of variation in how to space and plant your different vegetables in a garden. Each seed packet will come with instructions, but if you're totally harvesting from the wild, it's easiest to just examine the plant's natural growth. Look to see how much space the plant takes up before producing something to harvest, examine the seed dispersal methods, and experiment with different depths to plant the seeds.

Practicing observation techniques to see how certain plants grow naturally can help you incorporate those methods into your own garden, rather than using a trial-and-error method.

How to Protect the Garden from Wild Animals

Getting the garden up and running is a huge process. To have it completely destroyed by wild animals right away is a catastrophic attack on your resilience, making it difficult to turn around and start again. High-quality protection from wild animals is key to keeping your garden for yourself.

Fences tend to be the most effective way of keeping animals out of your garden. Get sturdy wire and be sure to bury it a few inches underground to prevent critters from digging underneath it. There are a few other techniques that work effectively to protect your garden.

- **Netting** - Draping nets above the garden helps keep birds from flying down and getting into the garden.
- **Companion Planting** - Certain plants are natural insect deterrents. Planting these alongside the vulnerable plants helps keep small insects and other critters away.
- **Scare Devices** - Scarecrows are the classic example of a scare device, but you can also use noise makers or reflective tape.
- **Traps** - Usually this is the last resort, but setting traps to protect your garden over the long haul is sometimes necessary after having issues with one animal over and over.

Usually, it's a combination of these tactics that works the best. Most gardens benefit from fences to keep large critters out, scare devices or netting to prevent the birds from coming in, and companion plants to help keep harmful insects away.

It's a lot to do, but it will save you the trouble of losing all of your crops after working so hard for them.

Seeding Mushroom Spores

Mushrooms are a fantastic food and medicinal source when you are starting a wild garden. They're easy to grow, and you can produce them in high abundance.

The most important thing about dealing with mushrooms is to be fully confident in your identification skills. The number of lookalikes and dangerous mushrooms out there is high, so it's important to be certain of what is picked and seeded.

Collecting Spores

When growing mushrooms at home, it can be as easy as ordering a mushroom growing kit from the internet and getting started. When tending the land and living fully self-sustained, you need to start from the very beginning. That means the first step is to collect spores from mushrooms you have harvested.

Collecting spores from a mushroom is a pretty easy process, but it is time consuming and delicate. Start by exposing the gills underneath the mushroom cap and fully removing anything in the way. Then set the cap with the gills down on a piece of paper. Cover the mushroom cap with a glass and leave it for 24 hours.

For mushrooms that have pores on the underside, like a bolete, simply remove the stipe and place the cap with the pores down, just like with the previous type of mushroom. These spore prints are also useful for identification.

When you come back, the mushroom will have dropped plenty of spores onto the paper that create a "spore print". This can be stored in a bag until you're ready to start cultivating. If you're ready to go, get to a clean space and start the process. I also harvest mushrooms in a basket so that their spores can spread as I walk around.

Cultivating Spores

Cultivating spores is a trickier process than collecting them. In this process, you are starting by rehydrating the spores with clean water. Then, add the mixture to a medium to help the spores begin to populate.

This process is typically done with a syringe in a more controlled environment, but in the wild, you need to be innovative. Try to keep water as clean as possible in a sterile container. If you have a straw, use that in place of a syringe.

Into a small glass, combine a small amount of fresh water and some spores that you scrape. Allow for the spores to hydrate and you may begin to see some spores floating on the surface. This mixture can be used to inoculate your medium.

The best medium for growing mushrooms in the wild is typically a rotten log that the fungi can feed on. If you have sawdust available, that works as a great medium for your spores to begin propagating.

Germinating Spores

Germinating spores is combining your spores with the medium and the nutrients inside it to make the spore spawn. This spawn will encourage the growth of mycelium, the small fungus fiber that is where mushrooms take their "root".

When you mix the spores and create spawn, you are injecting spores into something that they can feed upon. Mushrooms don't require sunlight; they need nutrient-rich, compostable material that they can slowly eat away at.

The better you mix nutrients with spores, the more mushrooms you'll end up with. Keep your logs that you are growing mushrooms on in a dark and humid place if you can. All you have to do is wait and keep them from drying out.

Seasonal Food Procurement

Growing food in the wild is a great way to feed yourself throughout the year, but part of sustaining yourself with food is making sure you have enough to last through the cold season when nothing will grow. This often requires learning how to store food for a long period of time without it going bad and developing a solid storage system that keeps critters out.

There are also parts of the year when you may find that your garden isn't producing as much as you expected it to. In these cases, you can start foraging for what is already growing naturally or start hunting.

Living in the wild is about making life work through a combination of different skills, not only perfecting a single one. It also requires getting to know the land as well as you know yourself. In this relationship, there is a give and take that allows for everyone to thrive and survive even in the difficult moments of low food production.

WILDERNESS BASIC FIRST AID

MEDICINAL PLANTS YOU CAN FIND IN THE WILD

In this section, we discuss 15 medicinal plants found in Europe (note that many of these plants are found worldwide). These plants include Calendula (*Calendula officinalis*), Lemon Balm (*Melissa officinalis*), Oak (*Quercus* spp.), Russian Comfrey (*Symphytum uplandica*), Arnica (*Arnica montana*), Corydalis (*Corydalis* spp.), Methuselah's Beard (*Usnea longissima*), Elecampane (*Inula helenium*), Peppermint (*Mentha piperita*), Marshmallow (*Althaea officinalis*), St. John's Wort (*Hypericum perforatum*), Mustard (*Brassica alba*), Rosemary (*Rosemarinus officinalis*), Chamomile (*Matricaria recutita*), and Yarrow (*Achillea millefolium*).

1. Calendula

Calendula (*Calendula officinalis*) Flowers

French Marigold (*Tagetes patula*)

Description: Calendula (*Calendula officinalis*) is also known as Pot Marigold, Common Marigold, Garden Marigold, Gold Bloom, Mary Bud, and Ruddles. This plant is native to Western Europe, Southwestern Asia, Macaronesia, and the Mediterranean, but is naturalized worldwide.

Calendula typically grows 1 to 2 ft. (30 to 60 cm) in height. It has sparsely branched, upright stems. Its leaves are oblong- to lancet-shaped, and each leaf is about 3 to 6 inches (7.5 to 15 cm) in length. The leaves have an aromatic smell. Calendula usually blooms from May to August. Its flowers are bright yellow to deep orange in color. It can have single or double flowerheads, with each flower measuring 3 to 4 inches (7.5 to 10 cm) in diameter.

Calendula (*Calendula officinalis*)

Poisonous Look-Alike:

French Marigold (*Tagetes patula*) contains tagetone and tagetes oil. Swallowing these can cause vomiting and/or diarrhea. You can tell the difference between the two as French Marigold flowers have a double row of petals while Calendula flowers have a single row. Calendula leaves are larger than those of the French marigold. French Marigolds typically grow higher than 2 ft. (60 cm) tall, while Calendula is typically shorter. Calendula flowers are more consistently yellow and orange while French Marigold flowers come in shades of red, burgundy, and two-color combinations.

Warning: Calendula should not be taken internally by anyone who is pregnant. To reduce the likelihood of an allergic reaction, do not use Calendula if you are allergic to Marigold, Ragweed, Daisies, Chrysanthemums, Chamomile, Echinacea, or other plants in the Aster/Daisy family.

2. Lemon Balm

Lemon Balm (*Melissa officinalis*) Leaves

Description: Balm (*Melissa officinalis*) is also known as Balm, Balm Mint, and Common Balm. It is native to southern Europe, but is naturalized in the eastern, midwestern, and Pacific northwestern United States.

Lemon Balm typically grows 2 to 3 ft. (60 to 90 cm) in height. Its stems are square and usually green, but can become slightly woody as the plant ages. The leaves are oppositely paired and aromatic, giving off a minty lemon-like odor. Lemon Balm blooms from June to August. Its flowers are very small, and they appear close to the stem. They are creamy white in color.

Lemon Balm (*Melissa officinalis*) Flower

Poisonous Look-Alike:

Foxglove (*Digitalis purpurea*)

Foxglove (*Digitalis purpurea*) is a very poisonous look-alike of Lemon Balm. It contains a chemical called digoxin which can cause severe harm and even death if ingested in small to moderate amounts. All parts of the plant contain digoxin, and even a small amount can be dangerous to children or pets. Symptoms of digoxin consumption include nausea, vomiting, diarrhea, headache, confusion, vision changes, and, in severe cases, coma and even death.

You can tell the difference between Lemon Balm and Digoxin with some careful observation. Lemon Balm has green, oval-shaped leaves with a slightly wrinkled texture. Foxglove leaves are much larger, pointed, and more oblong with a fuzzy texture. Lemon Balm has small, white or yellowish flowers that are arranged in whorls around the stem. Foxglove flowers are large and bell shaped; are white, pink or purple; and typically grow on a tall spike. Lemon Balm grows 1-3 ft. tall (30-90 cm) while Foxglove can grow up to 6 ft. (1.8 m) tall. Lemon Balm has a lemon-like scent when you crush it, while Foxglove has almost no odor.

Warning: Lemon Balm blocks thyroid stimulating hormone from binding to receptors in the body, effectively decreasing the body's production of thyroid hormones (T3 and T4). While this can be helpful in cases where the thyroid is overactive, people with underactive or sluggish thyroid function (e.g., hypothyroidism, Hashimoto's thyroiditis) should only use Lemon Balm with caution, and ideally under the care of a trained professional.

3. English Oak

English Oak (*Quercus robur*)

English Oak (*Quercus robur*) Fruit

Description: English Oak (*Quercus robur*) is also known as Common Oak, European Oak, French Oak, Pedunculate Oak, Polish Oak, and Truffle Oak. This tree is native to Europe, northern Africa, and western Asia.

English Oak typically grows between 40 and 70 ft. (12 and 20 m) in both height and width. It has a short, round, sturdy trunk. Its bark is grayish-brown to black and deeply fissured. It has alternate leaves that are 3 and 5 inches (7.5 to 12.5 cm) long. The leaves are dark-green, and each leaf is made up of 3 to 7 pairs of deeply rounded lobes, giving the outline of the leaf a wavy appearance. The tree begins to flower in spring as the leaves appear. It has greenish-yellow, slim, cylindrical clusters of petal-less flowers. The fruit (acorn) is oval-shaped and about 1 inch (2.5 cm) in length. The top ¼ to ⅓ of the acorn is covered by a cap that is attached to the tree by a long stalk.

Warning: English Oak should be avoided by women who are pregnant or breastfeeding. It should be used with caution in people with chronic constipation, because it can exacerbate this concern. People with iron-deficiency anemia and malnutrition should exercise caution when using English Oak because its high tannin content can block the absorption of nutrients.

4. Russian Comfrey

Russian Comfrey (*Symphytum uplandica*)

Description: Russian Comfrey (*Symphytum uplandica*) is also known as Blackwort, Borraja, Bourrache, Bruisewort, Buyuk Karakafesotu, Consolida, Consound, Consuelda, Gewone Smeerworte, Gum Plant, Healing Herb, Hirehari-So, Knitback, Knitbone, Liane Chique, Slippery Root, and Yalluc. This plant is native to watery areas of Europe, Great Britain, and parts of western and central Asia.

Russian Comfrey typically grows 20 to 40 inches (0.5 to 1 m) in height. Its stem is green and has rough hairs. Its leaves are alternate and elliptical. They are rounded at the attached end and more pointed at the free end. It blooms from June to August. Its flowers are drooping and bell- or trumpet-shaped. They can be lilac, pink, blue, or occasionally white in color.

Warning: Russian Comfrey should never be used topically on broken bones that have not yet been set or on deep wounds, as it heals wounds very quickly. It should not be used internally by pregnant or breastfeeding women. It should not be used by children or by anyone with liver disease or hepatitis. Anyone taking medication that is known to damage the liver should avoid using Russian Comfrey. In general, comfrey is best as an external/topical herb.

5. Arnica

Arnica (*Arnica montana*)

Description: Arnica (*Arnica montana*) is also known as Leopard's Bane, Mountain Arnica, Mountain Snuff, Mountain Tobacco, and Wolfbane. This plant is native to Europe, where it grows from Norway to the Balkans and from Spain to Ukraine.

Arnica typically grows between 0.5 and 2 ft. (15 and 60 cm) in height. Its stems are upright and hairy. Each stem has a single flower. The leaves are oblong to lancet-shaped and cluster together. The leaves that are attached to the stems are opposite. The upper sides of the leaves are hairy, and longitudinal veins are visible within the leaves. Arnica blooms in summer. Its flowers are 1 to 3 inches (2.5 to 7.5 cm) in diameter. The petals range in color from yellow to orange.

Poisonous Look-Alike:

False Hellebore (*Veratrum viride*)

False Hellebore (*Veratrum viride*) may be confused with Arnica. It contains many steroidal alkaloids that can cause severe gastrointestinal upset, cardiac arrhythmias, seizures, and even death in severe cases. This chemical is concentrated mostly in the leaves and roots. The leaves of False Hellebore are large and broad. They can grow up to 18 inches (46 cm) long while Arnica leaves are 2-3 inches (5-8 cm) long. False Hellebore produces tall flower spikes with tiny greenish flowers, rather than the yellow-orange daisy-like flowers of Arnica. False Hellebore can grow 6 ft. (1.8 m) tall, while Arnica is typically 1-2 ft. (30-60 cm) tall. False Hellebore is usually found in wetlands and marshes, but Arnica likes to grow in dry, rocky soil.

Warning: Arnica has a narrow therapeutic window, meaning that the difference between a therapeutic dose of Arnica and a toxic dose (when taken internally) is very small. Because it is very easy to take too much Arnica (which can be life-threatening), it should only be used internally with extreme caution. Arnica should not be used by pregnant or lactating women. Best used as an external/topical herb.

6. Cordyalis

Corydalis (*Corydalis lutea*)

Description: Corydalis (*Corydalis lutea*) is also known as Yellow Fumitory, Hollowort, and Yellow Corydalis. It is native to the southern alps of Europe.

Corydalis typically grows 6 to 20 inches (15 to 50 cm) tall. Its stems are fleshy, upright, and hollow. They can be single or branched. The leaves are pale green to blue-green in color, and the underside of the leaves has a waxy appearance. The leaves are pinnately compound, meaning they are divided into smaller leaflets that are arranged on each side of a central stalk. Corydalis begins to bloom in late spring. Each of the stems that rise above the foliage has 6 to 16 flowers. The flowers are bright yellow and trumpet-shaped. They are angled downward, and are 1 to 2 inches (2.5 to 5 cm) in length. Each flower has 4 petals.

Poisonous Look-Alike:

Bleeding Heart (*Dicentra spectabilis*)

Bleeding Heart (*Dicentra spectabilis*) contains several potentially harmful compounds, including isoquinoline alkaloids such as protopine, allocryptopine, and sanguinarine. They are most concentrated in the root, but are also found in the leaves. Even small amounts of plant material can cause symptoms such as nausea, vomiting, and diarrhea. In severe cases, ingestion of large amounts of the plant can cause convulsions, irregular heartbeat, and even death. You can tell Bleeding Heart apart from Corydalis in several ways. Corydalis has fern-like leaves, while Bleeding Heart has rounded, lobed leaves. Corydalis is shorter and more bush-like than Bleeding Heart, and it has a beak-shaped flower, while Bleeding Heart has a heart shaped flower that droops.

Warning: Corydalis should not be used by pregnant women, and its use is not recommended by breastfeeding women. Caution should be taken when using Corydalis along with medicines or drugs (e.g., alcohol, opiates, etc.) that depress the central nervous system.

7. Methuselah's Beard (Usnea)

Usnea longissima- Peter Pearsall U.S. Fish and Wildlife Service

Description: Methuselah's Beard (*Usnea longissima*) is also known as Beard Lichen or Old Man's Beard. This lichen is native to western Europe and North America.

Methuselah's Beard can be seen growing on and hanging from trees. It ranges in color from pale sage green to silvery green. Methuselah's Beard can be differentiated from other species of Usnea and similar plants of other genera because its cylindrical stems are largely unbranched, whereas the stems of other lichens are branched. This gives Methuselah's Beard an appearance similar to that of pipe cleaners or bottle brushes.

The stems of Methuselah's Beard are much longer than other Usnea species; it can be up to 10 ft. (3 m) in length. Usnea species also have a diagnostic white rubber-band like core that can be seen when fresh lichen is pulled apart.

Warning: There is a lack of data about the safety of Methuselah's Beard when used by pregnant or lactating women. People with liver disease should not use Methuselah's Beard.

8. Elecampane

Elecampane (*Inula helenium*)

Description: Elecampane (*Inula helenium*) is also known as Horse Heal and Elfdock. This plant is native to Europe and northern Asia, but has been naturalized in parts of eastern North America, from Nova Scotia to Minnesota south to North Carolina and Missouri.

Elecampane typically grows 3 to 6 ft. (1 to 1.8 m) in height. Its stems are straight and green in color. The leaves at the base of the plant are alternate and oval- to lancet-shaped with wavy edges, while the leaves higher up on the plant tend to be more lancet-shaped. The lower leaves are 6 to 16 inches (15 to 40 cm) long and 4 to 8 inches (10 to 20 cm) wide. The underside of the leaves is covered in velvety hairs, while the upper surface is covered in rough hairs. Each leaf has a central, white vein. Elecampane blooms from July to September. Its flowers are sunflower-like and are 2 to 4 inches (5 to 10 cm) in diameter. Each flower has 50 to 100 thin, scraggly-looking, yellow petals.

Poisonous Look-Alike:

Jacobaea vulgaris subsp.; Rasbak; CC BY-SA 3.0

Homer Edward Price - Tansy-Ragwort-leaves, CC BY 2.0

Ragwort (*Senecio jacobaea* or *Jacobaea vulgaris*) contains potentially harmful alkaloids that may cause liver damage and can be fatal if ingested in large amounts. There are ways to tell them apart. Elecampane is taller than Ragwort. It can grow up to 6 ft. (1.8 m) tall. Ragwort usually reaches a height of approximately 3 ft. (1 m). Also, Elecampane leaves are larger and broader and Ragwort leaves are pinnately lobed.

Warning: Because it stimulates coughing, Elecampane should not be used by people with dry respiratory conditions like a dry, hacking cough; it is better used by people with productive coughs to facilitate the expulsion of phlegm.

9. Peppermint

Peppermint (*Mentha piperita*) Leaves

Peppermint (*Mentha piperita*) Flowers

Description: Peppermint (*Mentha piperita*) is also known as Mint Plant. It is native to Europe and the Middle East.

Peppermint typically grows 1 to 3 ft. (30 to 90 cm) in height. Its stems are square and reddish-green in color. The stems may have fine hairs. It has lancet-shaped, green leaves that are 1-2 inches (2.5 to 5 cm) in length and 0.5 to 1 inch (1-¼ to 2.5 cm) in width. There are fine hairs on the undersides of the leaves. The plant blooms in the summer. Its flowers are small and arranged in little clusters around the stem. They range in color from pink to lavender.

Warning: Peppermint should not be used by people with gallbladder obstruction, cholecystitis, or severe liver disease. Caution should be taken in individuals with constipation, iron deficiency anemia, and malnutrition because the tannins present in Peppermint may impair absorption of nutrients.

10. Marshmallow

Marshmallow *(Althaea officinalis)*

Marshmallow *(Althaea officinalis)*

Description: Marshmallow (*Althaea officinalis*) is also known as Marsh Mallow Plant. This plant is native to Europe and North Africa.

It typically grows 3 to 6 ft. (1 to 2 m) in height. Its stems are mostly upright, with few lateral branches. Its leaves are oval- to heart-shaped, grayish-green, and soft. The upper surface and the underside of the leaves are covered in soft hairs, giving them a velvety texture. It blooms from August to September. Its flowers are pale pink and bloom either singly or in clusters. Each flower is about 1.5 inches (4 cm) in diameter.

Warning: There is insufficient data to determine whether Marshmallow is safe for use in pregnant and lactating women.

11. St. John's Wort

Harry Rose, *Hypericum perforatum* leaf, CC BY 2.0

Hypericum perforatum- C T Johansson; CC BY-SA 3.0

Description: St. John's Wort (*Hypericum perforatum*) is also known as Goatweed and Klamath Weed. It is native to Europe, western Asia, and North Africa, and has been naturalized to North America.

St. John's Wort typically grows 1 to 3 ft. (30 to 90 cm) in height. Its stems are upright and branched toward the top. They are reddish in color. Each leaf is about 1 inch (2.5 cm) long and ⅓ of an inch (0.8 cm) wide. The leaves are oblong and they do not have hair on them. It blooms from June to August. Each flower is about ¾ of an inch (2 cm) in diameter and has 4-5 yellow petals. Each flower also has 4-51 bushy stamens. The petals have small black dots on the margins.

Warning: St. John's Wort should never be taken by individuals who are experiencing psychosis or severe depression. Because it can cause sensitivity to light, those who are photosensitive should avoid it. Because it increases serotonin levels, St. John's Wort should not be taken while also taking medication that increases serotonin levels (e.g., antidepressants like the serotonin-specific reuptake inhibitors Zoloft, Prozac, and Paxil). Taking both increases the risk of a life-threatening condition called serotonin syndrome.

12. Mustard

Mustard (*Brassica alba*) Leaves

White Mustard, flowers-H. Zell;CC BY-SA 3.0

Description: Mustard (*Brassica alba*) is also known as White Mustard and Kedlock. It is native to many regions of Europe, and it is cultivated in the United States, Nepal, Russia, and Canada.

The plant typically grows 1 to 2 ft. (30 to 60 cm) in height. Its stems are branched and they usually contain coarse hairs.

Its leaves are alternate and are comprised of 3 smaller leaflets. It is easier to see the distinct leaflets on the leaves that are attached to the upper portions of the stems than those that are attached at the base. The leaves have coarse hairs and each leaf is connected to a stalk. It blooms from June to August. Its flowers are yellow and about ½ inch (1.5 cm) in diameter. There are 4 petals and 6 stamens on each flower.

Warning: Mustard should not be taken orally by individuals with inflammation of the gastrointestinal tract. It should not be used topically by people with peripheral neuropathy. When Mustard is used topically it can be very hot and cause blistering if it is applied to the skin for too long. Do not use topically for long periods of time without a break and take caution not to burn your skin.

13. Rosemary

Rosemary (*Rosemarinus officinalis*)

Common Juniper (*Juniperus communis*)

Description: Rosemary (*Rosmarinus officinalis*) is native to the Mediterranean, Portugal, and northwestern Spain.

This plant typically grows 4 to 5 ft. (1.2 to 1.5 m) tall. Its stems are soft and green when young and become woody as they mature. It has aromatic, needle-like leaves. The leaves are usually less than 1 inch (2.5 cm) in size. There are short, dense hairs on the underside of the leaf. Rosemary blooms in spring to summer. Its flowers are small and usually range in color from pale blue to purple to white. Some cultivated varieties may produce pink flowers.

Poisonous Look-Alike:

Common Juniper (*Juniperus communis*) is generally safe for humans in moderation but the berries can be very toxic to livestock or dogs. The berries contain a potentially toxic chemical called thujone that can cause gastrointestinal irritation and central nervous system depression if ingested in large amounts. If livestock or dogs consume large quantities of the berries, it can cause kidney damage, and in extreme cases, even death. You can tell the difference between Common Juniper and Rosemary because Rosemary has needle-like leaves that are dark and shiny on the upper surface and pale green on the underside. Common Juniper has scaly-looking leaves that are arranged in opposite pairs of three and are blue-green or gray green in color. Rosemary is a perennial shrub that grows up to 5 ft. (1.5 m) tall and 4 ft. (1.2 m) wide. Common Juniper is a small, evergreen tree or shrub that grows to 30 ft. (9 m) tall. Rosemary does not produce berries while Common Juniper produces small, round, dark blue berries that are about the size of peas.

Warning: There is insufficient data to support the medicinal (not culinary) use of Rosemary in pregnant and lactating women.

14. Chamomile

Chamomile (*Matricaria recutita*)

Description: Chamomile (*Matricaria recutita*) is also known as German Chamomile, Sweet False Chamomile, and Wild Chamomile. This plant is native to Europe, Africa, and Asia, and has been naturalized to North America.

It typically grows 1 to 2.5 ft. (30 to 75 cm) in height. Its stems are branched, upright, and smooth. Each leaf is light green in color. The plant is doubly pinnate, meaning that each leaf is divided into leaflets that are subdivided into leaflets. It blooms from June to August. Its flowers are daisy-like, and each flower features 10 to 20 white petals that surround a bright yellow domed center. Chamomile produces an aromatic smell.

Warning: To reduce the likelihood of an allergic reaction, do not use Chamomile if you are allergic to Marigold, Ragweed, Daisies, Yarrow, Chrysanthemums, Calendula, or other plants in the Aster/Daisy family. Chamomile is safe for use during pregnancy; however, high dosing during the first trimester of pregnancy warrants caution.

15. Yarrow

Achillea millefolium-Alpsdake;CC BY-SA 4.0

Poisonous Look-Alike:

Conium maculatum, Sylvain Piry, CC BY-SA 2.0 fr

Hemlock (*Conium maculatum*)

Description: Yarrow (*Achillea millefolium*) is also known as Common Yarrow, Devil's Nettle, Dog Daisy, Dog Fennel, Milfoil, Soldier's Woundwort, Thousandleaf, and Western Yarrow. Yarrow is native to Europe and North Africa and is naturalized throughout North America.

The plant typically grows 1 to 3 ft. (30 to 90 cm) tall. Its stems are green, aromatic, and hairy. Each aromatic leaf is narrowly oblong to lancet-shaped. The leaves are alternate and are composed of deeply divided leaflets. It blooms from June to September. Each flower is 2 to 4 inches (5 to 10 cm) in diameter. Yarrow produces many small flowers, and its petals are usually white, red to pink, or yellow.

Hemlock (*Conium maculatum*) contains the alkaloids coniine and gamma-coniceine. All parts of the plant also contain piperidine alkaloids. These alkaloids act as neurotoxins, impairing the normal functioning of the nervous system. This, in turn, leads to paralysis and death. Coniine is the most plentiful and the strongest alkaloid in Hemlock. No amount of Hemlock is safe to ingest. Here's how you can differentiate between this deadly plant and Yarrow. Hemlock grows up to 6 ft. (1.8 m) tall, while Yarrow only reaches 1-2 ft. (30-60 cm) tall. Hemlock has finely divided leaves arranged in an alternating pattern along the stem. Yarrow has feather-like, finely divided leaves arranged in a more of a rosette at the base. Hemlock's stem is smooth, hairless, and hollow with purple spots and streaks. Yarrow's stem is hairy and solid. Hemlock has small, white flowers that grow in umbrella-shaped clusters at the tip of the stem. Yarrow has flat-topped clusters of small white or pink flowers.

Warning: To reduce the likelihood of an allergic reaction, do not use Yarrow if you are allergic to Marigold, Ragweed, Daisies, Chrysanthemums, Calendula, or other plants in the Aster/Daisy family. Do not use Yarrow internally if you are pregnant as it could lead to premature labor.

TRADITIONAL USES

Bites and Stings

It is important to be able to address bites and stings using wildcrafted herbs. In this section, we'll discuss two herbs - Calendula (*Calendula officinalis*) and Lemon Balm (*Melissa officinalis*) - and how they can be used to address bites and stings. Note that Plantain is my #1 go-to for bites and stings.

Calendula (*Calendula officinalis*)

Calendula has anti-inflammatory, antiseptic, lymphagogue (promotes the production or flow of lymphatic fluid), and vulnerary (promotes wound healing) properties. It is commonly used alongside conventional treatment for bites, inflammation of the skin, wounds, cuts, abrasions, bruises, minor burns, skin ulcers, peptic ulcers, digestive inflammation, gastritis, gastroenteritis, and lymphadenopathy.

Recipes:

Calendula Tea (Infusion)

Ingredients	Instructions
3 teaspoons Calendula flowers	Bring water to a boil
	Add Cleavers to boiling water
	Allow to boil for 5 minutes then reduce to low heat and let simmer, covered, for 20 minutes
1 cup water	Allow to cool, then strain
	Repeat up to 3 times daily for a maximum therapeutic dose of 9 teaspoons per day

Calendula Salve

Ingredients	Instructions
1/2 cup olive oil	Combine Calendula and olive oil in a pan on very low heat
	Heat the oil and cayenne until it is warm
	Remove from heat and let sit for about 20 minutes
2 tablespoons Calendula flowers (add plantain for a more potent salve)	Return to heat and let sit for 20 minutes again
	Repeat as many times as desired (more heating leads to a more potent salve)
	Use a cheesecloth to separate the infused oil from the Calendula
1/2-ounce beeswax	Heat the beeswax until it melts
	Stir in the infused oil and combine
	Pour the mixture into a jar and let cool
	Label your salve container
	Apply to skin as needed to promote healing of wounds and bites

Lemon Balm (*Melissa officinalis*)

Lemon Balm has nervine (promotes optimal functioning of the nervous system), spasmolytic (reduces muscular spasms), carminative (promotes passage of gas out of the gastrointestinal tract), antiviral, diaphoretic (promotes sweating), thyrosuppressive (reduces hyperactivity of the thyroid gland), antidepressant, hypnotic (helps restore balance to the circadian rhythm in order to promote restful sleep at appropriate times), and sedative properties. It is commonly used alongside conventional treatment for bee stings, insomnia, restlessness, palpitations, hypertension, anxiety, excitability, hyperactivity, hyperthyroidism, colic, poor digestion, nausea, gas and bloating, colds, influenza, herpes simplex virus, and other viral infections.

Recipe:

Lemon Balm Tea (Infusion)

Ingredients	Instructions
3 teaspoons Lemon Balm leaves	Bring water to a boil
	Add Lemon Balm to boiling water
	Allow to boil for 5 minutes then reduce to low heat and let simmer, covered, for 20 minutes
1 cup water	Allow to cool, then strain
	Repeat up to 3 times daily for a maximum therapeutic dose of 9 teaspoons per day

Bleeding and Breakage

It is important to be able to address bleeding and breakage using wildcrafted herbs. In this section, we'll discuss three herbs - English Oak (*Larrea tridentata*), Russian Comfrey (*Symphytum uplandica*) and *Achillea millefolium* - and how they can be used to address bleeding and breakage.

English Oak (*Quercus robur*)

English Oak has astringent, styptic (decreases bleeding), and antiseptic properties. It is commonly used to treat inflammatory blood disease, oral ulcers, bladder ulcers, hematuria (blood in urine), menorrhagia, bleeding gums, hemorrhoids, diarrhea, anal fistula, bedsores, canker sores, pharyngitis, inflammatory skin conditions, and contact dermatitis.

Recipe:

English Oak Tea (Decoction)

Ingredients	Instructions
	Add cold water to plant parts and bring to a boil
3 teaspoons English Oak bark	Allow the herbal mixture to boil for 10 minutes
	Reduce heat and cover pot, then allow to simmer for 20 minutes
	Remove from heat and allow to sit for at least 5 minutes, covered
	Strain to separate the plant material from the liquid
2 cups water	Drink the liquid, refrigerating any unused portions
	Repeat up to two times per day for a maximum therapeutic dose of up to 6 teaspoons per day
	Discard if unused after two days

Russian Comfrey (*Symphytum uplandica*)

Russian Comfrey has vulnerary (promotes wound healing), demulcent (soothing to the mucus membranes, including the gastrointestinal tract), emollient (soothing to the skin), and astringent properties. It is commonly used topically alongside conventional treatment for cuts, skin abrasions, superficial wounds, ulcers, contusions, soft tissue injury, gastrointestinal ulcers, broken or fractured bones, tendon or ligament injury, and cartilage tear.

Recipe:

Russian Comfrey Soak

Ingredients	Instructions
5 tablespoons Russian Comfrey leaves and/or root	Bring water to a boil
	Add Russian Comfrey to boiling water
	Allow to boil for 5 minutes then reduce to low heat and let simmer, covered, for 20 minutes
	Allow to cool slightly to a tolerable temperature, then strain and pour into a basin or bucket
6 cups water	Submerge affected body part in the Russian Comfrey solution for 20-30 minutes
	Remove affected body part from the solution and pour tepid water over it
	Dry the body partv

Recipes:

Yarrow Salve

Ingredients	Instructions
1/2 cup olive oil	Combine Yarrow and olive oil in a pan on very low heat
	Heat the oil and Yarrow until it is warm
	Remove from heat and let sit for about 20 minutes
	Return to heat and let sit for 20 minutes again
2 tablespoons Yarrow flowers and/or leaves	Repeat as many times as desired (more heating leads to a more potent salve)
	Use a cheesecloth to separate the infused oil from the plant particles
	Heat the beeswax until it melts
1/2-ounce bees-wax	Stir in the infused oil and combine
	Pour the mixture into a jar and let cool
	Label your salve container
	Apply to skin as needed to promote healing of wounds and bites

Yarrow (*Achillea millefolium*)

Yarrow has styptic, diaphoretic (promotes sweating), venotonic (tonifies the veins), vulnerary (promotes wound healing), inflammation-modulating, astringent, antimicrobial, and anti-inflammatory properties. It is commonly used alongside conventional treatment for cuts, scrapes, inflammation, skin abrasions, wounds, illnesses that lead to bleeding, enteritis, maldigestion, hypochlorhydria, intestinal cramps, hematuria, urinary tract inflammation, reproductive tract inflammation, hemoptysis, hemorrhoids, and perineal tears.

Yarrow Soak	
Ingredients	Instructions
4 tablespoons Yarrow leaves and/or flowers	Bring water to a boil
	Add yarrow to boiling water
	Allow to boil for 5 minutes then reduce to low heat and let simmer, covered, for 5 minutes
	Allow to cool to a tolerable temperature, then pour into a basin or bucket
4 cups water	Submerge affected body part into Yarrow infusion for 15-30 minutes, as tolerated
	Remove affected body part from the infusion
	Pour tepid water over the area and dry them thoroughly

Pain Management

It is important to be able to address pain management using wildcrafted herbs. In this section, we'll discuss two herbs - Arnica (*Arnica montana*) and Corydalis (*Corydalis* spp.) - and how they can be used to address pain management.

Arnica (*Arnica montana*)

Arnica has analgesic, inflammation-modulating, vulnerary, and anti-inflammatory properties. It is commonly used alongside conventional treatment for pain due to soft tissue injury, bruises, hematoma, phlebitis, sprain or strain, sore muscles, injury, or abscess.

Recipe:

Arnica Compress	
Ingredients	Instructions
2 teaspoons Arnica flowers	Bring water to a boil
	Add Arnica flowers to boiling water
2 cups of water	Allow to boil for 5 minutes then reduce to low heat and let simmer, covered, for 20 minutes
2 clean, dry cloths, large enough to wrap the affected area	Allow to cool, then strain
	Saturate one clean cloth with the herbal tea and use the cloth to wrap the affected area
Pins or other means of securing the cloth after wrapping	Wrap the wet compress with another clean, dry cloth and secure it using pins

Corydalis (*Corydalis* spp.)

Corydalis has analgesic, sedative, and spasmolytic properties. It is commonly used alongside conventional treatment for chest pain, headache, abdominal pain, dysmenorrhea, gallbladder pain, cholelithiasis, musculoskeletal injury, muscle spasms, and insomnia.

Recipe:

Corydalis Tea (Decoction)	
Ingredients	Instructions
1 teaspoon Corydalis root	Add cold water to plant parts and bring to a boil
	Allow the herbal mixture to boil for 10 minutes
	Reduce heat and cover pot, then allow to simmer for 20 minutes
	Remove from heat and allow to sit for at least 5 minutes, covered
	Strain to separate the plant material from the liquid
1 cup water	Drink the liquid, refrigerating any unused portions
	Repeat up to three times per day for a maximum therapeutic dose of up to 3 teaspoons per day
	Discard if unused after two days

Infections

In this section, we'll discuss two herbs - Methuselah's beard (*Usnea longissima*) and Elecampane (*Inula helenium*) - and how they can be used to address infections. Note that Yarrow is also a very strong anti-bacterial. It is my go-to paired with Usnea for sinus, ear, and throat infections. For colds and flu I like to combine the herbs in this section with an internal Elderberry tincture.

Methuselah's Beard (*Usnea longissima*)

Methuselah's Beard has antimicrobial and immunestimulating properties. It is commonly used alongside conventional treatment for bacterial infections, colds, influenza, urinary tract infection, upper respiratory tract infection, gastroenteritis, impetigo, pharyngitis, skin infections, bronchitis, sinusitis, pneumonia, prostatitis, skin infections.

Recipe:

Methuselah's Beard Tea (Infusion)

Note that I prefer a dual-extracted alcoholic tincture if possible to make in the field.

Ingredients	Instructions
3 teaspoon Methuselah's Beard (whole lichen)	Bring water to a boil
	Add Methuselah's Beard to boiling water
	Allow to boil for 5 minutes then reduce to low heat and let simmer, covered, for 20 minutes
1 cup water	Allow to cool, then strain
	Repeat up to 3 times daily for a maximum therapeutic dose of 9 teaspoons per day

Elecampane (*Inula helenium*)

Elecampane has antimicrobial, anti-inflammatory, and inflammation modulating properties. It is also a stimulating expectorant (stimulates the body to expel phlegm through coughing) and a lung tonic (tonifies the lungs). It is commonly used alongside conventional treatment for acute and chronic bronchitis, pneumonia, productive cough, asthma, emphysema, indigestion, and poor appetite.

Recipe:

Elecampane Tea (Decoction)

Ingredients	Instructions
3 teaspoon Elecampane root	Add cold water to plant parts and bring to a boil
	Allow the herbal mixture to boil for 10 minutes
	Reduce heat and cover pot, then allow to simmer for 20 minutes
	Remove from heat and allow to sit for at least 5 minutes, covered
	Strain to separate the plant material from the liquid
1 cup water	Drink the liquid, refrigerating any unused portions
	Repeat up to three times per day for a maximum therapeutic dose of up to 9 teaspoons per day
	Discard if unused after two days

Digestive Upsets and Diarrhea

It is important to be able to address digestive upset and diarrhea using wildcrafted herbs. In this section, we'll discuss two herbs - Peppermint (*Mentha piperita*) and Marshmallow (*Althaea officinalis*) - and how they can be used to address digestive upset and diarrhea.

Peppermint (*Mentha piperita*)

Peppermint has carminative (promotes passage of gas out of the gastrointestinal tract), spasmolytic (reduces muscle spasms), diaphoretic (promotes sweating), antiemetic (reduces nausea), decongestant, rubefacient (increases circulation and produces redness of the skin), and anesthetic properties. It is commonly used alongside conventional treatment for intestinal cramps, gas, bloating, nausea, vomiting, motion sickness, colds, influenza, pharyngitis, bronchitis, tension headaches, neuralgia, toothache, and musculoskeletal pain.

Recipes:

Peppermint Tea (Infusion)

Ingredients	Instructions
2 teaspoon Peppermint leaves	Bring water to a boil
	Add Peppermint to boiling water
1 cup water	Allow to boil for 5 minutes then reduce to low heat and let simmer, covered, for 20 minutes
	Allow to cool, then strain
	Repeat up to 3 times daily for a maximum therapeutic dose of 6 teaspoons per day

Peppermint Steam Inhalation

Ingredients	Instructions
2 cups water	Bring water to a boil and remove from fire
	Add Peppermint essential oil to water
	Use a towel to create a tent over yourself and the pot, being careful not to burn yourself
3-5 drops Peppermint essential oil	Breathe deeply, inhaling and exhaling fully to clear nasal passages and fight respiratory pathogens
	Repeat multiple times per day as needed

Marshmallow (*Althaea officinalis*)

Marshmallow root has demulcent (soothing to the mucus membranes, including the gastrointestinal tract), vulnerary (promotes wound healing), emollient (soothing to the skin), and diuretic properties. It is commonly used alongside conventional treatment for gastroesophageal reflux disease, irritable bowel syndrome, leaky gut, hyperacidity, peptic ulcer disease, colitis, inflammatory bowel disease, gastritis, constipation, diarrhea, hemorrhoids, gastrointestinal infection, abscess, boils, ulcers, wounds, spastic cough, urinary tract irritation, kidney stones, cystitis, and gangrene.

Recipe:

Marshmallow Cold Infusion

Ingredients	Instructions
6 tablespoons washed and chopped Marshmallow root (leaves may also be added)	Combine plant parts and water in a pot or bowl
	Allow to infuse at room temperature for at least 8 hours to extract mucilage
1 cup water	Strain and drink
	Maximum therapeutic dose: up to 18 teaspoons of Marshmallow leaf and/or root per day

Taking Care of Your Feet

It is important to be able to address trench foot using wildcrafted herbs. In this section, we'll discuss three herbs - St. John's Wort (*Hypericum perforatum*), Mustard (Brassica alba), and Rosemary (*Rosemarinus officinalis*) - and how they can be used to prevent and treat trench foot.

St. John's Wort (*Hypericum perforatum*)

St. John's Wort is a nervous system trophorestorative (helps build up the nervous system), nervine (promotes optimal functioning of the nervous system), antidepressant, antiviral, vulnerary (promotes wound healing), and anxiolytic (reduces anxiety). It is commonly used alongside conventional treatment for wounds, nerve pain, skin abrasions, cuts, bruises, sprains and strains, contusions, and spinal injury.

Recipes:

St. John's Wort Oil

Ingredients	Instructions
1/2 cup olive oil	Combine St. John's Wort and olive oil in a pan on very low heat
	Heat the oil and St. John's Wort until warm
	Remove from heat and let sit for about 20 minutes
	Return to heat and let sit for 20 minutes again
2 tablespoons St. John's Wort flowering tops	Repeat as many times as desired (more heating leads to a more potent oil)
	Use a cheesecloth to separate the infused oil from the St. John's Wort particles
	Pour the oil into a jar
	Label and store your oil
	Apply liberally to promote wound healing

St. John's Wort Tea (Infusion)

Ingredients	Instructions
1 rounded teaspoon St. John's Wort flowering tops	Bring water to a boil
	Add St. John's Wort to boiling water
1 cup water	Allow to boil for 5 minutes then reduce to low heat and let simmer, covered, for 20 minutes
	Allow to cool, then strain
	Repeat up to 3 times daily for a maximum therapeutic dose of 3 teaspoons per day

Mustard (*Brassica alba*)

Mustard has rubefacient (increases circulation and produces redness of the skin), diaphoretic (promotes sweating), carminative (promotes passage of gas out of the gastrointestinal tract), and vesicant (tends to cause blistering) properties. It is commonly used alongside conventional treatment for mild skin irritation, inflammation, reduced peripheral circulation, cold extremities, muscle pain, joint pain, arthritis, bronchitis, pneumonia, and congestive headache.

Recipes:

Mustard Poultice

Ingredients	Instructions
1 part Mustard Seeds	Mix Mustard Seeds and flour
	Spread onto thin cloth
	Cover the area to be treated with olive oil or a salve to protect the skin
3-4 parts flour	Apply the cloth to the area
	Check periodically for reddening or blistering
	Apply for a total of 10-20 minutes
	Remove the poultice if it begins to feel uncomfortable

Mustard Foot Bath	
Ingredients	**Instructions**
1 teaspoon crushed Mustard seeds	Bring water to a boil
	Add Mustard seeds to boiling water
	Allow to boil for 5 minutes then reduce to low heat and let simmer, covered, for 5 minutes
	Allow to cool to a tolerable temperature, then pour into a basin or bucket
4 cups water	Submerge feet into Mustard infusion for 5-15 minutes, as tolerated
	Remove feet from the infusion
	Pour tepid water over feet and dry them

Rosemary (*Rosmarinus officinalis*)

Rosemary has circulatory stimulating, nootropic (increases blood flow to the brain and may enhance memory or cognitive function), antioxidant, antimicrobial, and inflammation-modulating properties. It is commonly used alongside conventional treatment for poor circulation, cold extremities, inflammation, pain, inflammation, low vitality, congestive heart failure, cardiac weakness.

Recipe:

Rosemary Tea (Infusion)	
Ingredients	**Instructions**
2 teaspoon Rosemary leaves	Bring water to a boil
1 cup water	Add Rosemary to boiling water
	Allow to boil for 5 minutes then reduce to low heat and let simmer, covered, for 20 minutes
	Allow to cool, then strain
	Repeat up to 3 times daily for a maximum therapeutic dose of 6 teaspoons per day

Hypothermia

It is important to be able to address hypothermia using wildcrafted herbs. In this section, we'll discuss two cooling herbs - Chamomile (*Matricaria recutita*) and Yarrow (*Achillea millefolium*) - and how they can be used to address hypothermia.

Chamomile (*Matricaria recutita*)

Chamomile has nervine (promotes optimal functioning of the nervous system), inflammation-modulating, spasmolytic (reduces musclular spasm), carminative (promotes passage of gas out of the gastrointestinal tract), hypnotic (helps restore balance to the circadian rhythm in order to promote restful sleep at appropriate times), mild sedative, vulnerary (promotes wound healing), and diaphoretic (promotes sweating) properties.

Recipe:

Chamomile Tea (Infusion)	
Ingredients	**Instructions**
3 teaspoon Chamomile flowers	Bring water to a boil
	Add Chamomile to boiling water
	Allow to boil for 5 minutes then reduce to low heat and let simmer, covered, for 20 minutes
1 cup water	Allow to cool, then strain
	Repeat up to 4 times daily for a maximum therapeutic dose of 12 teaspoons per day

Yarrow (*Achillea millefolium*)

Yarrow has venotonic (tonifies the veins), vulnerary, inflammation-modulating, astringent, antimicrobial, and anti-inflammatory properties. It is commonly used alongside conventional treatment for cuts, scrapes, inflammation, skin abrasions, wounds, illnesses that lead to bleeding, enteritis, maldigestion, hypochlorhydria (low stomach acid), intestinal cramps, hematuria (blood in urine), urinary tract inflammation, reproductive tract inflammation, hemoptysis (coughing up blood), hemorrhoids, and perineal tears.

Recipes:

Yarrow Tea (Infusion)

Ingredients	Instructions
2 teaspoon Yarrow flowers and/or leaves	Bring water to a boil
	Add Yarrow to boiling water
	Allow to boil for 5 minutes then reduce to low heat and let simmer, covered, for 20 minutes
1 cup water	Allow to cool, then strain
	Drink hot every hour when feeling feverish or ill

Yarrow Oil

Ingredients	Instructions
4 tablespoon dried Yarrow leaves	Place Yarrow in a heat-proof container
	Add enough oil to cover the herbs
	Fill a small pot about 1/3 full of water and bring to a boil
	Turn the heat down to a simmer
	Place the jar of oil and herbs into the water, preventing the water from getting into the oil container
	Use the water like a double-boiler to gently heat the herbs and oil for 2 to 3 hours, being careful not to overheat
½ cup olive oil	Allow the oil to cool, then filter through a couple of layers of cheesecloth
	Squeeze the cheesecloth to get all the oil
	Discard the herb and use the oil topically as needed

CRAFTING IN THE WILD

KNOTS THAT ARE EXTREMELY USEFUL IN THE WILD

Every level of survival and bushcraft requires an in-depth working knowledge of knots and how to use them in the wild. These skills come in handy out in the wild, whether you're camping, surviving, or even building a tree fort.

There are so many variations of knots and hitches out there that it's possible no one knows them all, and it's not important to know each and every one. Through practice and experience, everyone discovers their favorite knots for every situation. Some people may use a taut line hitch whereas others would use a trucker's hitch.

Here, various knots are presented to help get a start on what can take a lifetime to learn. By the end of the chapter, anyone should be able to head out and know what knots to use for what use in the wild. But, remember, there's always more to learn.

Uses for Knots in the Wild

In the wild, ropework is an art form that will come in handy every day. From the moment you wake up until you fall asleep, there are countless moments where knots will be required to get past whatever obstacle stands in your way.

You'll find yourself tying a plethora of different knots just setting up a shelter and preparing or shutting down camp. Stakes in the ground require a certain knot while connecting to a tree requires another. Hanging food to keep it from wild animals comes with its own set of knots.

When building a shelter, there are different knots to lash wood together and hold everything in place. Then, you can hang your clothes from a clothesline with a wide selection of different knots.

Fishing knots are of a completely different variety because of the nature of the line. Fishing line is small and very slippery. There's little-to-no friction to rely on with the line, meaning a lot of normal knots will slip out. There are a few knots that are perfect for fishing, and plenty more that experienced anglers would argue that they prefer.

Everyone needs knots out in the wild. You will find what works best for you through experience and trial-and-error.

All the Knot Lingo

As with everything in the wild, there's a level of lingo that comes along with knot tying. These are the basics you need to know before diving into how to tie each knot. Without these, it's hard to know what to do when people talk about different parts of the rope and different ways to maneuver it.

Parts of the Line

- Working or Running End - the end of the line in your hand that does all the work
- Standing End - the fixed side of the line that you aren't actively working with. This is often fixed to a point, such as a tree.
- Body - the middle of the line between the working and standing ends
- Tail or Tag - the very end of the rope on the working end. Also refers to the small section of the working end remaining once the knot is complete.
- Underhand Loop - a loop formed by placing the working end underneath the standing end
- Overhand Loop - a loop formed by placing the working end on top of the standing end
- Bights - a section of rope formed by grabbing a loose portion of rope without any rope crossing itself
- Turns - when rope goes completely around itself for one full loop

Dressing a Knot

"*A not neat knot is a knot not needed.*"

Hard to say, but totally spot on. Dressing the knot is the final important stage of tying any knot. When a knot isn't neat, it's possible that there are twists in the line that can add unnecessary stress to different parts of the rope.

Every knot tied into a line will reduce the strength of the rope used. This varies with every bend you make. For example, a bowline functions between 70-75% of the normal tested strength, while an overhand knot will only have 60-65% of the normal strength.

Dressing a knot allows you to get both the correct functionality of the knot, and the maximum strength possible from every knot tied.

Hitches vs. Knots vs. Bends

Hitches and knots are commonly mistaken for each other. More often, a hitch will be called a knot, but this isn't the case. Knowing the difference can help determine which to use in various situations.

The important distinction is that a knot will hold its form without the object it's being tied to. A hitch will fall apart when the tree, post, bolt, etc. is removed. For example, a bowline can be tied in a line and laid on the ground. A clove hitch will fall apart when laid down apart from the rod it is tied on.

A bend is still technically a knot because it only involves different lines. Bends are used to tie two different ropes together, often when trying to extend the length of one rope or haul one rope up with another (common in rock climbing).

The Best Knots for Use in the Wild

1. Canadian Jam Knot

Also commonly referred to as the arbor knot, the Canadian jam knot is a favorite amongst bushcrafters and anyone who spends time outdoors. It's easy to see why when you recognize the simplicity and functionality of this knot. It can be tied in a heartbeat and is easily undone when you no longer need it.

How to Tie It

- Wrap the working end around the object you are tying to.
- Bring the tail under the standing end and across both sections of rope.
- Form a loop around the standing end and pass the tail through, creating an overhand knot that holds both the working and standing end.
- Tighten this knot.
- Loop the tail around itself and pass it through the loop, tying another overhand in the tail and tighten.
- Now, pull on the standing end to jam the knot in the tail up against the first knot.
- The knot will tighten and hold tension around the object you tied to.

Best Uses

- Fishing (tying to the arbor)
- Holding gear or firewood bundles together
- Lashing shelter
- Connecting line to a fixed object

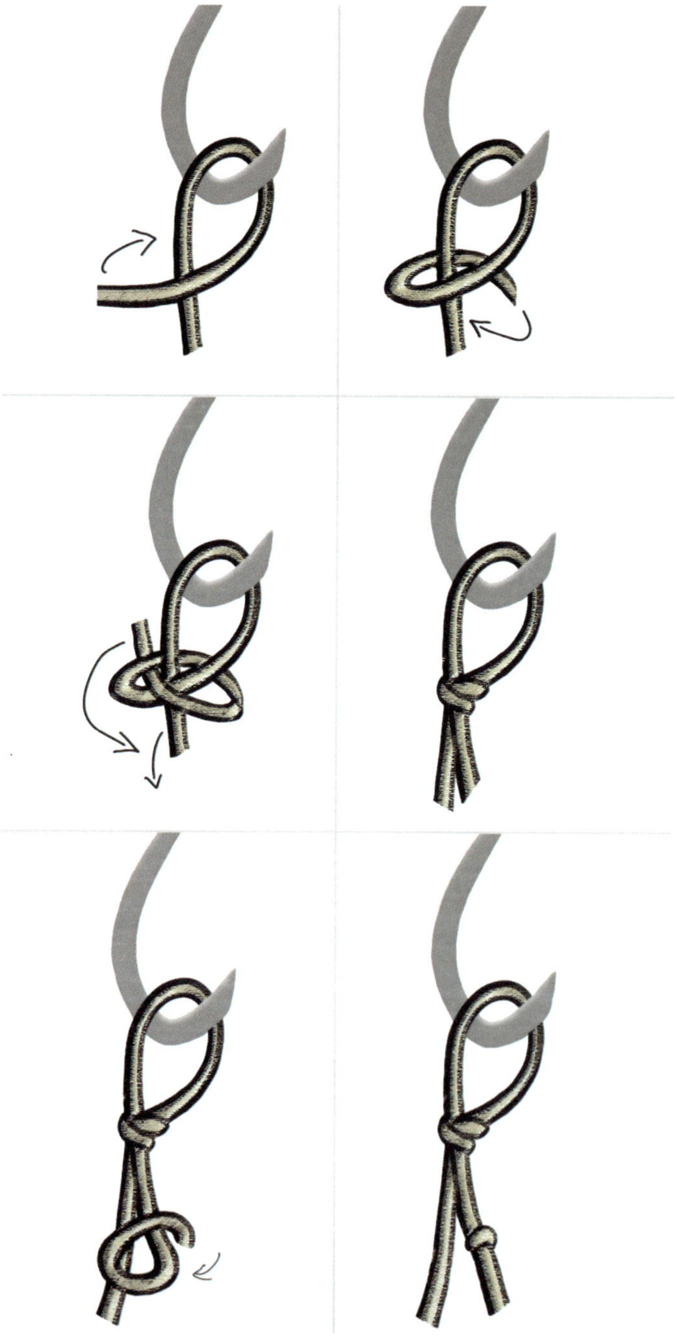

2. Square Knot (Reef Knot)

The square knot is a common knot used to tie two lines together when the line isn't bearing a heavy load. It's referred to as the reef knot, because it's used in sailing to reef the sail (lowering the sail and reducing the area put up).

How to Tie It

- Lay the two ends of the separate ropes parallel to each other.
- With one tail in each hand, place the right end over and under the left rope.
- Take the two tails and place the left end over and under the right end.
- "Right over left, left over right"

Best Uses

- Holding bundles together
- Connecting handmade cordage sections
- Joining short sections of rope
- Non-human weight-bearing loads (never trust your weight on a square knot!)

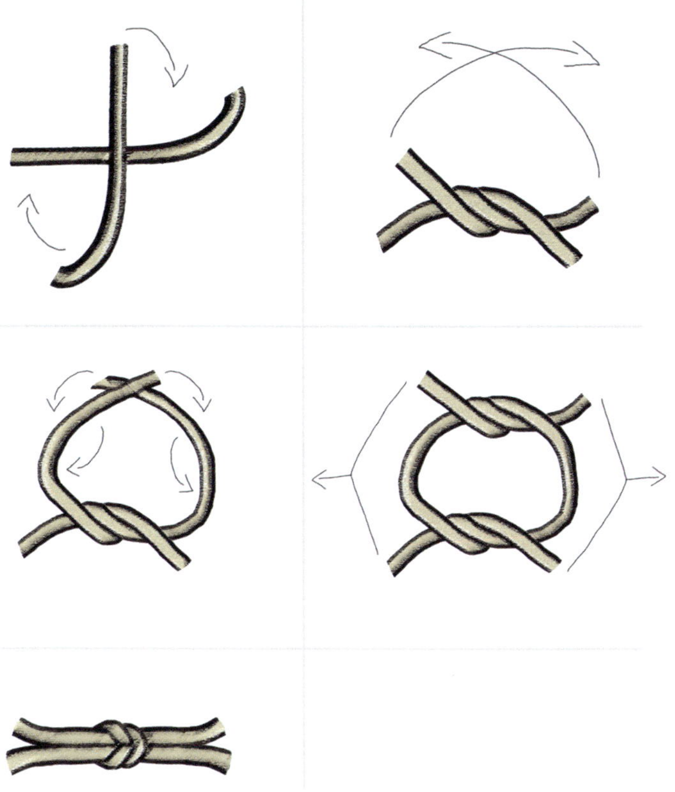

3. Sheet Bend

A sheet bend is a different way to connect two ends of different ropes, often used for two ropes of different diameters. This bend is much more substantial than a square knot, meaning you can use it for much heavier loads. When bearing heavier loads, many people will use a double sheet bend to ensure more security.

The double sheet bend adds kinks in the line, meaning it will reduce the strength of the line itself. So, while more secure, it's actually weaker than a single.

How to Tie It

- Create a bight with the tail thicker rope, creating a "J" shape.
- Bring the working end of the smaller line up and through the bight.
- Make one turn with the smaller tail around the larger.
- Bring the smaller tail around and under its own body. This is a single sheet bend.
- Create a double sheet bend by making a second turn around the larger line and bringing the smaller tail back under itself.

Best Uses

- Famous for tying two lines together of different diameters
- Can also be used to tie a guy line to a grommet on a tarp

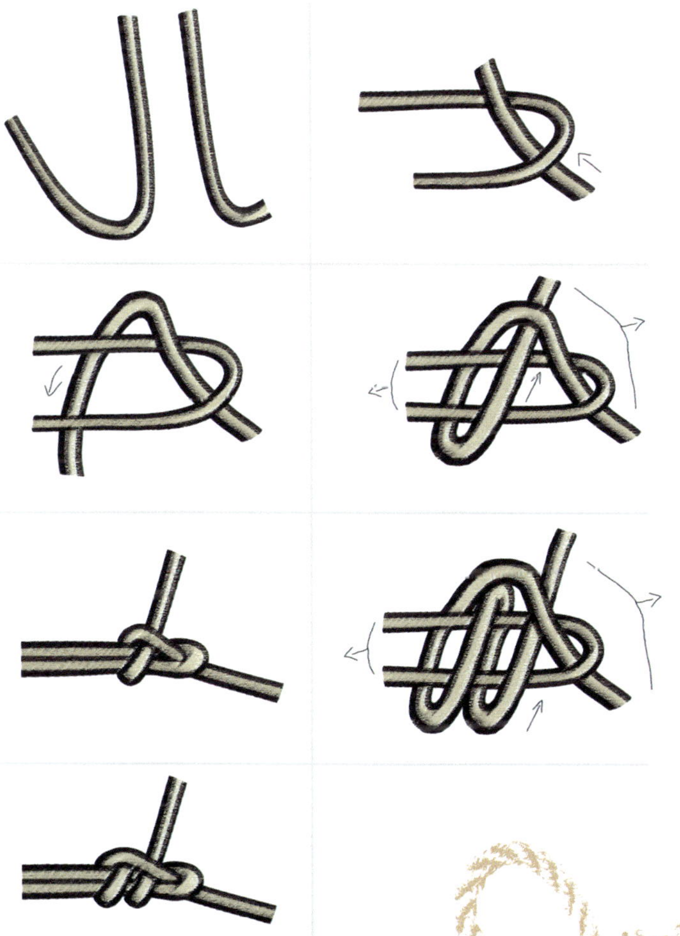

4. Bowline

Coming from boating (the bow-line), the bowline (pronounced the bo-lin), is a favorite for many while camping, boating, or practicing bushcraft. It's loved for its strength and inability to slip once tied correctly. It was used popularly as the primary knot for tying in while rock climbing. While it isn't used as commonly for this anymore, it's found everywhere else.

Once tied, the loop formed will not shrink or expand. It's a perfect knot for tying a line to any fixed object when you don't want it to move. Even after the knot is put under extreme tension, it is easily untied, which is one of the knot's best features.

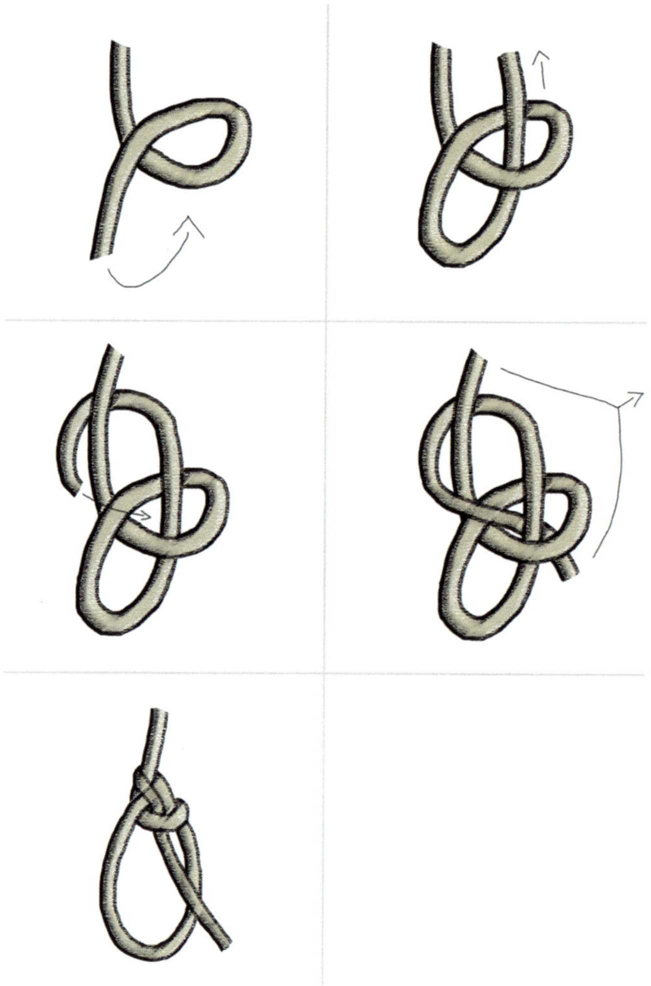

How to Tie It

- Create an overhand loop, leaving plenty of tail on the working end.
- Bring the working end up through to loop formed.
- Wrap the tail behind the standing end, around, and back through the loop.
- Pull tight and dress.

The idiom of a rabbit coming out of its hole is often used for this knot. The rabbit comes up out of its hole, runs around the tree, and jumps back into its home.

Best Uses

- Tying a line to a fixed object as an anchor
- Creating a non-slipping loop at the end of a line
- Rescue situations
- Attaching line to tarps

5. Fisherman's Knot

The fisherman's knot is exactly as it sounds, a knot loved by fishermen all around the world. It's the go-to knot for many to tie a line to a hook without worrying about the slippery line pulling out when a monster grabs onto the bait. While it may be used for other tasks, this is its primary use.

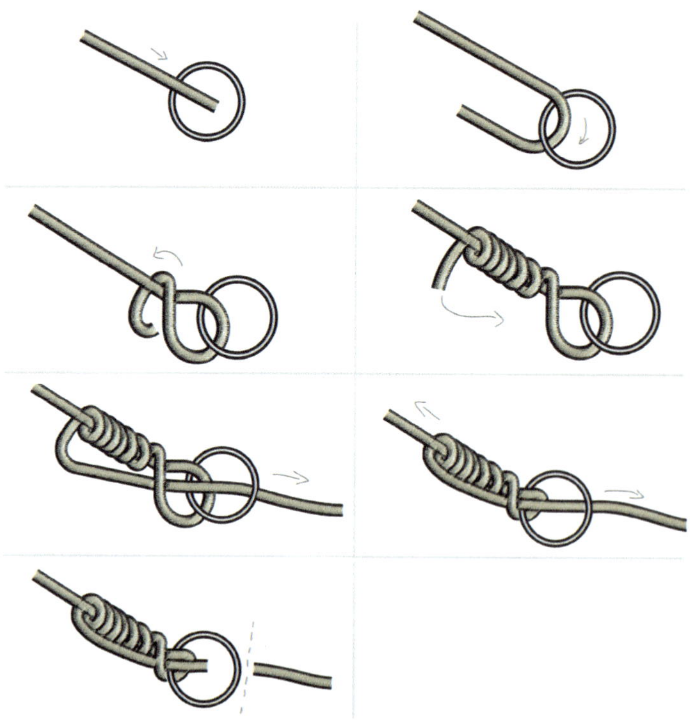

How to Tie It

- Pass the tail through the eye of a hook, or around the object being tied to.
- Wrap the tail around the other side of the line between 5-6 times.
- Pass the tail through the gap between the first wrap and the hook.
- Pull tight (using your saliva often helps tighten fishing line) and trim excess tail if used for fishing.

Best Uses

- Securing fishing line to a hook

6. Double Fisherman's

Technically a bend, and very different from the fisherman's knot, the double fisherman's is a great choice for tying two lines together. If you have two lines of a similar size, this bend will hold them together securely. When not under tension, the bend can be pulled apart to tighten a loop and adjusted again to loosen it.

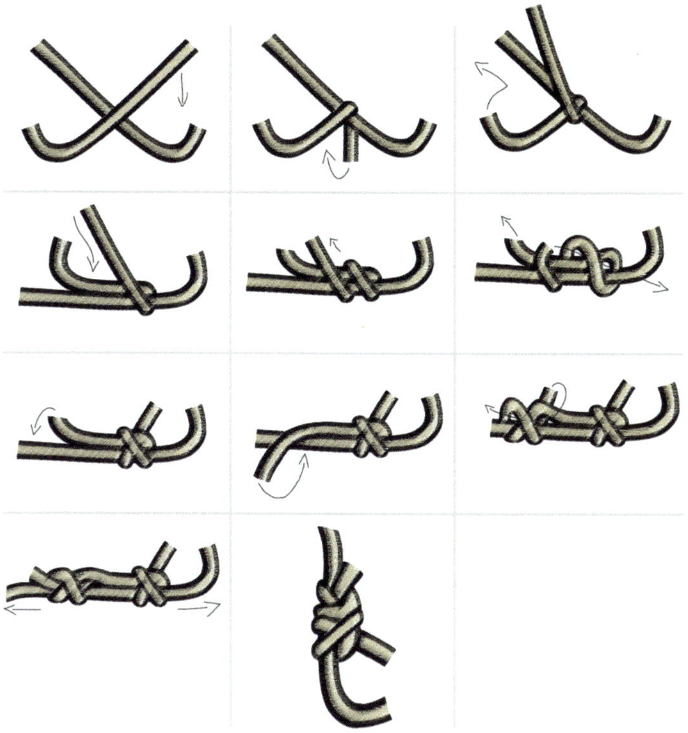

How to Tie It

- Lay the two lines parallel and create a "J" with each line, placing the tails away from the center where the two lines lay touching.
- Lay the two ends overlapping each other.
- Wrap one tail around both with two full turns and pass it back through the turns to pull tight.
- Repeat with the second tail.
- Pull the standing ends to bring the two bends together.

Best Uses

- Tying two ends of a similar line together
- Creating an adjustable loop in one line

7. Slipknots

Slipknots are simply knots that come undone when the tail is pulled on. Obviously, this can be great for many reasons and dangerous to use in others. When used correctly, it can make any outdoorsmen's life significantly better.

Oftentimes, it's useful to use the slipknot to finish tying other knots, making them easy to release after being under tension. Using a slipknot in combination with others can make tearing down camp a much quicker task. Especially in colder environments when dexterity is limited, it can be useful to simply pull and have a knot untie itself.

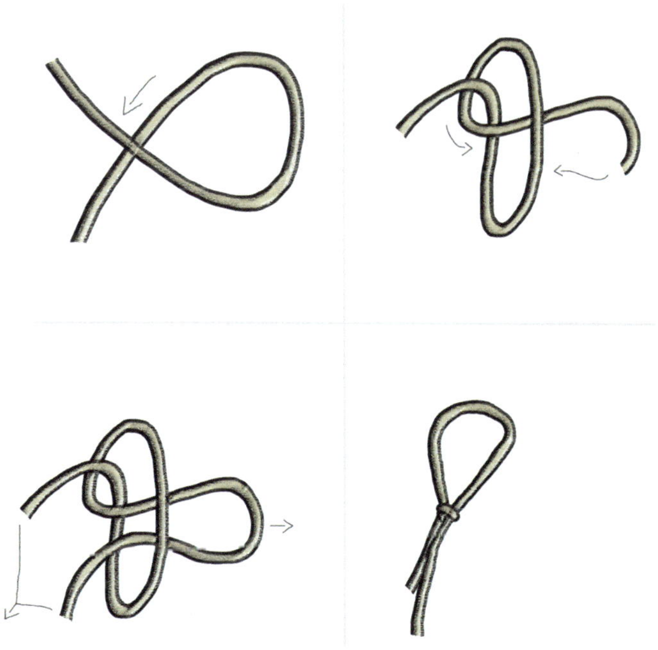

How to Tie It

- Form a loop near the end of the rope.
- Create a bight in the short tail end.
- Tuck the bight into the loop and tighten the loop down on the bight. Similar to an overhand, but passing a bight through the loop rather than the tail.
- To untie, pull on the tail and remove the bight.

Best Uses

- In conjunction with a trucker's hitch or other compatible knots
- Temporary stopper knot

The Best Hitches for Use in the Wild

1. The Clove Hitch

Along with the bowline, the clove hitch is one that is likely used the most often in the wild. It's the perfect hitch to secure both ends of the line that come out from the object it's tied onto, with neither end slipping at all. It proves to be incredibly useful in situations ranging from putting up a tent to anchoring yourself while performing a serious rescue.

How to Tie It

There are two main methods for tying a clove hitch. One is best for when tying it in the middle of a long rope onto an object that it can be slid onto. The other is best for working with a free tail end of a rope and tying to a longer object that you can't slip a loop onto.

Method One

- Holding a section of rope, create two loops by twisting two separate bights counterclockwise.
- Take the right loop and lay it over the left.
- Insert the object you are tying to through both loops.
- Pull both ends tight.

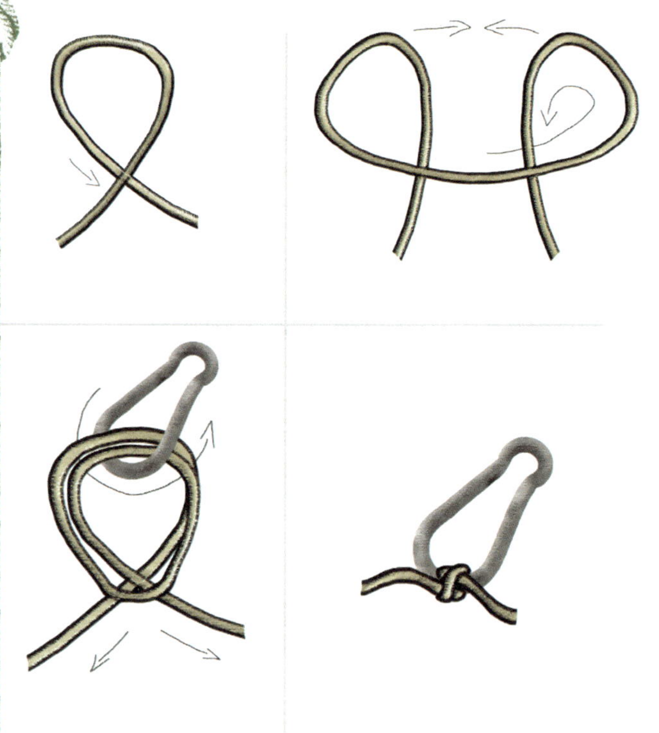

Method Two

- Pass the tail over the object you are tying to and back to the front.
- Make another pass over the object and the line, creating an "X".
- Bring the tail under the line and the object, then pass it below both sections of line through the center of the X.
- Pull both ends tight.

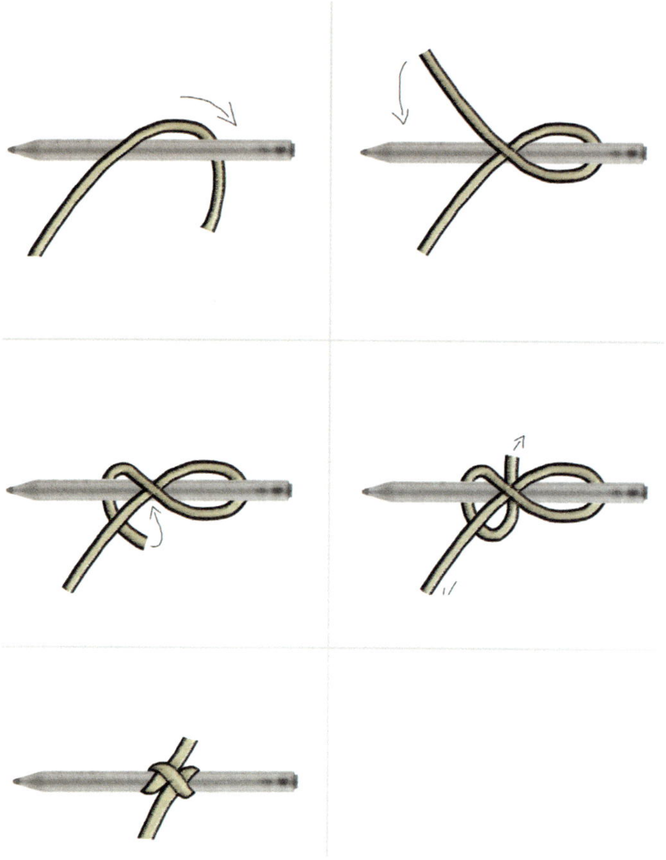

Best Uses

- Securing any point of a line to a fixed point
- Rescue scenarios
- Tying to stakes for a tarp or setting up a tripod
- Creating two fixed lines off of one point with a single rope

2. Prusik

Created by an Austrian mountaineer, Karl Prusik, this hitch was originally designed for ascending ropes while on long mountaineering expeditions. It connects a loop of cord to another rope or fixed object, using friction to wrap and grab onto the rope once downward pressure is applied.

This is a hitch primarily used in outdoor recreation while climbing, canyoneering, mountaineering, caving, etc., but is also used by arborists to ascend ropes into trees.

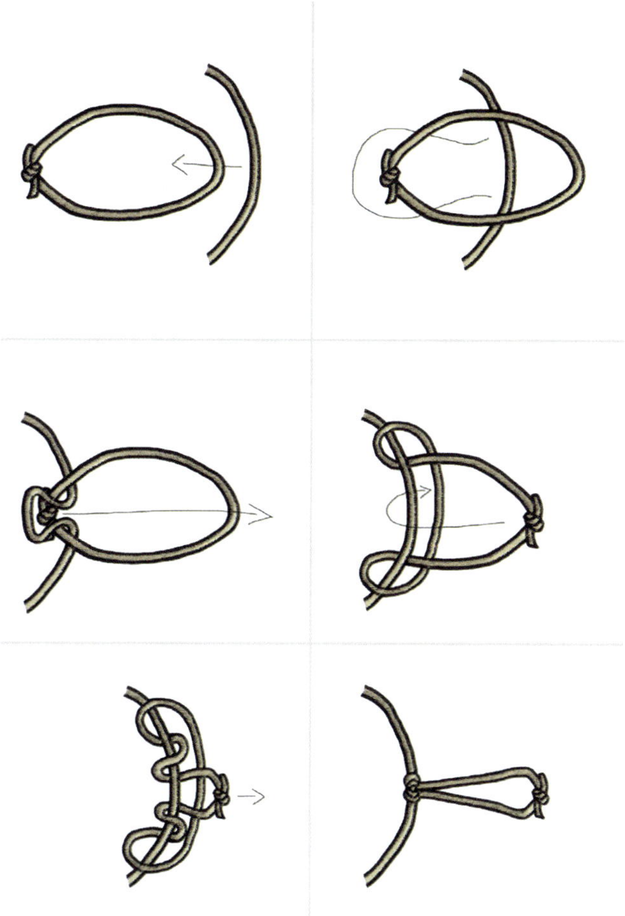

How to Tie It

- With a fixed loop of cord, lay it underneath the rope being tied to.
- Pass one bight of the loop over the rope and through itself.
- Bring the same section under the rope and through the same loop a second time.
- Pull this bight tight and work the remaining line to wrap tightly onto the rope.

Best Uses

- Ascending and descending on ropes
- Tying a load to a rope

3. Taut Line Hitch

Also referred to as the midshipman's hitch, the taut line hitch is an easy way to create a line that can be tightened easily by sliding the knot along the line. Many people love this hitch for its adjustability, being able to make a line tauter without much effort.

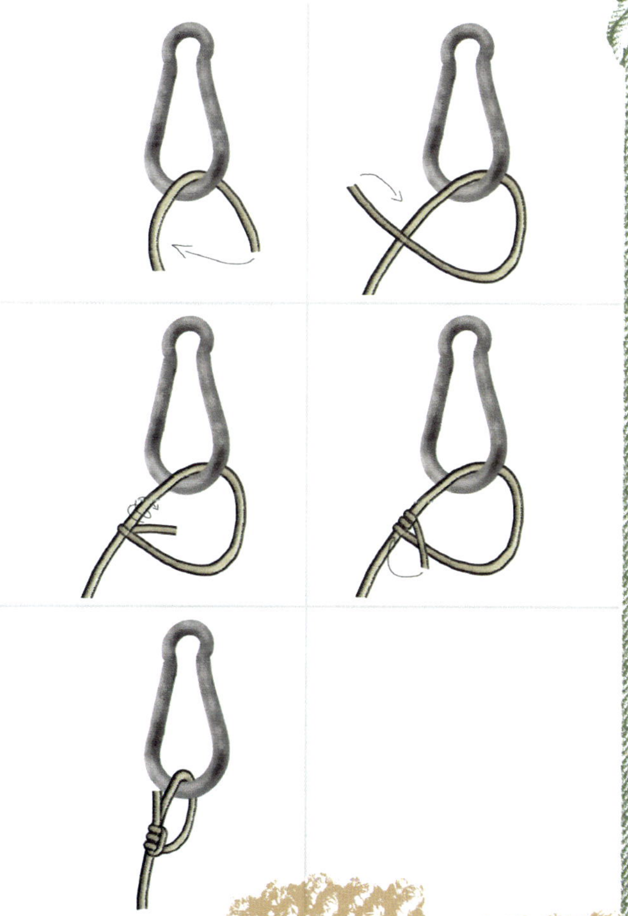

How to Tie It

Wrap the line around the object you are tying to.

Pass the tail around the standing end twice and tighten.

Bring the tail to the other side of where the line initially intersects the standing end.

Tie a half hitch (over the line and back under itself).

Best Uses

- Creating a line that can be pulled taut

4. Trucker's Hitch

Another hitch that is used to pull a line incredibly taut is the trucker's hitch. Technically, this is a compound knot because it requires tying multiple knots in the same line to form the trucker's hitch in the very end. The trucker's hitch utilizes the physics of a pulley system to pull the line taut, making it a go-to for putting up a tarp as a solid shelter.

There are several ways to tie this knot, using a variety of different knots as the first knot. The way laid out here is designed to be released easily, even after being under extreme tension.

How to tie it

- Wrap the rope around the object being tied to.
- On the standing end, create an underhand loop.
- Reach through the underhand loop and grab a bight from the working end's side and pull it through the loop creating a slip knot.
- Bring the tail through the loop created.
- Pull tension towards the object you are tying to.
- Pinch the line where it meets the loop to hold it in place.
- Tie a half hitch up on the new standing end up against the loop.
- To make it quick-release, pass a bight through underneath the line rather than the tail.
- Pull the half hitch tight.

Best Uses

- Creating a taut line to set up tarps
- Secure gear to backpack
- Create rope bridge across a gap

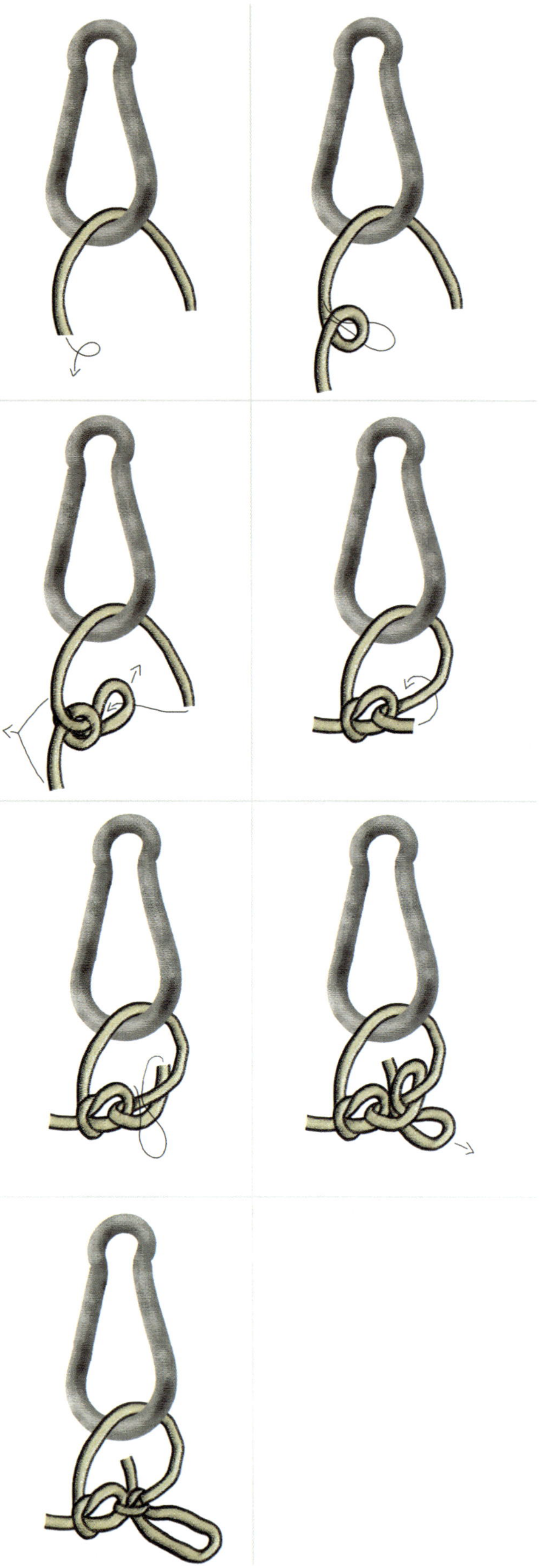

HOW TO CRAFT TOOLS AND WEAPONS IN THE WILD

Learning to create your own wild tools and weapons is not only interesting; it's a vital skill. This chapter outlines how to build them with materials you can find around you.

What Materials Can You Use?

Survivalists can seem like magicians as they harvest and manipulate natural resources into something usable. The truth anyone can do that as nature provides plenty of materials to make just about anything you want.

Stone

Using rocks for primitive tool building is as old a practice as any. They are plentiful, come in all kinds of hardness, and are a staple in creating any tool for your kit. Stones are generally used as cutting and skinning tools since they can be honed or knapped to a sharp edge.

Your kit should include several sizes of rocks, everything from pebbles to larger grinding stones. Using flint is a great way to create a spark for fires while also being sharp enough to skin the hide from an animal.

Antlers and Bone

Bones are unique in that they can take a sharp edge while also staying flexible. They are commonly used in projectile weapons, fishing hooks, and sewing needles. Try not to over-manipulate the shape of the bone, but instead, use its natural curve to your advantage. You can somewhat alter the shape of bone with hot water or steam.

Antlers are naturally shed by deer, as they grow new ones each year. They are extremely hard and make excellent hammers for flint knapping and rock shaping, good knife handles, and great buttons.

Wood

Wood is used in everything from fire making to building materials to weapons. It is commonly used in creating handles for tools and depending on the type and condition of the wood, can last for several decades.

Wood can be soaked and manipulated into the shape you want. Additionally, it can be charred or fire-hardened to increase its resilience against water and mold. If you're surrounded by a forest of healthy trees, then you have potentially unlimited resources to craft the tools that you want.

Shells

Seashells such as mussels and clams can give you an effective cutting edge with proper preparation.

If you find shells that are big enough, you can use them as primitive plates or bowls to hold food and water. Scallop shells can be carved to create teeth on the edges, providing you with the means to saw through materials like wood.

Plants

Plants that have stringy fibers can be twisted and woven into cordage that you can use to complete tools that you're making.

If you're making a primitive stone axe, you can use these fibers to secure the stone blade to the haft of the axe. Plant fibers can also secure an arrowhead to the arrow shaft. Vines are an excellent resource for tying things together as they are often sturdy and thin.

Some trees have inner bark that can be braided into rope. Basswood is a great example of a tree that can help you make cordage. Other plants that can be handy for making rope include stinging nettle, willow, and dogbane. See the cordage chapter for more information.

Primitive Tools You Can Make in the Wild

Now that you know a little about how you can take advantage of the free resources in the wild, it's time to put theory into practice. Below are the most common tools you can build in the wild. If you have your own modern knife or axe, even better, as you can use these to expedite the process of crafting.

Primitive Hafted Stone Axe

Stone axes have been around for as long as history has been recorded, and for good reason. It goes beyond smashing a rock to create a sharp edge with the addition of a wooden handle. The most common axes involve pushing a sharp rock into a hole created in the wooden handle as opposed to modern axes where the handle goes through the head of the axe instead.

1. Find a short to medium-length hardwood branch that looks and feels like it can support the weight of a stone.
2. Find a piece of hard stone for the axe head. The stone needs to be thick enough to withstand physical force. There should be a thinner side that can be used for rough cutting.
3. Split the thicker end of the branch using a knife or rock. The best way is to start batoning the branch with your knife and then use thin stones as wedges to force open the split. Using a sturdy piece of wood is good for hitting wedges.
4. Wedge the formed axe head into the widened split. You may need to smack it repeatedly to get it to fit.
5. Wrap the axe handle with natural fibers or paracord to act as a vise for the split. This will prevent the axe head falling out and helps protect the handle from breaking.

You can now use your primitive stone axe to split pieces of wood; however, trying to use it to cut down large trees might render it unusable.

Stone Knife

Much like making a primitive axe, a stone knife is a hand-held tool that can be used for anything a regular knife can be used for. You'll want to use a sharper rock such as chert, flint, or obsidian as the cutting edge needs to be keen enough to skin an animal.

1. Find or shape a flat, thin rock with a sharp edge. It should be flat on the top with a drop point shape if possible. It should be between 2-5 inches (5-13 cm) in length.
2. Find a short piece of dry wood about 2-3 inches (5-8 cm) in diameter. This will become the knife handle.
3. Form a split in the thicker end of the wood. You can widen the split using thin stones as wedges.
4. Push the rock into the split, ensuring the flat part is on the top and the "blade" is protruding. You can use another piece of wood to help smack it in a few times if needed.
5. To further reinforce the rock blade, wrap natural cordage or paracord around the split.

If you don't have string handy, you can use pine or spruce pitch glue to further secure the blade to the handle. Your knife is now ready to be used for cutting plant materials and skinning an animal if needed. If you notice your knife getting dull, then you can use another hard rock to help reform your edge.

Primitive Spear

The primitive spear was the weapon of choice for hunter-gatherer societies as they are easy to produce and simple to use.

Wooden spears are one of the oldest tools, dating back to 400,000 BCE. They are mainly used for hunting, hiking, and eliminating threats.

1. Find a straight, sturdy branch off of a dead-standing tree. You can use any length, but the general rule is that the longer the spear, the better it is for hunting animals and fish. Keep the diameter no more than 2 inches (5 cm) wide. Ensure you take off any small branches on the spear haft.
2. Using your knife or a sharp rock, form the tip of the spear into a sharp point. Keep the point thick enough that it won't break.
3. To harden the tip, pass it back and forth through a campfire. You don't want it to combust, but to form an outer layer of hardened carbon. This will help prevent the spear tip from breaking when thrown.

If you want to harden the tip even more, dip the end of the spear in some animal fat and plunge it into the fire. Afterward, use a stone to rub it until it has a glossy look. Your spear tip will then be properly hardened for throwing.

The straighter the spear, the straighter it will fly. However, if there is a slight bend or curve in the stick that is fine as well. As the spear spins the centrifugal force will keep it flying true to your target.

Atlatl

An atlatl is a throwing spear that has a handle on one hand and a hook on the other. This additional leverage allows you to not only throw the spear a lot further, but with much more force. Throwing the atlatl is much like throwing a ball at something. If you want to throw the dart like a fast ball, then you need to get your entire body into the motion. In the case of launching the dart from an atlatl, the speed and distance will require a full body throw.

You'll want to grip the atlatl with your fingers by first letting the dart shaft rest on your knuckles. Your fingers should be gripping the dart from the side and the dart should be resting on the launcher. If your fingers are over top of the dart then it won't launch when you go to throw it.

Here are some tips for throwing an atlatl:

1. Lean back and balance on the foot that is on your dominant hand. For example, if you're using your right hand then balance on your right foot.
2. Take a step forward and shift the weight to your left foot.
3. Throw the arm holding the atlatl forward, keeping the dart pointed at your target.
4. Right as your arm is completely extended you want to snap your wrist down hard.
5. Ensure the 2nd, 3rd, and 4th steps are in one fluid motion and that you release in a straight line toward your target.

The atlatl spear is like a cross between an arrow and a spear. The lightweight dart can be thrown over 100 yards (90 m) if properly constructed. It is one of the best weapons you can craft in a primitive environment and should be a staple lesson for survival enthusiasts.

1. Locate a medium-sized branch between 1-2.5 inches (2.5-6 cm) in diameter. The length of this branch doesn't matter at this point. The important thing is that you'll want a lateral branch protruding at around a 40-degree angle at one end of the branch.
2. Using a saw, cut the lateral branch so there is a 1–2 inch (2-5 cm) nub protruding from the main branch. Sharpen it with a knife until it has a slight point.
3. Cut the main branch, so that it is about 1-3 inches (2-8 cm) longer than your hand. This will be the atlatl handle.
4. Next is your projectile. Look for a thin branch that is as straight as possible to make the atlatl dart (projectile). If available, river cane or bamboo make the best darts, but any stick should be fine as long as it's light and straight.
5. At one end of the dart, you want to use a rock or knife to carve an indent into the material. This indent is what the lateral nub will rest in when you go to launch the dart.
6. Sharpen the other end of the dart as it's the piercing tip. You can even push an arrowhead or piece of glass into the tip to make it better for penetration.

Throwing an atlatl takes some practice. To help increase accuracy, fletch the butt end of the dart with feathers, much like an arrow.

Wooden Utensils

While eating with our hands is a cultural tradition all around the world, having some basic utensils makes eating a lot less messy. The most common utensils include a spoon and bowl. All of these utensils are easily created using the forest around you.

Spoon

1. Find a 2-inch (5-cm) diameter stick or split a log a few times so that you have a 2×2 diameter piece to work with.
2. Using a knife, whittle one end so that it isn't round, but flat.
3. Place a hot ember on the flat part you just carved. The burning ember will help weaken and carve out the spoon shape. You may also carve it out using a knife or carving tool.
4. Using a rock or knife, continue carving away the depression in the wood until you have a suitable curvature.
5. Shape the handle of the spoon by carving it with a knife. The final design is up to you.

Bowl

A bowl may be carved or burnt out of a piece of wood. You can use wood that you've split yourself or a piece of driftwood that you've found in the wild.

1. Find a suitable piece of wood that is not rotten or still green. You'll want it roughly 6-9 inches (15-23 cm) across and 5 inches (13 cm) wide. Avoid resinous wood such as pine or spruce and stick to hardwoods such as white birch, maple, or oak. Cottonwood also works well and is easy to carve.
2. Using hot embers from a fire, carefully place them on the area that you want to use as the bowl. Gentle blow on the embers to get them hot enough that they start to burn down into the bowl.
3. Use a knife or a stone with a sharp edge to carve out the charred bowl depression. Stop when you get to your preferred depth. If you have access to sandpaper or sandstone, you can sand your bowl.
4. Rinse out the bowl with water and let air dry.

Primitive Needle

A needle is handy in the wilderness because it enables you to punch holes in hide and leather. From there, you can use sinew or another natural cordage to sew together fabric and hides to make clothing. These needles are extremely easy to make as long as you have access to animal bones or thorns from different plants.

1. Look for small animal bones that can easily be splintered into shards.
2. Use a rock to break up the bones into smaller pieces, these will be fashioned into the needle. You want the length of the needle to be between 3-4 inches (8-10 cm) long.
3. Take your knife and start to whittle down the bone so that each end has a sharp point that can puncture hard materials.
4. If you want to attach sinew or fishing line through the needle, take the sharp point of your knife and poke a hole through one end of the needle. In this case, one end will be pointed while the other end is whittled flat so that you can poke a hole through it.

Primitive Bow and Arrows

Using a bow for hunting is one of the best ways to get food. A good bow should be lightweight and flexible in order to handle the force of shooting an arrow. The ability to fashion a survival bow from raw materials around you is one of the most important skills you can learn.

Each limb of your bow should flex evenly and gradually so as not to introduce too much physical stress throughout the bow. Before you pick a tree to start creating the bow stave, you can do a simple test to see if it's suitable for the job.

Get a branch from the tree about the circumference of your pinky. Bend it slightly and see how it snaps back. If it snaps back quickly, that's a good sign; if it's sluggish to return to its shape, then move on.

If it passed that first test, then try to bend it into a "C" shape. If it snaps back into place, then you have a good tree to choose from; if it breaks, then you'll want to choose a different tree.

Your branch should not have knots or a lot of other smaller branches coming off of it. These introduce weakness into the limb and can cause a critical failure when you go to pull back on it.

Bow

1. Begin by finding a suitable tree for your bow. A sapling made of maple, ash, yew, or oak will work well. It should be 3 inches (8 cm) in diameter and about 6 feet (1.8 m) tall with no knots or lateral branches.
2. Find the middle of your sapling and cut a mark into the bark.
3. Place your hand around the bow with the top of your hand on the ark you made. If it looks centered, then mark the bottom of your grip. This will be your riser.
4. On either side of your marks, whittle down the wood gradually until there is a consistent taper from the middle to the end. It should go from 3 inches (8 cm) to 1 inch (2.5 cm) in diameter.
5. Place one limb of your bow on the ground and push into the handle while holding the top tip. This will show you how much of a bend your limbs have. Both ends should bend in an even arc.
6. Cut a notch into the end of each limb at a 45-degree angle and deep enough that it can hold a bowstring.
7. To fashion the bow string, you can use any form of strong cordage you have handy. The less stretchy the material, the better, as you want to keep the tension taut. Natural string such as dogbane, nettle, and sinew work best, but you can use synthetic materials such as paracord.

Arrows

1. Find any straight stick from trees such as maple, ocean spray, or dogwood. You want them as straight as possible with no knots. Ensure that there is also a slight taper to the arrow or you'll have to whittle it yourself.
2. Scrape the bark from the stick and, if there is a slight bend, run the arrow over a hot fire to help straighten it out. Simply heat the crooked spot, bend it back just past the straight point, and let it cool. It should set up pretty straight once fully cooled down.
3. Sharpen the edge of the stick to a point or, if so inclined, cut a cross notch into the arrow tip and insert an arrowhead made of glass or stone.
4. Cut a notch into the non-projectile end to make your arrow knock. This is what keeps the arrow clipped on the string. Ensure that the knock is deep enough that it has a snug fit onto your bowstring.
5. Fletch your arrow using either a bundle of pine needles or feathers with their quills strapped to the arrow shaft. Secure the fletching using sinew or another lightweight cordage.

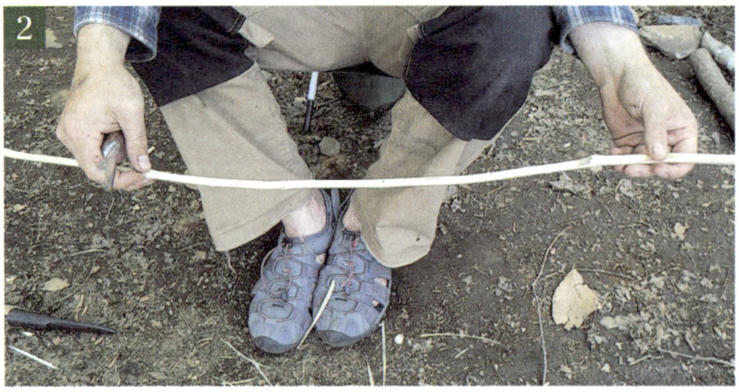

Walking Stick

A walking stick is crucial for hiking on uneven terrain or in inclement weather. However, choosing any old branch as your walking stick is not the best idea.

For example, choosing a pine tree for your walking stick might leave your hands a sticky mess as the resin leaks out. An old limb from a balsam fir has rough bark and can easily cause blistering to occur on your hand.

1. Choose a sturdy branch or tree root for your walking stick. Look for 2-3 inches (5-8 cm) in diameter, up to your chin for height, and no major deformities in the wood.
2. Remove all of the bark from the branch. You should be left with smooth wood that is not rough on your hands.
3. Using a saw, cut the very bottom inch off the walking stick so that it is flat. Use a knife and round it out so that it makes good contact with the ground. It'll help when you are walking up hills or over rocks and need good traction.
4. With the general shape of the walking stick done, you can customize it by carving designs into the wood or even topping it with a rock or something unique from the landscape.

The Ancient Sling

Much like a slingshot, the sling is a primitive weapon that launches a projectile such as a pebble or glass marble. It consists of cordage with a small pocket in the middle that houses the projectile made of leather or hide.

The slinger swings the sling and launches it at a high velocity at the target. It has been used since ancient times and is even depicted in some famous stories, such as the one with David and Goliath. It takes practice but can be quite accurate and deadly.

1. The best material to use for your sling is leather. Find a piece that is 2-3 (5-8 cm) inches wide and 5 inches (13 cm) long in a rectangular shape.
2. Fold the leather in half lengthwise. Cut out two holes with your knife on either end of the leather, this is what you'll use to pass the cord through.
3. Pass your cord through the folded leather so that when you unfold it, it looks like it looped through.
4. On one end of the cord, create a figure 8 knot so that it doesn't slip back through the holes.
5. On the other end of the cord, tie the same knot but with a loop at the end so that you can slip your finger through it for more comfort.
6. Hold the sling and ensure that the pocket is level as this will greatly affect your accuracy.

1

2

3

4

5

6

Final Sling

Slingshot

The slingshot is an excellent hunting tool for small game and fruit that is out of arm's reach. The materials needed are few and you can craft it with a little bit of rubber tubing and a Y-stick.

1. Find a strong "Y" shaped stick from a dead-standing tree or off the ground. The handle portion should be around 2-3 inches (5-8 cm) thick, enough for your hand to hold comfortably.
2. Cut the handle to about 3 inches (8 cm) in length. Do the same for each of the load-bearing arms so that they are each 2-3 inches (5-8 cm) in length.
3. Clean off the outer bark and set your Y-stick near a fire to dry. This causes the wood to shrink so that your fitted strap won't loosen.
4. Cut a notch into each of the slingshot's arms all the way around the wood. This is to stop the binding from slipping.
5. Attach the rubber strap or tubing to each end of the load-bearing fork and secure it by wrapping the ends in cordage.
6. Cut a small piece of leather and then cut a hole into each end of that leather patch. You will then run your rubber and or tubing through these holes and secure them by wrapping cordage around them. You now have your pocket for holding small pebbles or marbles.

Digging Stick with Hook

A digging stick comes in handy when you don't have a shovel or pickaxe. The addition of a hook at the end helps you reach things higher up in trees and other areas. In essence, it's a versatile tool that only needs a good branch to be effective.

1. Choose a sturdy branch that is roughly 2 inches (5 cm) in diameter and about 3-5 feet (1-1.5 m) in length. If you are digging in rocky soil, then you may want a stick that is skinnier, about 1.5 inches (4 cm) in diameter to penetrate between the rocks. Try to find one with a lateral branch protruding from one end so it can be fashioned into a hook.
2. Using your knife, whittle one end down until it is flat, like a shovel head. Don't make it too thin or it will break when you use it. This end is used for digging in dirt and loose rocks.
3. The other end that has the lateral branch can be shaped using a saw and knife to fashion a hook. It should be about 5 inches (13 cm) long. It can be used to reach high up or to lever heavy rocks out of the way.

Bow Drill

A bow drill is used to help create fire by friction. This friction generates an ember that can be transferred to a tinder bundle for ignition. Essentially, you are grinding two combustible materials past their auto-ignition points to create the small ember.

There are four main parts of a bow drill and it's important to find the right wood for each job. The parts include the drill/spindle, hearth board, bow, and bearing block/ handhold.

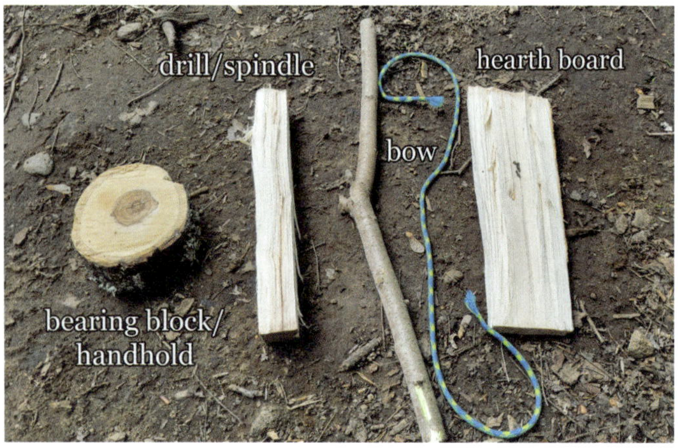

It's best to use materials that are commonly found and easy to identify for a higher chance of success. The spindle and hearth board must be created from dead, dry wood as any moisture will significantly reduce your friction generating capability. Look for dead standing trees that are upright, angled wood tends to catch more water when it rains.

Additionally, the spindle and hearth board should be made from the same species of wood, ideally the same tree. You can try and use two different species but there may be too many issues when it comes to creating friction.

Ensure that you choose the correct hardness for the spindle and hearth board. If the wood is too hard then it becomes harder to generate the wood dust needed. If it's too soft then you'll just eat through the wood. Dig your fingernail into the wood and if you can barely make an indent in it without bending your nail, then it should be fine.

Keep an eye out for these species of trees to use for building the spindle and heart board:

- Cedar (a good option as long as it's not raining out, as it is a moisture absorber)
- Yucca (by far the best choice as it requires little physical effort to generate dust)
- Willow
- Maple
- Alder
- Birch
- Cottonwood
- Basswood
- Aspen

The bow should be made of stiff and light wood. Ensure that the bow is slightly curved with minimal flexing. If it is too flexible the cordage will slip on the drill. If you follow these criteria then the species of tree does not matter.

The bearing block can be made of the hardest wood you can find. If that isn't possible then you can find a rock with an indent. In most cases, however, finding the hardest piece of wood you can use is much easier than finding the rock. Use green wood for the bearing block as it will minimize friction where it shouldn't be.

As a side note - it is best to avoid using resinous soft woods for any part of the bow drill set. It can cause a convective cooling effect that will stop an ember from being created.

1. Find a branch around 8 inches (20 cm) in length and about 2 inches (5 cm) in diameter. This will be your spindle.
2. Using a knife, whittle one end of your spindle into a blunt point. The other end can be sharpened to a thick point.
3. The bearing block (handhold) can be any square piece of hardwood that fits comfortably in your hand. If you can't find any suitable hardwood, you can use a rock with an indent or a hole drilled in it, a deer kneecap or ankle (talus) bone, which also has a natural indentation, or a piece of antler. It needs to comfortably hold the pointy end of your drill (the spindle).

Ankle (talus) bone

4. Find a block of wood that is the same wood as the drill/spindle or one that works well with your spindle choice and is about as thick as the drill. It should be about 12 inches (30 cm) in length. This will be the hearth board and where the ember will be created.
5. Using the blunt end of your drill or a rock, carve a slight depression into the hearth board, close to the edge. You want the indent to touch the edge of the board.

6. Use your knife and cut a "V" notch at the edge of the indent on your hearth board. This is where the hot ember will fall onto your tinder board.
7. The bow can be made of any wood you can find, just make sure that it is slightly curved, like a bow. Notch both ends for your bowstring.
8. For the “bow string” you can use any cordage you have, including paracord, a shoelace, or string. Simply attach your string to the ends of the bow and make sure it's taut.

To make a fire, wrap your bowstring around your drill. The pointed end of the drill will be facing up to work with your bearing block as you hold it. The blunt end will be in your hearth board.

Moving the bow back and forth causes the drill to turn. Do this fast enough and you'll create some wood dust as the drill grinds against the hearth board. Make sure it is level.

Do this long enough and you'll generate heat through friction, which ignites the dust and gives you an ember. Use your knife to carefully drop the ember down the "V" notch and onto your tinder board or bundle. Give it some air so that it may ignite your tinder bundle.

It takes practice but is a great way to start a fire if you find yourself without other means of ignition.

WILDERNESS POTTERY AND CONTAINERS

When you are out in the wild, having the ability to create functional containers is a game-changer. Containers provide you with a way to carry water, transport food, and even serve as a tool for cooking.

In this chapter, we will cover two types of containers you can create in the wilderness - birch bark containers and clay pots.

Birch Bark Containers

Birch bark, particularly from the White/Paper Birch tree (Betula papyrifera), serves as an incredibly versatile material for creating containers in wilderness settings. Not only can a birch bark basket hold various items, from foraged food to small tools, but it can also withstand the heat of hot coals or added hot rocks in water, making it feasible to boil water or even cook in it.

The ability of birch bark to resist decay and its natural waterproof qualities further bolster its application as a durable container. Note that birch bark is highly flammable, so keep it away from direct flame.

Step-by-Step Guide to Making a Birch Bark Container

By following the steps outlined below, you will be able to craft a versatile, durable, and waterproof birch bark container, essential for wilderness survival.

Step 1

Source a Sheet of Birch Bark

Begin by finding a birch tree. Look for loose bark that you can gently peel off. Aim to get a sheet approximately 12 inches by 18 inches (30 cm x 45 cm). If there are no loose sheets, you may have to cut one. Use a sharp knife to make a shallow, horizontal incision about 1/8th of an inch (0.3 cm) deep, being careful not to penetrate deep into the tree's cambium layer so as to prevent permanent damage. Then, peel the bark sheet back slowly until it separates from the tree.

Step 2

Warm the Birch Bark

Birch bark becomes more pliable when it's warm. Hold the sheet of bark near your fire (not directly in the fire), and warm it evenly. Be careful not to burn or damage it.

Step3

Fold the Birch Bark

Once the bark has warmed up, it's time to shape it. Fold the bark into a roughly rectangular shape with the smoother side facing inward. This shape will form the body of your container.

Step 4

Make 'Clothespins'

Find two straight branches that are about as thick as your thumb. Split these down the middle to about halfway.

Step 5

Secure the Folds

To hold your folded bark in place, use the split sticks as 'clothespins'. Slip one half of a stick inside the container, and align the other half on the outside. Do this for both sides of the container. The pressure between the two halves will hold the birch bark in the desired shape.

Step 6

Let It Cool

Allow the container to cool in this position. The bark will harden as it cools, solidifying the shape of your container.

Tips for Making a Birch Bark Container

Crafting a birch bark container can pose unique challenges for beginners, particularly in the stages of sourcing and shaping the bark. Novices may struggle with finding a suitable birch tree and effectively warming and molding the bark without causing it to crack or break.

Here are some tips to help you build your container:

- Keep a sufficient supply of birch bark sheets on hand, as beginners may need a few attempts before successfully crafting a container.
- Be patient while warming the birch bark. A slow, even heat prevents the bark from burning or becoming too brittle.
- Choose your 'clothespin' branches wisely. They need to be strong enough to hold the container's shape yet flexible enough not to snap under pressure.
- Let the container cool naturally. Trying to speed up the process may cause the birch bark to crack or lose its shape.

Alternative Bark Materials for Containers

While birch is the go-to bark for many crafters, there are many trees with bark suitable for basket making. Elm bark, known for its flexibility and strength, is commonly used in basket weaving.

Similarly, the fibrous inner bark of the basswood tree, often referred to as bast, makes it an ideal choice for crafting sturdy containers.

Western Red Cedar is renowned for its lightweight and rot-resistant bark, and is used to make hats and baskets. Additionally, willow trees, with their flexible and strong shoots, are traditionally used in basketry. Cattails and tule rushes are other good options for weaving.

Clay Pots

Clay pottery has been an integral part of human civilization, tracing back to the dawn of human creativity and ingenuity. Ancient societies worldwide have utilized clay's versatility, molding it into functional containers that have stood the test of time.

These earth-born materials, when skillfully manipulated, provide various uses in the wilderness, from cooking pots to water storage. This long-standing tradition of clay pottery offers a practical solution when navigating the challenges of living in the wild.

Dry Clay Harvesting

Harvesting dry clay involves locating a source of clay in the wild, typically by looking for areas where the soil has a dense, sticky texture. Clay-rich soil often has a distinctive reddish-brown or orange color. Once a potential source is found, the next step is to extract the clay.

Extraction involves digging out the clay-rich soil and then using a process of levigating, whereby water is added to the soil and thoroughly mixed until it forms a slip. The slip is then allowed to settle, and the clear water on top is poured off. This process is repeated until only pure clay remains. The clay is then dried prior to use.

Clay Soil from Panchkhal Valley, Krish Dulal - Own work, CC BY-SA 3.0

Wet Clay Harvesting

In this section, I provide a step-by-step guide to equip you with the necessary knowledge and techniques to successfully harvest wet clay from a creek or riverbank.

Step 1

Locate Clay Deposits

Look for a creek or river bed where the water body makes a bend. These bends are often rich in clay deposits. The soil in these areas tends to retain water and appears slick and shiny when wet.

Step 2

Prepare Your Tools

You'll need a bucket (or a similar container you have with you in the wild) and a small shovel to harvest the clay.

Step 3

Extract the Clay

Use the shovel to dig down under the first 2 inches (5 cm) of silt and then feel with your hand for the clay underneath. Start grabbing it with your hands and toss it into your bucket.

Step 4

Store the Clay

If you're using the clay right away, make sure to keep it covered with a damp cloth. Add water to the clay if it starts to dry out. Otherwise, keep in an airtight container to stop any oxygen from getting in.

Remember, while wet clay harvesting is relatively straightforward, always respect the natural environment from which you are extracting the clay. Avoid causing unnecessary damage to the landscape and always clean up after yourself.

Getting Clay from Soil in the Absence of Riverbanks

In areas where riverbanks are scarce, you can extract clay from ordinary garden soil, though the process is more labor-intensive. The first step involves gathering a significant amount of soil from your garden or a local field - the more soil you have, the more clay you can potentially extract.

Once you've gathered your soil, place it into a large bucket and fill the bucket with water. Stir the mixture vigorously to help separate the clay particles from the rest of the soil. After stirring, let the bucket sit for 2-5 minutes. The rocks and silt will fall to the bottom and the clay will stay suspended in the water since it's finer.

Next, drain the clay water from the bucket, being careful not to lose any clay in the process. The clay will be in a partially liquid form, similar to heavy cream. Pour this liquid clay into a cloth bag and hang it in a place where it can drip dry.

As the water drains, the remaining material will harden into clay. This process can take several days to a week, depending on the climate. Once the clay has reached the desired consistency, it's ready to be used for pottery.

Making a Pinch Pot with Freshly Harvested Wet Clay

Now that you have your freshly harvested clay, let's dive into one of the most fundamental pottery techniques: creating a pinch pot. This method is considered the simplest form of pottery, making it an excellent starting point for beginners.

Follow the steps below to create a pinch pot using your fresh wet clay and a campfire:

Step 1

Prepare Your Work Area

Start by cleaning a flat surface where you can work with the clay. It could be a wooden table, a slab of plywood, or a flat rock.

Step 2

Make a Ball of Clay

Take a piece of your harvested clay and roll it in your hands to create a ball about 4-6 inches (10-15 cm) in diameter.

Step 3

Create a Well

Press your thumb into the center of the clay ball to about halfway down, creating a well.

Step 4

Form the Pot

With your thumb in the well and your fingers on the outside, slowly pinch the clay to create the walls of the pot. Work your way from the bottom to the top, turning the pot as you go to maintain an even thickness.

Step 5

Smooth the Pot

Once you have the desired shape and thickness, smooth the surface of the pot with a wet finger or a damp cloth.

Step 6

Let the Pot Dry

Allow the pot to dry in a safe, dry place for about 24-48 hours. This step is crucial as too much moisture in the clay can cause it to explode in your fire. The pot should be leather-hard before proceeding to the firing stage. It should no longer feel cold or damp to the touch.

Step 7

Prepare the Campfire

Gather enough dry wood to create a decent-sized campfire. Light the fire and let it burn down until there is a bed of glowing embers.

Step 8

Place the Pot in the Fire

Carefully place your pot in the middle of the embers. Cover it with more wood and let the fire blaze.

Step 9

Let It Fire

Allow the pot to fire for about 2 hours. The exact time will depend on the size of your pot and the heat of your fire.

Step 10

Cool the Pot

After 2 hours, let the fire die down and allow the pot to cool inside the fire pit. Do not attempt to remove the pot until it is completely cool to avoid cracking.

Step 11

Clean It Up

Once the pot is cool, clean it with a damp cloth to remove any ashes. You now have a beautiful pinch pot made with your harvested clay.

Creating a Coil Pot with Fresh Wet Clay

Utilizing fresh wet clay, it's possible to craft coil pots of various shapes and sizes. This technique offers immense flexibility and creativity, permitting the artist to mold anything from small, intricate designs to large, elaborate pieces.

Let's explore the step-by-step process to create your own unique clay-coiled pot.

Step 1

Prepare Your Clay

Start by kneading your wet clay to ensure it is smooth and easy to work with. This process, known as wedging, removes air pockets and ensures a uniform consistency.

Step 2

Create the Base

Roll out a slab of clay that's about 1/4 inch (0.6 cm) thick. This will serve as the base of your pot. The size and shape of the base will determine the eventual size and shape of your pot.

Step 3

Roll the Coils

Take a small amount of clay and roll it into a coil. The coil should be about the thickness of a pencil.

Step 4

Attach the First Coil

Score the edge of the base where the first coil will be attached. Apply some slip (a mixture of clay and water) to the scored area and then press the coil onto the base.

Step 5

Add Additional Coils

Continue rolling and attaching coils, one atop the other, using the slip and score technique to attach each one.

Step 6

Shape the Pot

As you continue to add coils, you can begin to shape the pot to your desired design. You can create a wide base and narrow neck, a straight-sided cylinder, or any other shape you choose.

Step 7

Smooth the Coils

Once all the coils have been attached, use your fingers or a tool to smooth the coils together, both on the inside and outside of the pot. This will help to create a seamless and sturdy structure.

Step 8

Let the Pot Dry

Like the pinch pot, allow your coiled pot to dry until it's leather-hard. This can take 24-48 hours depending on the thickness of your pot and the humidity in your environment.

Step 9

Fire the Pot

Follow the same firing instructions as for the pinch pot. Remember that the fire should not be rushed, and allow time for the pot to cool before handling.

Step 10

Clean and Polish

Once the pot is cool, clean it with a damp cloth to remove any ashes. Your coiled pot made from fresh wet clay is now complete.

Handy Clay Tips for Beginners

As you embark on your pottery journey, there are a few key tips and tricks to keep in mind. These insights will help to simplify the process and ensure that you achieve the best possible results.

- **Identifying Clay:** Clay suitable for pottery typically feels sticky and will hold its shape when molded. If it forms a firm shape and doesn't easily crumble when dry, you've likely found clay.
- **Preparation is Key:** Before starting with your pinch or coiled pot, ensure all tools and materials are within reach. This includes your clay, a water source, scoring tools, and a cloth or sponge for smoothing surfaces.
- **Patience with Drying:** Allow your pot to dry naturally; avoid rushing this process. Hastening the drying-time can lead to cracks.
- **Smooth Transitions:** When attaching coils in a coil pot, make sure the transitions are as smooth as possible. Uneven coils can lead to structural weakness.
- **Firing Safety:** Always follow safety procedures when firing your pot. The temperatures involved can be dangerous, so it's crucial to pay attention to your campfire.
- **Practice Makes Perfect:** Don't be discouraged if your first few attempts don't turn out. Clay pottery is an art form that requires practice. Keep trying, and with each pot, you will see improvement.

Mastering these pottery techniques can be a game-changer in survival situations, providing an essential skill for creating practical tools and containers.

HOW TO BUILD A STONE OVEN IN THE WILD

While the premise of creating an oven in the wild may seem simple, actually crafting it with the resources around you can be challenging. There are many ways to make it; this chapter focuses on using rocks as the main building material.

How Does a Stone Oven Function?

A stone oven, being wood-fired, generally needs two compartments to work properly. The bottom compartment, known as the firebox, is where you build the fire that provides the heat.

The upper compartment, the oven itself, is where you put the food that is being cooked. The reason for the separation is that you don't want the direct flame of your fire touching your food. This will cause scorching and inevitably ruin whatever you're trying to cook.

Essentially, you want to build the fire underneath a layer of rock. Hot rocks can maintain their temperature for a long time as they slowly release the heat into the oven.

The dry heat from the fire will radiate throughout the oven compartment providing even heating for your food. An opening in between the two compartments will allow smoke to vent out as it rises and runs along the roof of the oven. You can use clay to seal up any air cracks but if the fire is hot enough then having some air gaps can help control the temperature in the oven.

The Benefits of Using a Stone Oven in the Wild

You could argue that the main benefit of a stone oven is that it gives you the ability to cook hot meals in any weather. However, the construction and use of a stone oven instead of a traditional clay or brick oven make it the ideal choice in most survival situations for other reasons as well.

The Design Can Be Easily Modified

Initially, the design of a stone oven consists of stacking several rocks on top of each other to build up a hearth. This means you can use pretty much any shape of rock to get the same result.

Even the rock type can be modified based on what's around you. If you don't have a lot of rocks then you can substitute with clay from a riverbed. These mud-based materials require a "firing in" to set it. In a survival situation, you must keep construction simple and not time-consuming so that you don't waste any excess energy.

Doesn't Require Tools to Build

To build one of these stone ovens all you'll need are your hands to stack the rocks. Depending on the size of the oven you don't even need a lot of physical strength to complete it.

If you are looking to turn this stacked stone oven into a long-term solution, having a shovel as a tool is indeed helpful to gather mud or clay to fill in the air gaps.

They Hold Heat for a Long Time

Rocks have been used as portable radiant space heaters in survival and camping for as long as history can remember. Since rocks have a large thermal mass, they can store a lot of heat. The rocks will slowly release the heat over time providing consistent heat.

Dense rocks such as granite will hold heat much longer than something like shale. In an oven, you will have a continuous source of heat but the rocks will help regulate the temperature.

What You'll Need to Build the Stone Oven

A stone oven is going to need stones and lots of them. If you're a fan of stacking games like Jenga or Tetris, then you'll love interlocking all of the rocks to make the perfect oven.

Other than that, all you'll need is a pair of gloves (optional) to ensure you don't beat up your hands too much. Some rocks have sharp edges, which can easily cut you. Additionally, you can damage your hands while you're rummaging around to find the perfect stones.

How to Build a Survival Oven in the Wilderness

This type of survival stone oven is appropriate for all forms of cooking. You can bake bread, roast wild game, and even slow-cook a stew. Ensure you make the oven part large enough to accommodate whatever it is you're going to cook or you'll have to make modifications.

As a word of caution, it is best to avoid using rocks that have been submerged in water. Some rocks such as limestone and sandstone are porous, meaning water can get stored inside. If these stones are heated too quickly then the water will turn to steam, potentially causing the rock to explode.

Although you can use sandstone and limestone to build an oven in survival situations, try to find rocks that have not been submerged in water. Granite or quartz are better options since they are conductive and hold heat well.

To be clear, any rock can explode if the circumstances are just right. However, in most situations, you shouldn't have a problem as long as the rocks aren't soaked.

Step 1

Find a Suitable Location

Finding the best location for your stone oven depends on how far you want to carry your rocks. Ideally, you want to be in a location where resources are readily available.

It is best if you build your stone oven on top of rock since that will help keep the heat inside the oven. Building it on grass or dirt will cause some of the heat to be absorbed into the ground.

Build your oven in an area that is suitable for cooking. For example, having a stream or river nearby will make it easy to transport water.

Step 2

Create the Fire Box

The first part of the actual construction is to gather as many rocks as you think you'll need to create the three main walls. It's best if you can find a rocky piece of ground to build the oven on, but you can also sit it on a large piece of rock.

Use the largest of the rocks to build the side and back wall for the firebox since it will be holding most of the weight of the oven. You'll also want to find some longer pieces of stone that will be used to separate the two compartments.

Fit the stones together in an interlocking pattern. If you cannot do that with the rocks at hand then try to stack them as close to each other as possible. The idea is to minimize the number of air gaps that could potentially cause heat loss in the oven.

The size of your firebox should reflect the ledger and capstone size that you'll be using on the oven. If the walls are farther apart than the large piece of stone you'll lay across them, then you'll have to restack them.

The height of these side and back walls should be no higher than 16 inches (41 cm); between 10-16 inches (25-41 cm) is the sweet spot.

Step 3

Attach the Ledge Stone to Make a Platform

After you have built up enough of a foundation it's time to place the ledge stone. This is the barrier between the fire and the oven. It needs to be large and relatively flat so that food can rest on it. It should also overlap past your walls to provide additional stability.

Place your ledge stone so that there is a 4-inch (10 cm) gap between it and the back wall. This gap will act like a vent to help get the smoke out of the oven through the top portion of the oven. It also helps the oven develop a convection-style action where the heat is now being circulated throughout the oven instead of the fire just heating the ledge stone.

Ensure you are filling in most (if not all) gaps with interlocking stones as when you go to build the oven compartment it becomes quite difficult to fill in these areas afterward.

Step 4

Construct the Oven Compartment

Building this part of the oven requires more rock stacking. You'll want to stock these rocks so that they are overlapping the ledge stone you placed in the last step.

These side walls are important as they will help direct the radiant heat as well as provide the necessary support for the large stone you will place on top.

You'll want the height of the oven compartment to allow for food to be placed inside but not too high to disperse the heat. Anywhere between 5-10 inches (13-25 cm) in height is appropriate for most applications.

Step 5

Capping the Top of the Oven

As you near the finish line for completing your oven you'll need to place a second ledge stone, also called a capstone. This is to become the top of the structure and will be what keeps the heat inside your oven.

This stone should also extend to the edges of your built wall on all three sides. Test the oven for sturdiness and shore up any loose rocks to ensure that it doesn't collapse while you're using it.

You can take this time to fill in any large cracks with mud or clay if you want. This step isn't entirely necessary unless you are looking to make a more permanent fixture. As long as there aren't any huge holes the rocks should do the job just fine.

Step 6

Start a Fire in the Fire Box

Start a fire in the firebox using your favorite firestarter and some kindling. Smoke will most likely leak out the front until the fire gets hot enough and the draft kicks in.

You'll know you're successful when you see the smoke being pulled through the gap you left between the oven and fire compartment in the previous steps.

Of course, each oven will have its unique quirks and it may take time to figure out how to get it running as efficiently as possible.

HOW TO BUILD A SMOKEHOUSE IN THE WILD

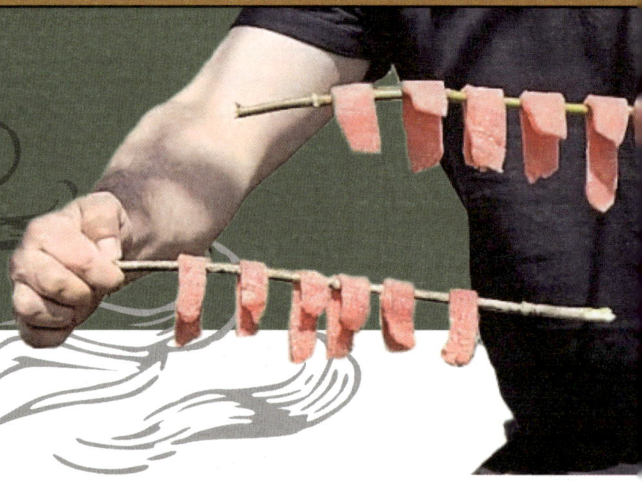

If you hunt a deer or some other large animal in the wild, keeping your food from spoiling is as important as obtaining the food itself.

So, what do you do without refrigeration? Submerging a bag of sealed meat in a cold river is one quick trick. But that's not always a safe option.

Smoking and drying food on the other hand is areexcellent alternatives for food preservation without a fridge.

You can build a smokehouse using nothing but the resources around you. This chapter will teach you about the fundamentals of smoking meat for preservation and show you how you can build your own wild smokehouse.

How Does a Smokehouse Work?

The main function of a smokehouse is to provide a chamber that captures the smoke from a fire and keeps it inside. Meat and other items are suspended on a shelf that sits in the smoke. How well your smokehouse works is based on its ability to hold in heat and smoke.

Using natural materials, it will be impossible to get 100% efficiency, but you can get it pretty close. Commercial smokers have gaskets and other sealing methods to keep all of the smoke inside the chamber.

Hot Smoking vs. Cold Smoking

There are two main types of smoking: hot and cold smoking. For this smoker, we will be focused on the hot smoke technique, but it's a good idea to understand both methods.

Generally, most people dry their food using hot smoke. This is a combination of low heat and smoke to dehydrate the food. The type of wood will determine the final flavor that is imparted to what you're smoking. The temperature range should be between 160°-275° Fahrenheit (71°-135° Celsius).

Cold smoking is much different in that the food should already be cured or cooked. The temperature range is around 68°-89° Fahrenheit (20°-32° Celsius). By curing the meat before cold smoking, the added phenols will create a hostile environment for bacteria.

Understanding How to Have an Efficient Fire

Temperature regulation is important when using a smokehouse. If the temperature is too high, then you'll end up cooking your meat before the smoke can penetrate it.

Creating smoke involves not only using good firewood but also managing the different aspects of building a fire. A fire needs oxygen, fuel, and heat to work efficiently.

Fire uses oxygen to build up energy, so you'll need a clean feed of air to help make smoke. Fuel is needed to keep the fire going and it's best to find dry, seasoned wood. Old, punky wood burns at a lower temperature and can impart a nasty smell. The last part of the equation is the heat itself and how to keep it from getting too hot. Managing the oxygen and fuel will help you regulate the heat and give you the optimal temperature.

The Benefits of Using a Smokehouse

Most people might assume that smoking is only something that you can do in your backyard with the right equipment. However, all you need is a well-maintained campfire, an enclosure, and some time. The benefits of using a smokehouse are as follows.

Preserves Food

Imagine you had a great day of fishing and you have several fish that need to be prepared and cooked. Those fish will spoil within a day or two if left uncooked and in a warm location. Even if you cook the fish, without refrigeration, they will spoil within a few days after cooking.

Smoking eliminates any residual moisture inside the meat and acts as an antimicrobial agent since the environment cannot support bacterial life. Suddenly, your shelf life of two days turns into two weeks, under proper conditions. Using a smokehouse is an effective way to preserve large amounts of food so it doesn't go to waste.

Materials Are Easily Obtained

As long as you have a forest near you and some paracord or wire, you can easily build your smokehouse over a small campfire. The skill required to build it is minimal as long as you can make some tight knots (please see our chapter "Knots That Are Extremely Useful in the Wild" on page 133).

The important thing to remember is to find good quality building materials. Rotting wood is weak and may not support the items you're trying to smoke. As with most bushcraft projects you want to try and stay away from live trees and stick with dead standing trees.

Helps Keep the Biting Bugs Away

The warmer months of the year are the best time to use a smokehouse, largely due to the colder months acting as refrigeration. Coincidentally, the warmer months are when mosquitos and black flies start to get annoying.

One of the best ways to mitigate these insects is to build a smoky fire using wet wood or leaves. The primary function of a smokehouse is to create smoke and that will also help keep the bugs out of your way. It's just another incentive to frequently check your fire during the smoking process.

What You'll Need to Build a Smokehouse in the Wild

If you're an avid bushcrafter, then you might be able to do this project without any tools, however, for most people, there are some simple tools you can bring to make the job easier.

Items you should have on you to help build a smokehouse include:

- Paracord
- A saw
- A hatchet
- A sharp knife
- Your fire kit

A note on using paracord. If you don't have a lot with you, then there is a neat trick you can use to make more of it. Slice the paracord casing to expose the individually braided strands and then separate them into individual strings. The casing can still be used to lash the tripod poles together.

Use the Right Wood

We've already mentioned that rotten wood will produce subpar smoking results. However, using the right "seasoned" wood matters as well.

For example, many people use pine and spruce to start their fires because the resin inside is extremely flammable. But using that type of wood is not wise for cooking since the resin produces a thick black smoke of unburned carbon that will ruin the taste of the meat. It might even make you sick if you eat too much of it.

Generally, dry hardwoods will work best. These woods include:

- Oak
- Maple
- Birch
- Cherry
- Hickory
- Apple

Hardwoods will burn hotter and much longer than softwoods. They also impart their unique flavors into the food that you're smoking.

How to Build a Smokehouse Step-by-Step

It shouldn't take you too long to build a smokehouse using natural materials. The hardest part is picking a location that has everything you need, including a supply of firewood.

Step 1

Picking the Right Location

Picking the optimal spot for your smokehouse depends on available materials in your vicinity. You want to ensure that you have access to plenty of wood to keep the smoke production high.

Don't build your fire on wet ground or you'll have a problem maintaining a nice toasty bed of coals for your hardwood pieces; at least until all of the moisture has been drawn out of the ground near your fire.

Try to pick a location that doesn't get a lot of wind. Wind will move the smoke around too much. Instead of drafting upwards, it might be pushed around out of the entrance. You can choose to be sheltered by a dense forest or up against a rock face.

Step 2

Building the Tripod

The tripod will be the foundation for your smokehouse so it will need to be sturdy. To build it, you'll need to find three saplings that are about wrist-thick and 4-6 feet (1-2 meters) tall. The saplings should be as straight as possible to ensure that the tripod has enough stability to hold the meat.

Using your paracord, create a lashing where all three tops meet and tie them securely together. If you can find saplings with a "Y" at the top this will help interlock the top of your tripod.

You'll have to play around with it a little to ensure it is stable and able to stand on its own. However, don't worry about spending too much time on this as you will be securing each section of the tripod with a horizontal support stick.

Step 3

Build the Supports

Choose three horizontal sticks to connect each of the tripod legs. It's best to lay the tripod over your fire pit to see how far apart the legs need to be. Ideally, the smokehouse rack should be a couple of feet up from the fire to avoid cooking the food too much.

Once you've figured out how far apart your tripod legs need to be, cut the proper lengths of wood that you'll need to lash between the legs. The sticks don't need to be very thick, about the size of your thumb. Once these supports are connected, you can start to build the rack in your smokehouse.

Step 4

Build the Smoking Rack

The smoke rack is simply thin sticks that cross the gaps between the horizontal supports you built in the last step. The individual sticks can be lashed to the side supports using paracord if needed.

These sticks can be as thick as your index finger and are designed to hold the food that you are smoking. Larger sticks will cause more of a buffer between the smoke and your meat.

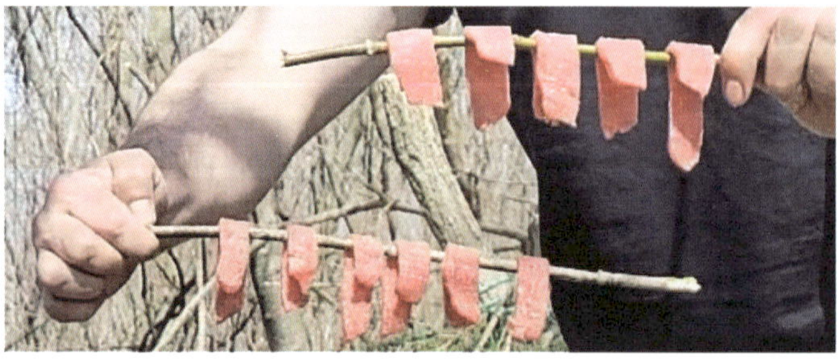

Step 5

Start Up Your Fire

Move your tripod away from your fire pit and begin work on building the fire. You can start the fire off with a softwood to get it really hot and then, once you have a bed of coals, throw on some hardwood to start the smoking process. Once you have coals developing, it is a good idea to put the tripod back on the fire pit.

To protect your fire from the elements, you can dig a hole in the ground and have the fire below the surface. Not only will this help direct the smoke upwards, the fire won't be as affected by the wind. Once your fire is going strong, you can add green wood to help produce the smoke needed to dry your food. Dry wood will work as well but ensure that you don't have too much fuel going at once.

Step 6

Covering the Smokehouse

For this smokehouse, spruce or cedar boughs work best as they can trap a lot of smoke. All you need to do is cover the outside of the tripod with interlocking boughs. At this point, you have to be very careful and work fast. The reason for this is simple. If you don't cover your contraption, the smoke will vanish into the open air.

You want enough to cover down to the smoking rack that you made in step 4. If it falls underneath it, then use your knife to trim away the excess material so it doesn't catch on fire. Ensure that you keep part of one side open so you can access the food and fire.

You might need to lash some of the boughs with paracord to ensure they stay in place.

Step 7

Arranging Your Meat or Other Food

There are two ways you can arrange the meat on your smokehouse rack. Draping them over the sticks so that they are hanging in the air is the best option. Remember to rotate the meat periodically so that it dries evenly.

Some people create a secondary rack that skewers the meat, allowing for easy flipping during the smoking process.

Step 8

Maintaining the Fire

You should have a large amount of hardwood stocked nearby to keep the fire going. Throw on a piece or two every time you see the previous wood turning to coals. You don't want to add too much wood at once or the fire will get too hot and cause flare-ups.

The Underground Smokehouse Variation

Often, in windy situations, having a fire aboveground can cause flare-ups or be difficult to start. For these conditions you can use a variation that involves building everything just below the surface of the ground.

To begin, dig a hole at least 3 feet (1 meter) deep and 1 ½ feet (0.5 m) in diameter. The hole needs to be deep enough to accommodate the smoky fire as well as the ingredients you are drying.

Build your fire at the bottom of the hole and light it. Once you have the flame established, start to add some green wood to make it smoky. Construct a wooden grate with small, green sticks that will lie over the smoky fire. The wooden grate needs to sit between 1 and 1½ feet (0.3 and 0.5 m) above the smoking fire.

Lay your meat in thin strips across the wooden grate. Afterwards, cover the hole with wooden poles and boughs. This is to help hold in the smoke during the drying process.

Check on your meat every couple of hours. You'll know it's done when it is dry, brittle, and has a dark color.

HOW TO CREATE CORDS AND STRINGS FROM PLANTS

Strings and cords are "must-haves" during any long-term wilderness living scenario. They serve as the base for fishing nets, bowstrings, and line for snares and other traps. While most people pack a hefty amount of paracord or nylon rope, those who practice wild survival with nothing but the clothes on their back and the natural materials found there must know how to make their own rope.

Survival Uses for Cord and String

Fishing Nets and Line

One of the best uses of natural cordage is for fishing nets and fishing line. These two tools can be necessary for survival when a fish is on the line, meaning the cordage must be made well and with the right materials.

Most plant materials will hold together better when submerged in water than any cord made from animal sinew, catgut, or rawhide as these unravel and stretch when wet.

Iris leaves, which provide only two usable fiber strands per leaf, were commonly used for fishing nets and lines in the Pacific Northwest because of their strength. The process to get enough material is laborious and takes a long time but is necessary to keep your dinner on the line.

Lashing

The lashing together of large branches is a necessary survival skill in many parts of the world. If you are building a shelter, rope becomes a vital part of your shelter system.

Trap Triggers and Snares

A large handful of traps (most deadfalls including the commonly-used Paiute Deadfall) and all snares require some form of cordage or rope. If you're looking to catch small game, making cordage is one of the first steps. For this use, most cordage doesn't need to be perfect so you can often use pieces that are from your early on trial-and-error days of making cordage as long as they're spliced together well.

Bowstrings

For hunting and starting fires with a bow drill, you need cordage. Most bowstrings for hunting bows were traditionally made from sinew or rawhide, but many were also made with hemp or flax cordage.

For a bow drill bow, you need a continuous piece of cord that can put up with a lot of friction and movement. Plants like nettle and dogbane are often used for bow drill fires, although you can use just about any natural material for this application.

What to Use for Cord and String

Cordage can be made from almost any part of a plant, from the leaves all the way down to the roots. Some plants offer great cordage from their stems, while others will make the strongest cordage from the inner bark of small limbs.

Start by looking for native species in your area. Get to know your local plants, so that you can practice specific techniques and master the use of local species.

Roots

Roots often make good natural string and cordage. Species that grow in sandy or loose soil are often the best choice as the roots will grow straighter, making it easier to get long strips of fibers to make cordage with.

Natives to the Great Lakes region often used the split roots of spruce trees to sew their birch bark canoes, proving its strength and top-tier performance in water environments.

Other species that provide great material for cordage from their roots are:

- Junipers
- Walnut
- Butternut
- Wild Cherry
- Osage Orange

Trunk and Limbs

Moving up the tree you hit prime territory for gathering materials. The trunks, and especially the small limbs, of certain tree species are the most common and debatably the best pick for cordage. This is mostly because of the ease of collection and you are more likely to get long, continuous strands of fibers to use from small limbs and the trunk.

It's preferred to look for already downed material or recently dead trees to allow the plant to continue to thrive in its environment. If you're in a true survival scenario, harvesting can still be done in a way that allows for the tree to stay alive. When gathering from the trunk, ensure that you don't cut all the way around, as this cuts off all the movement of nutrients upwards in the tree. Rather, harvest thin strips from many trees to minimize the damage.

The fibrous cambium layer between the outer bark and the wood is what you're looking for on both tree trunks and branches. If you're working with live trees, this is always the easiest to do in the spring when the sap is flowing steadily through the cambium layers, softening it up.

While most species of deciduous trees will provide enough fibrous material underneath their bark for cordage, some trees are better than others. For example, both willow and tuliptree (commonly referred to as tulip poplar or yellow poplar) have a lot of inner cambium that can be easily peeled and worked into cordage.

Species that are good to harvest from include:

- Willow
- Tuliptree
- Basswood
- Cedar
- Elm
- Mulberry
- Juniper
- Maple
- Cottonwood

Leaves

While less common, using leaves to make cordage is a viable option. Many people use the long leaves of the Yucca plant to create strong cordage that can be used for any purpose. It's an incredibly straight and strong source that only requires proper preparation to use effectively.

Stems and Grasses

There is a wide variety of other species that make strong, usable cord and string. Different grasses and other perennial plants have the capacity to grow long and straight with plenty of fibrous material to use for cordage.

Stems and grasses have a slightly different processing method, but the strength of the cordage you create can be impressive.

Different species of plants in which you can harvest cordage from the stem include:

- Nettles
- Dogbane
- Velvet leaf
- Milkweed
- Prairie Flax
- Thistles
- Fireweed

Grasses that work well for making cordage include:

- Sweetgrass
- Dunegrass
- Certain reeds

Animal Sources

Materials harvested from animals are used for string and rope as they allow one to use all parts of an animal, and the cord strength is impressive. Sinew, rawhide, and catgut are commonly turned into cord after processing the rest of the animal. I often use these and thin long strands of buckskin for sewing.

While these materials are great for strong rope, they don't work well when wet, as they will stretch and unravel easier than plant material. It also takes a lot more energy to get the material than harvesting plant materials, but there are plenty of benefits to using animal material.

Collecting and Processing Natural Material

Once you've identified the plant material you hope to harvest, it's time to start collecting. The process for collecting the material is often simple, but processing takes more time and effort.

When collecting from trees or woody shrubs, the material you're after is the fibrous cambium layer just below the outer bark and on top of the wood. In the months of May to August, sap tends to be moving through the tree and will soften this layer up, usually making it easier to peel fiber from the limb.

In colder months, you're likely using more rigid, drier fibers that can be tricky to work with and to keep in longer strands. Even if the material tends to break apart, splicing shorter cords together allows for almost any length or thickness of cord to be made.

First, separate the outer bark from the limb you're working with to access to the useful cambium layer. This layer will peel smoothly away from the bark (easier on some species than others). The slower and more intentionally you move, the longer yours strands. Take your time and focus on getting longer strands.

Processing Stems

When working with stems from plants such as nettles and fireweed, gathering the fibrous material can be more time consuming. Some plant species (a lot of grasses) are easily broken down by a process called "buffing". Buffing simply involves rolling the plant back and forth in your hands to break apart all of the plant material and get the fibers down to a thinner and stringier material. Another option is to roll the material on your thigh so you can get more strength and power into the action.

The end goal of buffing is to have a lot of thin, fluffy, and stringy fibers that will be worked together during the final stage.

Retting

Some plants are more resilient, requiring another process that uses both human force and a natural process to get strong fibers. For starters, work with a dulled rock or piece of wood to smash apart the stem. This is easily done by rolling the rock carefully across all parts of the stem. Be sure to use rocks without sharp edges, as fibers are easily cut in this stage.

When you have better access to the fibers, you can separate them out and set them aside for the next step in the process.

Retting is a process in which fibrous material is soaked in water for multiple days. During this process, the pectic material breaks down, releasing the fibers from the rest of the heartier, "woody" parts of the stem.

Soak the stems in water for multiple days, allowing enough time for the plant cells to swell and burst while pectin breaks down. The softening of the tissue that surrounds the fiber strand will make for a much better material to work with. Check on the material daily to see if the fibers have separated yet, as soaking for too long can do more harm than good.

During the retting process, you'll start to notice a strong, putrid smell. This smell means that the retting is working. During the breakdown, butyric acid, methane, and hydrogen sulfide are produced, leaving a malodorous scent. It is after all just a quicker process of rotting the materials. This smell signifies that your material is either ready, or getting very close.

Once the retting process is complete, you can jump straight into making cord and string. Many people like to work with wet material as it is more flexible and malleable, but it isn't necessary. Just be sure to remove all of the material from the water when retting is complete or it will continue to sit and rot, quickly becoming no good.

Step-by-Step Instructions on How to Make Cordage

You can make cordage by cleaning and drying your fibers, carefully separating them and grading them, or making 3 or 4-ply cordage. However, if you are new to this, you can simply start with this simple but strong two-ply cordage that can be done with green or dry plant material.

Here's how to do it:

1. Use a knife or pruning shears to help with harvesting, or a shovel for the roots.

a. **Stems and leaves** - simply cut them as close to the base as possible

b. **Bark** - use a knife to flake away the outer bark and expose the bast fiber just below it, then cut into that about ¼" (0.6 cm) and peel upwards to extract the fibers. For trees with fibrous outer bark (false cedar, certain junipers), you can simply strip pieces of the outer bark.

c. **Roots** - you will need a shovel or a digging stick, preferably only harvest from a fallen tree with exposed roots. Choose thinner roots that are easier to work with.

2. If you have leaves and stems with thick, juicy tissues like certain yucca, kudzu, many vines, and others and you have the time to spare, harvest them first to help remove the plant material. It takes a week of immersing the fresh materials in water in a bucket or the edge of a still body of water for about a week to allow them to decay partially. Then, when you pull them out of the water, the extra plant material should start falling off the fibers. It will smell bad, but this is normal. If you don't have time to spare or have drier plant material, skip this step and try pounding.

3. Pounding works best for drier materials, but you can also do this on green vines or leaves. Just be prepared to be splashed by the plant juices as you pound greener, wetter material.

4. Pounding involves using a smooth rock to pound the material on a piece of wood ideally, but you can also use another rock as your base. Be careful not to use too much force when using two rocks together, or you could break your fibers.

5. Pound the material until the fibers become fully visible.

6. Next, separate the fibers by pulling them apart by hand. If you have the time, spend a few minutes cleaning out bits of non-fibrous plant material, dead parts, etc., to make a finer-looking finished product. Rinsing in water helps remove the little bits. As long as the fibers are more or less separate, move to the next step.

7. If the material is green or you used water to clean it, you should lay your fibers out for about an hour to dry slightly, making them easier to work with. Again, if you don't have time, you can proceed to the next step.

8. Pick your longest fiber(s) and fold it/them loosely in half. If you have very large fibers, you only want one strand, but you may want at least 5 or 6 strands at a time for fine fibers like the yucca leaf fibers in the photos, depending on how thick you want your finished cordage.

9. Then, start twisting one half towards you, to the left, until it folds over on itself. That fold will become the end of your cordage.

10. Pinch that fold in your left hand and hold it. With your right hand, twist the right half of the fiber towards you (to the left) until it becomes tight, but not until it folds over. One or two twists are enough.

11. Lift the left half, take it together with the right half you just twisted, and twist them both together once to the right, away from you (in the opposite direction of the first twist).

12. Take the left half and twist it towards you, then take both halves and twist them together away from you. Keep repeating this step. Note that you can also do this in the reverse direction (spinning right first), whatever feels natural to you. The key is to spin one half in one direction, then spin both halves in the opposite direction to lock it in place. Which direction you start with does not matter; the key is consistency. Keep the twists nice and tight by pinching the cordage in one hand while twisting with the other.
13. Once you feel your cordage is getting thin, it's time to splice another piece in. Depending on the length of your fiber, you may need to splice roughly every 3 - 6 twist cycles.

14. There are different ways to splice. They involve taking another fiber or bundle of fibers about the same size as the first bundle, folding it loosely in half so that one side is a little longer than the other (so both sides don't run out simultaneously), and splicing it in.

a. One method is to put the new half with the fold tucked up into the crotch of the cordage you are working on and work one half into the left strand and the other half into the right strand, then proceed with your twisting one strand towards you then both strands away from you.

b. Another method that is a bit more forgiving is to take your new fiber(s) and lay it/them across the cordage you are working on where it is to be spliced and simply grab half of it into the left half and half into the right half and keep working. One half should always be longer than the other so you don't run out on both sides simultaneously.

15. Continue splicing more material in until you reach your desired length.

This method works great for all light and medium-duty uses and sometimes even heavy-duty loads, depending on the strength of the original fibers.

To make even stronger cordage for heavy-duty loads, you can double-ply your cordage. Simply take two strands of finished cordage and twist them together in the opposite direction as the original twist, making it thicker, stronger, more durable, and less likely to unravel.

Methods of Making Cord and String

There are multiple methods of turning all of this fibrous natural material into cord or string, but the method you choose depends highly on how strong you want your final product to be.

A Simple Wrap

This method of wrapping your cordage is the quickest way to get some cord. While it may not be the strongest, strength might not be your end goal. There are plenty of different tasks in which you may want something quickly, rather than for it to be able to hold up to a lot of pressure.

For a simple wrap, grab a bundle of the fibers that you've processed and lay them on your thigh. The amount of fibers you want will highly depend on how thick you want your rope to be. The fibers will tighten up together, but they are also doubled over on each other by the end of the process. Trying this method with different quantities is the best way to understand how thick of a rope different fiber will make.

Take the bundle and start to roll it in a singular direction, pressing lightly down with your palms enough to roll the fibers. Do this along the entirety of the bundle's length until it starts to fully twist on itself in a singular direction. It can help to hold one end of the strands, then use that same hand to "lock" the twist in place as you move down the strands.

When the entire bundle has been twisted in a singular direction, grab both ends of the strands and lift it up. The fibers should kink near the middle when there is enough twist in the bundle. Bringing the two ends together with the new kink becoming the end of your cordage, the strands will naturally twist around themselves creating a thicker, stronger, cord.

At the end of any cordage process, tie off the ends to keep the cordage from fraying and lock the twist in place. This can be done with a simple overhand knot, being careful not to break the fibers in the process. Wetting them before tying often helps.

Reverse Wrap

The reverse wrap, also known as twining, will result in a significantly stronger length of cordage that can be used for heavier duty tasks. This more meticulous and intentional twisting compacts much more fiber into one chunk of the string, which is what gives it so much more strength.

To use the reverse wrap, grab a bundle of fibers small enough to work easily between your fingers. As you become more practiced you will feel more confident managing larger bundles, but for starters it is best to understand the movement and rhythm of the process with smaller quantities.

To begin the wrap, twist a section in the center of the bundle until it kinks. This is the best and easiest way to make your starting point as it provides you with a solid loop to hold on to without it coming apart like frayed ends can. Pinch this small loop between your thumb and your index finger of your non-dominant hand, making sure the two strands are coming out towards your dominant side.

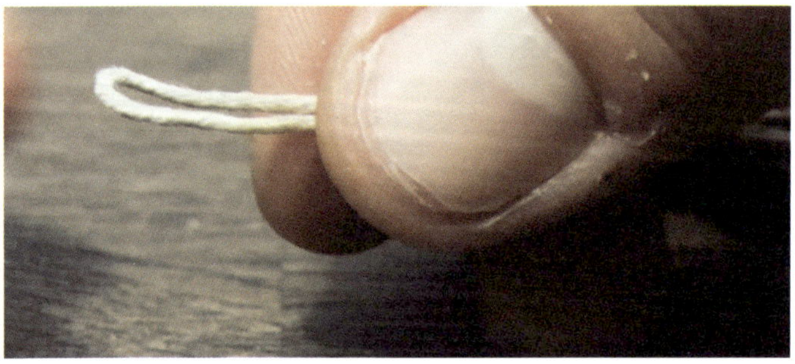

Now, with your dominant hand, pinch the top strand between your other index finger and thumb, then roll the fibers between your fingers away from you. You want to twist the fibers enough to make the cord tighter, but there's no use in twisting so much that it kinks. After the roll forward, bring the top strand in front of and under the bottom strand to switch their positions. Move your other hand over to pinch the new twist and lock it in place.

Then, simply repeat the process. The entire rope-making process is built on taking the two strands and rolling them in the same direction, but combining them both in the opposite way. In this example we are rolling the individual strands forwards (clockwise), and moving the two strands backwards (counterclockwise) to combine them.

The key here is to move your locking hand with each new twist put into the cordage. This holds everything tightly together and if you get behind, you will see the cordage fight to unwind rather than stay put.

This process can be tricky to grab ahold of at first, but with more practice you will find the flow and be able to make long strands of rope without much time put in.

Thigh Roll

Thigh rolling natural cordage is a great choice for when you're making thicker rope that's too large for pinching in between your fingers.

The general method is similar to a reverse wrap, but both strands are being done simultaneously.

Start by creating a kink halfway in your fibers, just like with the reverse wrap. Then, lay out the two halves on your bare leg (skin provides more friction), slightly separated but close enough together that your hand can cover both strands.

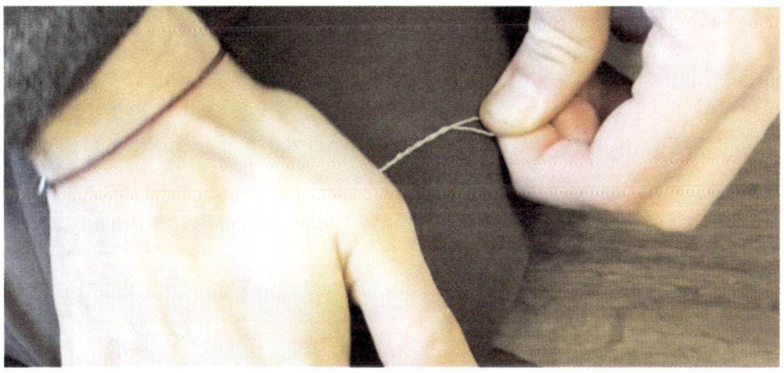

Hold both strands under your palm and roll them forward simultaneously. Continue to roll and twist both strands forwards until the cords are fully wound. Once both of the strands are twisted forward, bring them together and switch directions, rolling the two together back towards yourself. This will bring the two strands together and join them.

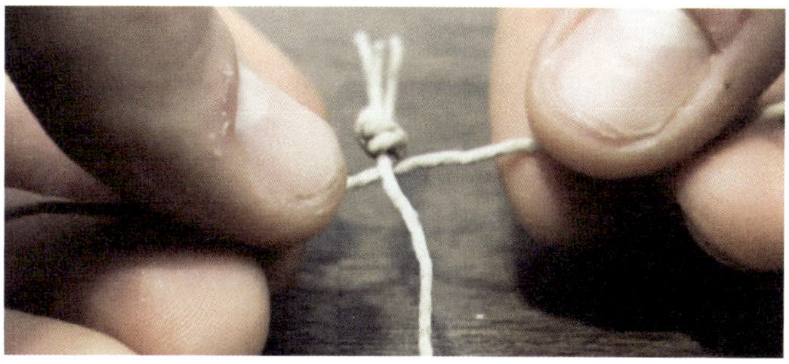

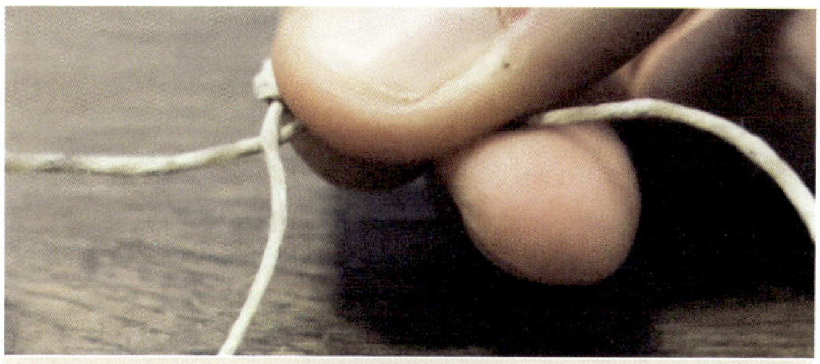

Braiding

While much less common, braiding is an option for making natural cords and strings from plants. This is traditionally done with flat material, but can be done with almost anything.

The main drawback of braiding is strength. Twining significantly increases the strength of the fibers, whereas braids are less strong.

Braiding cord is exactly like braiding hair, you need three strands and will tie them together with a simple overhand at one end. Then, with the three strands, start with the outside strand on the left or the right and bring it over and across the middle strand so that it now becomes the middle strand.

Move to the opposite side, and cross it over the middle strand, placing it in the middle. Repeat this back and forth, always switching sides. Once you're at the end, simply tie it off and you have a usable length of cord for lighter uses.

Splicing

Now, you've gotten to the end of your cords, but you don't have a long enough cord for your purpose. Splicing is the process of adding additional material into the cord while still twining. This allows for you to make a rope of almost any length without sacrificing much strength.

For starters, if you know ahead of time that you will need to splice additional material into your cord because you need something longer than about a third of your cord's length, make your first kink in the twining process so that one strand is longer than the other. This will help reduce the chance of splicing both strands at the same point, producing parallel splices, and significantly reducing the strength of the cord at that point.

To splice additional material into the cord you are twining, simply take a second strand and overlap it with the side needing to be extended with a few inches of material. Work this into the cord as if it were one piece, and after a few turns it will naturally hold itself in place.

Doubling

While single reverse wraps are significantly stronger than the fiber on its own or a simple wrap, you can further strengthen the rope when it's needed to take on a heavier workload.

To double your cord, simply twine two different cords together, or fold one in half and twine it just like you made it in the first process. In theory, this can be repeated over and over to make stronger and stronger cord. If you're using cord to take on bodyweight, this will be an important step in your process.

SAFETY

HOW TO PROTECT YOURSELF FROM BEARS, BOARS, AND OTHER WILD ANIMALS

Protecting yourself from wild animals is a vital set of skills to learn if you spend time in the wilderness. For most people, the fight or flight response is strong and quick to activate when presented with a confrontation with a wild animal.

It's important to learn both how to protect yourself and learn animal behavior because panicking in these situations does more harm than good. These strategies will help keep you calm, focused, and formidable in the eyes of wildlife.

General Wilderness Protection Strategies

To begin, the best protection against wild animals is a robust deterrent. Most wild animals are not used to humans and would only attack if they perceive you as a threat or are hungry. It is due to our foreign nature that scaring them off (when needed) is much easier than you would think it would be.

These general strategies are meant to arm you with the knowledge to avoid potential negative animal encounters. They work on most wildlife and should be the first tactics to use. Staying calm and letting the animal know that they are safe and that you are there in peace (known as animal communication) has worked extremely well for me in the wild. If that fails, some defensive techniques are useful in scaring the animal away.

- Research the local wildlife: In most cases, the best offense is knowing what the potential animals are in your area. There is plenty of research material available online and offline that can teach you what animals are in your current region while giving you tips on habitats, diet, behaviors, and even methods to deter them.
- Animals don't like the sound of metal: The sound of metal and machinery are not generally heard out in the wilderness and is something that can make even the largest predators run away. The best way is to hit a metal cup or bowl with a metal utensil repeatedly while making loud noises.
- Be intimidating: Predators are often large animals, which add to their intimidation factor. It contributes to the animal's decision on whether this target is viable. Standing tall with your arms extended while creating a loud, booming noise with your voice will signal to them that you are not to be messed with.
- Don't turn your back on a wild animal: Predatory instinct demands that the prey is chased until taken down. If you turn your back on an animal during a confrontation, it could identify you as prey and they may chase you. It is difficult to regain the intimidation factor after this point, so it's best to never lose it.
- Store food away from camp: Animal attacks at camp are usually caused by food. People usually make one of two mistakes: they either cook too close to their shelter or have food left in the vicinity.

  Human food tends to have a very strong smell that acts like a beacon for nearby animals. With a strong wind the scent of your food can be carried several kilometers from your location.

  Keep your food 300-600 feet (100-200 m) from your camp and elevated above the ground. This can be done by putting the food in a bag, tying it with a length of rope, and then throwing the rope over a branch to hoist the bag up. Make sure that the location on the branch is far enough from the tree trunk that an animal can't climb to get it and high enough off the ground.
- Arm yourself: The last resort in any animal encounter gone wrong is to use lethal force to defend yourself. For example, in bear country, it is not uncommon to see people armed with rifles that can be used as both a deterrent and weapon.

  Additionally, bear spray is a commercially available product that causes a strong irritation when sprayed in the face. It's an effective deterrent for charging bears.

  Having a knife or hatchet on you is sufficient for close-quarters defense. The idea is that the tool should be quickly deployable and able to inflict enough damage to stop an attack.

Species-Specific Protection Strategies

Encountering wildlife in European nature is not uncommon. While many encounters can be peaceful, being prepared for unexpected encounters with wild animals is something people may not always consider. Luckily, species you may encounter have specific strategies for protection, and having easy-to-follow tactics can allow you to make smart decisions when the need arises.

Wild Boars

Wild boars are abundant across Europe, particularly in woodlands and rural areas. In most cases, the species you'll encounter is the Eurasian wild boar. Generally, this species is not aggressive towards humans but can become dangerous if they feel threatened or cornered, especially sows with piglets.

- If a wild boar crosses your path, remain calm and slowly back away. Don't try to run away as this can cause them to charge you.
- Make sure to give the animal plenty of space to retreat.
- If a boar charges, try to climb a nearby tree or use a large object as a barrier.
- Avoid feeding wild boars, as this can lead to habituation and increased aggression.

European Brown Bears

European brown bears are found in the forests and mountainous regions of Europe. These creatures are generally quite peaceful but can be dangerous if surprised or if a mother bear perceives a threat to her cubs.

- Make loud noises and travel in groups to avoid surprising a bear.
- If you see a bear, do not approach it. Slowly back away in small increments, while keeping the bear in view. Do not turn your back to sprint away or try to climb a tree, as these bears can follow you up.
- In case the bear decides to attack, using a bear spray can be effective. However, if the bear is not bluff charging and you're knocked down, playing dead might persuade the bear to lose interest.
- Secure food and waste away from campsites to prevent bears from approaching.

Wolves

Wolves, specifically the Eurasian wolf, are making a comeback in many parts of Europe and are commonly found in forests and fields. They are generally wary of humans but may pose a threat if cornered or if emboldened by hunger.

- Do not run if you encounter wolves. Stand tall, make yourself appear larger, and make loud noises.
- If approached by a pack, back away slowly while facing the animals.
- Use sticks or any weapons available to deter them if they come too close.
- Wolves are more likely to attack if they perceive weakness, so stay composed and assertive.

Lynx

The Eurasian lynx is a reclusive species that typically avoids human presence and predominantly inhabits wooded regions. These solitary creatures are rarely seen, making encounters with them uncommon. Nonetheless, it's useful to understand how to respond if you happen to come across this elusive predator.

- If you spot a lynx, maintain your distance and do not approach.
- Make loud noises and raise your arms to appear larger if it comes closer.
- Back away slowly, ensuring the cat has an escape route. It will run away unless you threaten it.

Moose

In places like Finland, moose are commonly seen, especially in deep woods where you might be hiking. While these massive animals are not usually aggressive, they will fiercely protect their young and are known to trample people who get too close.

- If you encounter a moose, remain calm and don't approach it.
- Give the moose plenty of space as they can be unpredictable.
- Avoid sudden movements or noises that could startle the moose

Elk

Elk can be found in some European countries, such as Poland. They are essentially larger versions of deer and can become aggressive when they feel cornered or threatened. For protection, they respond to many of the same cues as moose, and similar techniques work for both.

- Avoid approaching or disturbing any elk and keep a safe distance if you encounter one.
- Give elk plenty of room to retreat, and never attempt to feed or provoke them, as this could lead to dangerous situations.

European Bison

European bison, also known as the wisent, are the heaviest surviving wild land animals in Europe. They are primarily found in forested areas and grasslands, where they typically graze. While generally peaceful, their large size and powerful build mean they can pose a threat if they feel cornered or if encountered during their mating season.

- Keep a safe distance and avoid sudden movements.
- Do not approach or attempt to feed them.
- If a bison charges, find cover behind a tree or large object.

Red Fox

Red foxes are medium-sized omnivores with a distinctive reddish coat, bushy tail, and pointed ears. They are adaptable and thrive in various environments, from forests to urban areas. They are generally considered not a threat to humans, but can carry diseases like rabies, which makes it important to learn how to mitigate any potential aggression. If you are bitten, you should go seek medical attention as soon as possible.

- Do not attempt to feed or touch foxes.
- If a fox approaches, make loud noises to scare it away.
- Secure food and waste to prevent attracting them.

European Adder

The European adder is a small, venomous snake that can be identified by its zigzag pattern along the back. It is commonly found in a range of habitats, including woodlands, wetlands, and grasslands. These snakes don't go looking for trouble, so bites are rare. However, the European Adder should be taken seriously due to its venomous nature.

- Wear thick boots and long trousers when walking in areas where adders are present.
- Use a long-forked stick to keep the snake away from you if necessary
- If you see an adder, give it space and do not attempt to handle it.
- In case of a bite, seek medical attention immediately.

European Hornet

European hornets are large, social wasps (meaning they live in colonies) with brown and yellow banded abdomens. They build papery nests in secluded locations, often in wooded areas. Despite their intimidating size, they are less aggressive than other wasp varieties, unless their nest is threatened.

- Avoid disturbing hornet nests. If one gets aggressive then the rest will follow.
- If hornets are nearby, remain calm and move away slowly. Running will trigger their defensive nature.
- If a swarm is on you, crouch low to make it harder for them to target you. Cover your face with your arms to protect it.
- In case of a sting, treat with antihistamines and seek medical help if allergic reactions occur.

Mouflon

Mouflons are a subspecies of wild sheep with a reddish-brown coat and distinct curved horns. They inhabit mountainous and forested regions and are considered the ancestors of domestic sheep. Generally shy, they prefer to avoid human interaction and are more active during the early morning and late afternoon. It is still wise not to bother them as they can charge you.

- Observe from a distance and do not attempt to approach.
- Avoid making loud noises that could startle them.
- If you encounter a mouflon, give it space to retreat.

HOW TO BECOME INVISIBLE IN THE WILD

In the wild, perfecting camouflage techniques is a very-important skill.

But as the environment changes, so will your camouflage and your methods.

This chapter discusses various ways in which you can stay hidden in the wild, from basic camouflage to building a blind to hunt from or to disguise your shelter. Each technique can easily be adjusted to your own environment depending on what resources are readily available.

How to Live in the Wild and Remain Untraceable

As humans, we naturally leave a trail behind no matter how hard we try to tread lightly. Our trails can easily be found and followed. If you are trying to live in the wild without being found, it's necessary to take each step with intention, leaving nothing behind.

This is often a lot easier said than done. There are countless movies in which stealth rangers move through the woods, convicts jump through rivers to lose tracking dogs. The reality is never that simple, and every step you take in the wild is going to leave an impression. The goal is to minimize your impact and make your trail nearly impossible to follow.

In camp, it's unlikely that you'll move around without leaving a trail. However, if you are able to establish a camp and get rid of any signs that could lead someone there, you can remain untraceable.

Human foot print

That means no broken twigs, no overturned dirt, no pieces of gear, no stepping in the mud, nothing at all.

Take the time to practice walking with intention and carefully moving as if every step will have a great impact.

Because it does.

Start by centering yourself and bringing your focus to all of your surroundings. This will allow you to be more aware of everything that's going on, so you can evaluate the impact of each step you take.

Take your time moving. Even if you take a minute between each step, you can choose your next spot carefully. Moving with haste will always leave a trail. Pay attention to how the ground feels underfoot. Try wearing shoes with soft soles or walking barefoot in order to get a better read of the ground, so you know exactly how to move.

Take steps leading with your toes and then slowly lowering your heel, rather than striking with the powerful heel and rolling forward onto your toes.

Above all else, try to walk without making any noise. The noises you hear while walking, broken twigs, crumpled leaves, etc., all signify a physical trail left behind. The less you hear while walking, the less of a trail there is to follow.

How to Cover Your Tracks

No matter how hard you try to walk without leaving any tracks, you'll likely need to cover them at one point or another. This can be helpful if you are trying to move in a rush or need to make sure that there is absolutely no trace.

Covering your tracks can be difficult because the process itself can leave its own tracks that someone can follow. The goal is to cover your tracks in a way that leaves the ground looking untouched, or as if something else had moved through there.

The best way to start is by covering your shoes in order to soften the surface that is contacting the ground, and to get rid of any obvious tread that could be left behind. Using an old piece of cloth, or even moss, can be a great choice in the wild.

If you are moving intentionally, through areas with little mud or brush, you can cover your tracks easily by dragging a makeshift broom behind you as you move. A large branch with plenty of leaves can work to erase any marks that you are leaving behind by turning over new leaves.

This can be a great way to cover your trail, but any serious tracker will be able to notice the trail of disrupted plants, stones, and dirt. It would be best to leave this for a time in which you don't have other options.

Camouflage

Camouflage is one of the most common methods to become invisible in the wild. Most people in the outdoors will have an array of camouflage clothing.

In the wild, you need to make your own camouflage from natural materials that you find around you. In fact, using natural materials can be even more effective than using things like camouflage clothing and store-bought face paint. If you're trying to blend in with the natural environment, it's always best to use things that come straight from it.

Shape and Outline

Many wild animals can recognize you by your silhouette before you get very close. The human shape is an uncommon one in the wild, and if you are trying to catch a wild animal, you need to trick it into thinking you belong there.

The first part of camouflage is breaking the shape and outline of your silhouette. This can be easily done by utilizing branches and leaves that protrude from your body. With enough sticks and twigs, you can transform into a shape that will be unrecognizable and won't cause distress.

Color and Texture

Next, work on the color and the texture of what you are wearing. Many colors that we use in our clothing aren't found easily in the wild, so you need to change to fit in with the earth-tone colors around you.

One of the best ways to do this is to use a base layer of mud to cover the flesh-tone of your skin, depending on your skin color. This will help provide a background to the rest of your camouflage that you can apply on top.

Camouflage using a base layer of mud

To add more color and texture, use leaves and small twigs to lay over the base layer of thick mud. You don't need to cover every last bit of your body but work to cover the majority of your skin.

By applying camouflage, you can move through the forest with more ease, without startling every creature that you come across.

Building a Blind

The last thing that you want to consider making invisible is your shelter. This can be a sign to creatures that something out of the ordinary is present, so it's best to find a way to make it blend into the background.

Many natural shelters such as debris shelters ("How to Build a Debris Shelter", page 17), lean-tos ("How to Build a One-Month Shelter", page 21), and other long-term shelters ("Long-Term Shelter for Living in the Wild", page 29) are prime for using as camouflage. These utilize natural materials to provide protection from the elements, but also will easily hide you from anyone looking.

If you are utilizing a tarp or tent, you may need to construct a blind to cover the majority of the human-made shelter from plain view. This can be easily done using wild items you already have around you.

Natural shelter

Start off by positioning your tarp or tent in a location that will allow you to build a blind around it. Your blind won't rely on the tarp or tent to hold the camouflage in place; you will construct a blind fully around it.

Collect a large number of sticks and branches that have a substantial area of leaf coverage in order to provide the most coverage possible.

Build a rough outline of a shelter around the area that your tarp/tent is in with sturdier branches that are thick enough to support the weight of what you will be adding afterwards.

If needed, and if you have it with you, use a bit of rope or cordage to tie all of these branches together at the main connection points in order to provide more support.

Once the general skeleton is built, use smaller branches to fill in the space. This process is similar to building a shelter, but you don't need to worry about the elements if you already have a tarp with you. If you are building this without a tarp, lay thick layers of leaves so that water will run down them and to the base of the shelter.

The more leaves and general cover, the better. As you build the blind up, add more and more layers, so it can withstand the elements over time. This is a great method to keep yourself hidden when in the wild for the long term.

This same method can be used to build a small blind that can be used for hunting and lying wait for prey to come by.

HOW TO TRACK AND USE BIRD LANGUAGE IN THE WILD

Often, people are surprised to learn that bird language is a survival skill. Bird language helps with knowing where potential danger lies as well as finding wildlife for pleasure or for food. When hunting, it is possible to outsmart a predator or prey by using this universal bird alarm network. You can use bird language to track animals from long distances. This long-lost art can help awaken your deepest primal instincts.

Bird language uses body language & vocalizations made by birds in order to locate aerial & ground animals in their natural habitat. For instance, if a bobcat is moving through the forest, birds react to this. They gather around the cat and fly in circular umbrella-shaped patterns, making repetitive, distinct vocalizations. To a bird language practitioner, the bird alarms for a bobcat are obvious even through thick bushes and from many yards away.

Five Voices of Birds to Listen For*

As you keep your eye on birds, practice listening for the five voices they use throughout all four seasons:

- **Song:** Their beautiful tweets, whistles, and songs are used for courtship and claiming territory.
- **Companion/ Feeding Calls:** These sounds are soft and rhythmic and are often heard between friendly birds or flock members. They can be quite quiet so listen carefully.
- **Territorial Aggression:** These sounds are often loud and aggressive. They are made by birds that are defending their territories from rivals. Sometimes you see birds flying at each other or physically attacking each other. This is usually a sign that no dangerous predators are in the area.
- **Juvenile Begging:** These are the frantic calls of baby birds receiving food from mom or dad. Baby birds are easy targets for predators as they don't know yet how to listen for danger. Bird language learners shouldn't confuse these sounds as coming from adult birds, as it might throw you off a trail of an alarm.
- **Alarms:** These calls and sounds are associated with predators that may pose a threat. Most birds have multiple types of alarms corresponding to different types of danger. Some alarms are even silent, meaning they are non-vocal. Examples are a woodpecker that drums on wood and other objects, owls that snap their bills together, or pigeons as well as owls that use wing-clapping to signal alarms.

How to Understand Bird Language

As a beginner, quietly sit and watch the birds for at least 20 minutes at a time, daily if possible. Each time, take note of what the birds are doing, and observe their vocalizations and behaviors. Over time, this will reveal how birds respond when watching for predators, feeding, mating, and nesting.

1

Adopt a Sit-Spot

Stay in one place to learn about the birds in your local area. Visit the same location regularly until you get to know the birds individually (this robin versus a robin). You'll learn where they like to sit, their feeding habits, and their attitudes toward predators and competitors. As the birds get to know you, you will disturb them less. Listen closely, learning the sounds of calls, songs, and alarms.

2

Try and Focus on 5 Local Species to Start

Start off growing your audio and visual skills by watching 5 common birds. Get to know these 5 very well. The more you get to know them, the easier it will become to recognize their different behaviors. Take note of what they do when they are alarmed, where they hide, how they ward off intruders, and other aspects of their behavior.

5
Common Bird Types in Europe

Common Wood Pigeon, Rohitjahnavi - Own work, CC BY-SA 4.0

Male Blackbird, David Friel, CC BY 2.0

Dunnock, Tim Felce, CC BY-SA 2.0

Chaffinch, Male, Arad, Ryoutou - Author, CC BY-SA 3.0

A male Eurasian Blackcap, Tony Hisgett from Birmingham, UK, CC BY 2.0

3

Learning the Birds' Vocalizations

Many bird species use different alarm calls for the different predators they encounter. Like American Robins, Eurasian Blackbirds (Turdus merula) will sound an alarm when they detect predators, including ground predators like cats or aerial predators such as hawks. Their alarm calls are sharp and loud, often described as a repetitive "chink" or "pink" sound, intended to warn other birds in the area of potential danger.

4

Learn the 'Shapes' of Alarm

Following are examples of bird 'shapes':

- **Ditching:** This is when birds ditch suddenly into thick bushes to escape a predator.
- **Bird Plows & Bullet:** You will see birds scattering very fast to get away from a predator such as a Cooper's hawk.
- **Sentinel:** Take note of birds that sit high on posts to get a good view from a safe distance.
- **Parabolic alarms:** When birds mob other predators such as owls, cats, hawks, snakes, and other birds that rob nests.
- **Tunnel of silence and oppression:** Silence in the area where dangerous hawks are on the prowl.
- **Popcorn alarms:** Quick brief outbursts made by a bird or birds when a fast-moving ground predator is in the area.

Each of these different alarm scenarios is associated with certain body language from the birds, as well as their vocalizations, and can occur in thousands of birds or just one bird.

5

Start to Practice What You Have Observed

Learning bird language is similar to how you would think about your own instincts when faced with a predator. The adaptation of birds to the environment is responsible for how a bird looks, why it behaves as it does, and the bird language it uses. Learn to observe the beak shapes of different birds, why a certain bird is alone, or why other birds like sparrows are in a flock.

Many people who live in the wild, like the San Bushmen of the Kalahari Desert, one of the last indigenous peoples who still often live as hunter-gatherers, are very astute in the bush; they are extremely skilled at bird language. Bird language keeps them alive by knowing where danger lies, it allows them to find prey when hunting, and it keeps them connected to the natural world and each other.

Bird Tracking

Toe Orientation (Dactyly)

The ancestors of modern birds had four toes, and most birds retain this trait (although one or more of these may be reduced or fused). However, the proportions and arrangement of the toes are quite variable, the product of millions of years of evolution and adaptation. The arrangement of toes around the tarsus (sole) is called dactyly, and the vast majority of bird tracks display one of a relatively few categories: anisodactyl, tridactyl, and zygodactyl. The presence or absence of webbing between toes is a further distinction, and webbed tracks are described as either lobate, semipalmate, or palmate, depending on the extent of the webbing.

Before discussing these track types in detail, a note is in order on how bird feet are classified. Most birds have feet with three forward-facing toes and one rear-facing toe, called the hallux. The toes in a track are always numbered consistently, beginning with the hallux. The other three rows are numbered 2, 3, and 4, starting with the innermost toe in the track. (This is the case even for tracks in which the hallux is absent: the three visible toes will still be toes 2 through 4.)

Anisodactyl (Perching Bird) Tracks

Unless you live on the beach, the vast majority of birds whose tracks you are likely to encounter will leave anisodactyl ("unequal toes") tracks. Anisodactyl tracks are designed for grasping twigs or branches: the hallux points straight backward, while the other three toes all point forward. The hallux is often, but not always, significantly longer than toes 2, 3, and 4, giving the bird a better grasp on its perch.

Anisodactyly is common to many families of birds, so an anisodactyl arrangement will not, in itself, tell you very much about the bird that made it. The overall length and spread of the track will go a long way toward winnowing the list of candidates; the relative lengths of the toes is also often distinctive. In many cases, however, a specific identification will come down to some idiosyncrasy particular to the foot of the bird that made it. In the tracks of chickadees (genus Poecile), for example, the first and second toe are exactly opposite, or nearly so, forming a single straight line.

Tridactyl (Game Bird) Tracks

A subset of anisodactyl tracks, tridactyl tracks look like classic anisodactyl tracks without a hallux, and are thus apparently three-toed. I say "apparently" because the hallux, while sometimes absent in tridactyl birds, is often present, but either elevated or reduced to the point that it does not register in the substrate. As can be imagined, tridactyl feet are unsuited to perching in trees or bushes, but well-adapted for walking and running.

Because of this, tridactyl tracks are often called "game bird" tracks - and many, if not most, well-known upland birds leave such tracks: turkeys, pheasants, and quail, among others. Many species of waterfowl — including ducks, gulls, sandpipers, and coots — all spend a great deal of time walking, and leave tridactyl tracks as well. Because of their distinctively webbed feet, they are classified separately below.

Zygodactyl

Less common than anisodactyl tracks, zygodactyl ("paired toes") tracks are still quite common, and seen in a wide range of birds. Zygodactyl tracks are easily identified by the backward-pointing fourth toe, giving the track a rough "X" shape (or in some birds, a "K" shape). Zygodactyly is a convergent rather than a conserved trait, meaning that it has evolved a number of times in unrelated families of birds: parrots, woodpeckers, and cuckoos are some of the more common. Because it is so widely distributed among different bird families, the context of the track can be of great help in identifying the bird.

A related arrangement, often treated as synonymous with zygodactyly, is ectropodactyly, in which the fourth toe is flexible. Owls and ospreys leave ectropodactyl tracks, and are often lumped in with zygodactyl tracks; the only real difference between the two is that the overall shape of the track is closer to a "K" than an "X".

Palmate Tracks

In palmate tracks, some or all of the toes are webbed, giving their tracks a broad, hand-like outline Palmate tracks almost always indicate a bird that spends most of its time in or near the water: the tracks of gulls, ducks, and geese are all palmate, as are those of many seabirds.

Palmate tracks may show a distinct hallux, but it is often either greatly reduced as in game bird tracks, or raised so high that it doesn't leave an imprint. Its presence or absence can be useful in distinguishing birds of similar habits: for example, diving ducks like teals leave tracks with short but distinct hallux prints, while dabbling ducks like mallards, which forage closer to shore and spend more time walking on land, are tridactyl.

Many long-legged shorebirds - sandpipers, plovers, and egrets - have toes that are only partly webbed; such tracks are called semipalmate. These tracks can be difficult to distinguish from tridactyl or anisodactyl tracks because the webbing may not make a strong impression. (Incidentally, this is sometimes the case even for birds that have fully webbed toes: if the substrate is coarse or resistant, or if the tracks are weathered, the webbing may not be obvious.)

In most palmate tracks, only toes 2, 3, and 4 are webbed; in totipalmate tracks, however, the hallux is rotated toward the inside of the track, and all four toes are webbed. This gives the print an asymmetrical shape that is quite distinctive, and quite rare: only a few fish-eating birds like pelicans, gannets, and cormorants have totipalmate feet.

Least common of all among waterfowl are lobed tracks, which have webbed pads on the feet that don't connect any two feet together. Coots and grebes are about the only common birds that leave such tracks, so they're quite distinctive — of the two, coots have much more obviously lobed toes, while grebe tracks are more subtly widened.

Gait

As noted above, the shape of a bird's track is rarely distinctive enough to identify the species, and often isn't even enough on its own to narrow it down to a genus or family. By observing the gait implied by the tracks, however, you may get a lot closer.

A bird's gait is simply the way it moves along the ground, which naturally will show in the track it leaves. To an expert tracker, a bird's gait speaks not only of its identity but its activity, its health, and even its age. Even a beginner can learn a great deal about a bird from how it behaves (or behaved) on the ground.

With allowances for individual variation, gaits fall into a few general categories: walking, running, hopping, and skipping. Keep in mind that unlike foot shape, a bird's gait is not set in stone: the same bird may use two or more of these gaits depending on the activity, the terrain, and the perceived danger of the environment.

Walking

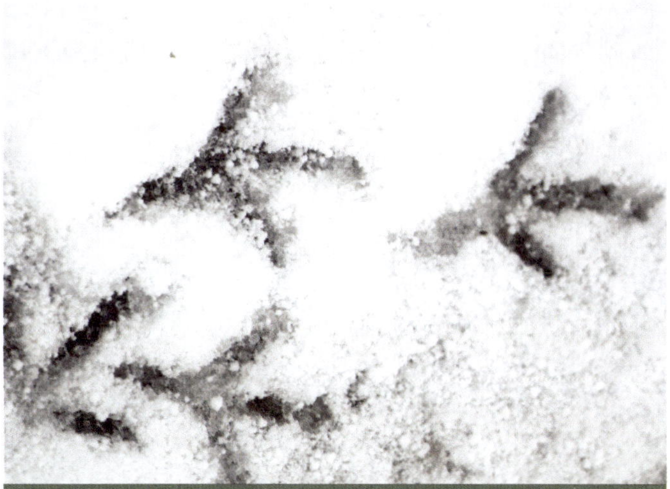
Pigeon walking gait in the snow

Unless they're very small, birds that spend a lot of time on the ground tend to prefer walking. A walking bird leaves a series of tracks much like that of a walking human: the individual tracks are evenly spaced, and relatively close together (although this can be hard to judge in isolation). Pigeons and starlings walk; crows and ravens walk; herons and storks walk.

The placement of the bird's feet is an important characteristic of a walking trail: it may be so narrow as to make the trail a straight line, or it may be rather wide, making more of a zig-zag trail. The width of the trail is called its straddle, and is measured from the tip of the third toe on the left track to the tip of the third toe on the following right track (or vice versa).

Running

Robins running gate

Some birds that usually walk will run when they sense danger, but this isn't the main reason birds run (it's easier and safer just to fly away). Instead, birds that run are often hunters, especially of insects or small, swift vertebrates like snakes or lizards: robins are perhaps the most obvious example, but we could add mockingbirds, roadrunners, and some shorebirds. A running gait looks much like a walking gait, but the distance between tracks is longer, and the straddle sometimes narrower.

However, these are highly relative: the difference between a walking gait and a running gait can often be determined only by comparing them in the same species. The relatively short-legged robin has a running gait of only two or three times the length of its track, while the gait of the similar-sized but longer-legged mockingbird may be up to five times the track length.

The best way to get a sense of these distinctions is simply to observe birds in the real world, and note how their gait appears to change when they switch from walking to running (or vice versa).

Hopping and Skipping

Sparrow footprints

Hopping and skipping are both mainly seen in smaller birds, and they produce tracks that may appear similar, but each uses different muscles and implies a different lifestyle, so it's worth distinguishing them. A hopping bird leaves a trail in which left and right track are always paired, just as a hopping rabbit or human. Some birds that are commonly seen hopping include blackbirds and blue jays, but many birds will use some combination of walking, running, and/or hopping, depending on what they are doing.

The stride of a hopping trail is measured from one track to the next, as with a walking or running trail, but because the tracks are paired, the same track (left or right) is used, rather than alternating tracks. The straddle is measured at the paired tracks' widest point - usually the fourth toe.

Skipping birds leave trails that appear intermediate between running and hopping, with the tracks clearly paired but not adjacent. However, skipping is more like running than it is like hopping, in the sense that it is designed to cover ground quickly. Usually, it is preferred by small birds that spend significant time both in trees and on the ground: sparrows and other small, ground-foraging songbirds will usually skip over open ground.

A skipping trail's length is measured the same way as a hopping gait, using successive tracks of the same foot. The straddle is measured horizontally, from the outermost toe of one track to the outermost toe of the other; you will find that skipping trails are much narrower than hopping trails, and usually have a fairly long stride as well - more like running trails.

Other Useful Features

The physical characteristics of bird tracks — their size, shape, and gait — do not appear in isolation: the substrate and ecological context of a track can tell you a lot about the bird. (For example, a zygodactyl track in desert sand is much more likely to be made by a roadrunner than a woodpecker.)

Birds may also leave imprints with parts of their bodies besides their feet: evident wing and or drag marks, for example, are common in the tracks of some species, and there may be peck marks if the bird was foraging. In some unusual cases the bird's entire body may be visible in the substrate - as in the case of an owl strike, which in snow leaves an unmistakable open-winged impression.

Other Bird Sign: Scat, Feathers, etc.

Birds often leave much more than merely footprints as they make their way through the world: these traces are collectively called sign or spoor, and can be just as useful as footprints in identifying or tracking a bird.

Owl pellet

Bird scat is one of the most commonly encountered types of bird sign, and depending on the species may be quite distinctive: owl pellets are probably the best-known and easiest to interpret examples of scat, but owls are far from the only birds that produce pellets: hawks, shorebirds and wading birds, and some corvids (such as crows & jays) all produce pellets, or casts, each of which can be identified both by shape and contents.

Bird droppings can also be an incredibly rich source of information about birds, as many hunters know: take, for example, the changes in the appearance and content of grouse scat over the course of a year, or the distinctive ring of droppings left by bobwhite quail (which feed in circles for safety).

Bird feathers can also indicate the presence of a bird, but don't assume that tracks and feathers found together belong to the same bird: the bird that left one may have preyed on the bird that left the other - or they may simply have shared space. However, feathers may be, and ought to be, part of an overall picture or gestalt that includes all the visible signs of a bird's passage through its environment, and in this context are one more piece of evidence that may prove conclusive.

* *Thank you to the bird language work of Jon Young - my friend and expert tracker.*

Tracking Other Animals

Common Animal Tracks

Below are some common tracks and signs you may find in the wild. It is prudent to familiarize yourself with these as this will make living in the wild much more pleasurable. In addition, it will help you find food, identify who might be trying to steal yours, and know when predators are in your area. I always recommend taking a tracking course or joining a local tracking club to acquaint yourself with local signs and tracks.

Eurasian Beaver

(*Castor fiber*)

Eurasian Beaver

Beaver-eaten tree

Footprints and tracks of Eurasian beaver

Eurasian Lynx

(*Lynx lynx*)

Eurasian Lynx

Eurasian Lynx excrement

Eurasian Lynx tracks in the snow

Eurasian Otter

(*Lutra lutra*)

Eurasian Wolf

(*Canis lupus lupus*)

Eurasian Otter

Eurasian Wolf

Eurasian otter spraint

Footprint of a Eurasian Wolf in wet mud

Eurasian otter footprints in the mud

Red Fox paw tracks in mud

European Badger

(*Meles meles*)

European Badger

Footprint of a European badger in wet mud

European badger hole; Carol Rose, CC BY-SA 2.0

European Bison

(*Bison bonasus*)

European Bison

Bison tracks in hot spring mud

Bison track in dry mud; Squidocto; CC BY-SA 3.0

European Hedgehog

(*Erinaceus europaeus*)

European Hedgehog

A hedgehog footprint in the sand

The feces of a hedgehog in the forest

European Mole

(*Talpa europaea*)

European Mole

Mole tunnels

Mole hole

Wild Boar

(*Sus scrofa*)

Wild Boar

Wild boar droppings in the forest

Footprints of wild boar

European Red Fox

(*Vulpes vulpes*)

European Red Fox

Red fox scat

Red fox tracks in the mud

Roe Deer

(*Capreolus capreolus*)

Roe Deer

Footprint of a roe deer in deep snow

Roe deer droppings on the ground

European Rabbit

(*Oryctolagus cuniculus*)

European Rabbit

European rabbit footprints in the snow

Rabbit scat on the grass

Brown Bear

(*Ursus arctos*)

Brown Bear

Bear scat

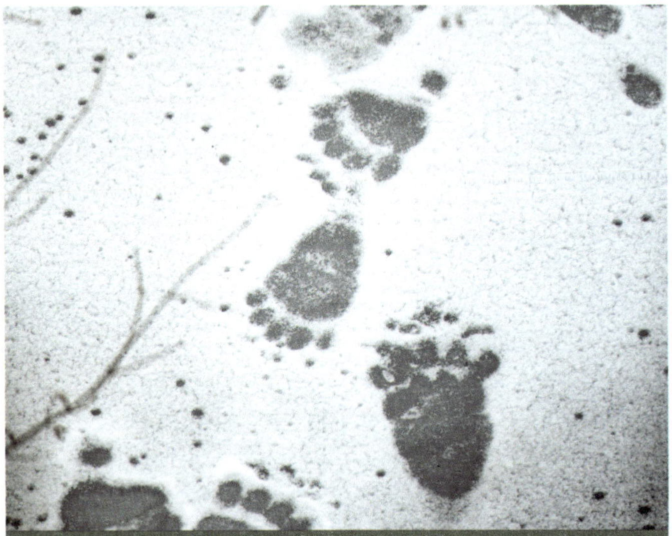

Brown bear footprints in the snow

European Hare

(*Lepus europaeus*)

European Hare

Feces of the European hare

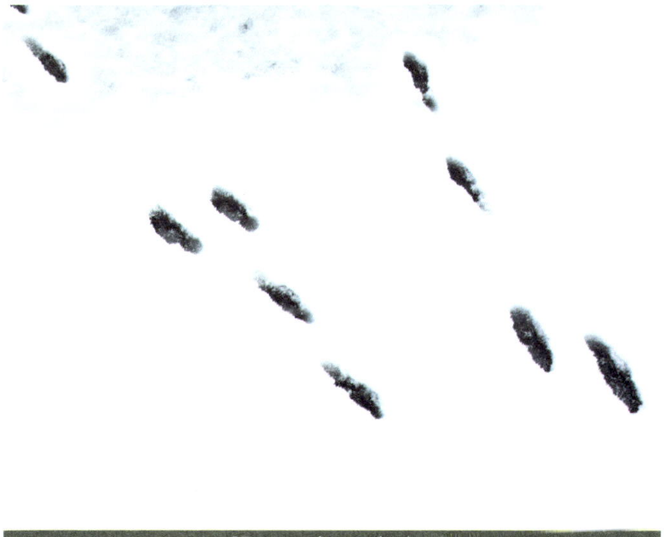

Hare tracks on the ice

European Wildcat

(*Felis silvestris silvestris*)

European Wildcat

Trail of bird feathers after a pigeon was killed by a wildcat

Wild cat footprints in the snow

Eurasian Magpie

(*Pica pica*)

Eurasian Magpie

Magpie nest

Magpie footprints in the snow

PERSONAL HYGIENE

CRAFTING WILD SOAP, TOOTHPASTE, AND OTHER ITEMS

There is no reason why we can't be clean just because we are "roughing it" or living "off-grid" in the wilderness. Some people may bring soap and body care items to stay fresh and clean, while others may not, thinking staying clean in the wilderness is unnecessary. In fact, keeping ourselves clean in the wilderness is more important than elsewhere. If we do not, we could get a stomach or intestinal infection or fungal or bacterial skin conditions that could cut our adventure short if we require medical attention.

Whether you run out of supplies, didn't bring any, or found yourself lost, unprepared, and concerned about your personal hygiene, you can stay clean in the wilderness using simple, natural ingredients that you find around you, no matter your environment.

Making Wilderness Soap

Using Mechanical Plant Processing to Release Natural Saponins

Many plants contain natural saponins, biochemicals with cleaning properties similar to soap. They even lather a little, some more than others. Even without visible lather, you can still feel the saponins, and they will clean well enough for most purposes. Keeping the plant fibers with the saponins will also help scour while the saponins help clean.

Some good choices are Soapwort (*Saponaria* spp.), a Eurasian native widely introduced elsewhere, and Clematis (*Clematis* spp.), found natively and introduced worldwide. You can crush their leaves and flowers and use them for natural soap.

To use natural saponins, simply bruise the plant material by crushing it between two rocks, mix it with water, and use it along with the plant fibers to wash and scour.

If you are still looking for something with a little more cleaning power, read on to learn how to make your own real soap in the wilderness.

Making Soap Using Chemical Processing of Animal Fat and Wood Ashes

You can make your own wilderness soap using three simple ingredients: water, ash, and fat (or oil). Since it's made with all-natural ingredients, it's biodegradable and safe for use near water, unlike chemical detergents from home.

Step 1

Rendering Your Fat

Always start with rendering your fat because this process takes the longest. Skip this step if you brought lard, beef tallow, olive oil, or vegetable oil from home; simply heating those fats is sufficient.

However, you may have brought raw animal fat or hunted a deer, moose, bear, or waterfowl and gotten fat that way. You can even use the fat from the tail of a beaver or alligator. Rendering is simply the process of boiling the fat to remove water and organics. This also makes fat shelf-stable.

To render it, cut your fat into small pieces, put it in a pot of water, and boil it. The smaller the pieces, the less time it will take. Boil it for anywhere from 1 - 6 hours, depending on your temperature, the fat, and how small you cut your pieces. Once lots of liquid fat is visible in the pot, strain it through a cloth to remove any unwanted particles, keeping the liquid fat in a container to use when needed. It will solidify once it cools.

Step 2

Making Lye from Wood Ashes and Creek Water

You only need a campfire and clean water to make lye for soapmaking.

Hardwood ash makes the strongest lye because it's higher in potassium and sodium. Good choices include maple, hickory, beech, and ash. Softwoods like pine, spruce, or fir don't contain enough potassium and sodium. If you only have conifers, then burn leaves and bark, which have higher mineral levels than wood. If you are in grasslands without wood, you can also use the ash from grasses.

Sometimes, people use charcoal, the black chunks in a fire not yet reduced to ash. If you use charcoal, you must crush it into a powder first.

Mix your ash or crushed charcoal with roughly equal parts of clean water from a creek, river, or collected rainwater. Do not use stagnant or highly alkaline water because the minerals and other compounds can interfere with saponification.

Next, boil it down over the fire or camp stove using a stainless-steel pot for 5 - 20 minutes, depending on how fine your ash is and how much water you add. It is critical to use stainless steel or another non-reactive metal rather than aluminum, which will react with the lye, dissolving aluminum into your lye and ruining your pot.

The longer you boil it, the more concentrated the lye will be. Making too strong of lye can make your soap harsh, but too weak will make your soap less effective. Since we lack the tools we would have at home, do your best and experiment a little.

After boiling, strain it, and you will be left with murky gray lye water.

Step 3

Preparing Your Additional Ingredients (Optional)

You can add additional ingredients to your soap for disinfectant properties, scouring, fragrance, or all of the above. Fresh pine needles or juniper leaves smell amazing in soap while also giving some scouring action and additional disinfectant properties. Juniper berries also smell amazing and are great for the skin; just pop the seeds out first. You can also use mint, sage, creosote bush, flower petals, or horsetail. Adding fine clay makes a great shaving bar. Cut whatever you use into small pieces that will easily disperse throughout the soap, then set it aside.

Step 4

Saponification - Mixing the Lye and Fats

Now for the fun part. Saponification is where you mix lye and fatty acids together to make soap.

You want your strained lye and your rendered and strained fat at roughly the same warm (not hot) temperature. Mix your lye and oils in your stainless-steel pot and return it to the heat.

Bring the mixture to a boil and boil it down. Depending on the heat and the size of your pot and soap batch, you may need to stir constantly at first to ensure it doesn't boil over. Boiling speeds up saponification and helps remove excess water. The amount of time this takes can vary enormously, but usually boiling it for 20 - 60 minutes will suffice. You will notice the mixture thickening, the boiling sound will change (listen for it), and then it's ready to pour.

Step 5

Pouring and Hardening Your Soap

Have a mold ready. It could be any stainless steel, glass, or thick plastic (never use thin plastic) bowl, cup, pot, etc. You can even use natural molds like seashells or hollowed-out gourds. You can line your mold with a cloth to help separate the soap and any remaining water as the bar solidifies, or just pour it directly into your clean mold.

Just before you pour, add your optional ingredients if using them, and stir well. Then, remove your soap from the heat and pour it into your mold.

Allow your soap to cool and harden for 12 - 24 hours. Once hardened, pop it out of the mold and break it into appropriate-sized chunks. Pour off any excess water that may have pooled on the bottom.

Using Your Wilderness Soap

Your finished soap may be hard, soft, or nearly liquid. It depends on how strong your lye was, the amount of potassium versus sodium hydroxide, what kind of oil you used, how long it was processed, etc. Even if it is soft and squishy, it will work more effectively than saponin-based plant soap rubs.

It becomes harder and increases in quality if allowed to sit for a while before use. However, since you are out in the wilderness and likely need it, it can be used immediately. Use it to wash your hands, body, hair, clothes, dishes, dog, or anything else.

Making Wilderness Toothpaste

Oral hygiene is just as important in the wilderness as it is at home. Fortunately, even if you left your supplies at home or ran out, you can make your own essentials to keep your teeth clean.

Twig Toothbrushes

Making a toothbrush is far simpler than most people imagine. People have been doing this for thousands of years with Miswak (*Salvadora persica*) twigs in Asia and Africa, and in North America good trees include maple (*Acer* spp.), oak (*Quercus* spp.), and birch (*Betula* spp.). Other good sources include willow (*Salix* spp. - very bitter but also helps with headaches), dogwood (*Cornus* spp.), and Neem (*Azadirachta indica*), but any non-toxic hardwood works.

Choose a small, living, semi-hardwood twig roughly ¼ inch (0.6 cm) in diameter. Older wood is too hard and may break, and younger wood is not rigid enough. Dead twigs tend to crumble.

Cut a 4–6 inch (10-15 cm) length of stick and pound one end a few times between two rocks. When you see some separate visible fibers, brush off the bark and other loose pieces, and it's ready to use.

Then, brush your teeth with it just like you would a toothbrush. The mechanical action alone will clean your teeth sufficiently. However, you can also add one of the following pastes.

Baking Soda or Salt Toothpaste

If you happen to have baking soda or salt, you can use those on your brush to help clean your teeth. But what if you don't have baking soda or salt? No worries, as other options are available.

Charcoal Toothpaste

Charcoal is antimicrobial and makes a great toothpaste. It also helps whiten teeth and remove toxins.

Take some charcoal from your fire and carefully grind it to a fine powder. The finer the powder the better, because it will be gentler on your teeth and gums. Next, you need to rinse your charcoal because otherwise, it can be very caustic (remember, we used this to make lye). Simply pour it into hot water, stir it, and strain it through a cloth. You should repeat this again to ensure the lye has been fully leached out.

Then, take your toothbrush twig, dip your stick into the wet paste or dried powder, and clean your teeth.

It may seem counterintuitive because it turns your teeth black. However, charcoal is a known tooth whitener and is sometimes added to commercial toothpaste. The trick is to rinse very well when done, and your teeth will be just as clean and white as if you used your toothbrush and whitening toothpaste at home.

A note of caution - charcoal is abrasive. Using it long-term could damage the enamel on your teeth, so limit its use to once weekly.

Mint or Birch Toothpaste and Mouthwash

If you have wild mint or birch trees, you can pop the leaves in your mouth and chew on them, rubbing them on your teeth with your tongue. You can also bruise the leaves between two rocks and use the resultant paste on your twig toothbrush.

Mint leaves

You can also make a mouthwash with mint or birch by making tea and rinsing with it. The mint and birch have antimicrobial and antibacterial activity, help with inflammation and pain, taste great, and freshen your breath. You can also use a saltwater rinse after brushing your teeth; it doesn't taste as good, but it works.

Nature's Toothpicks

Need a toothpick? Plant thorns make the best toothpicks. Some excellent choices are any cacti, Mesquite, Thorn Trees, Buckthorns, Hawthorns, and Honey Locust. If you can't find a thorny plant, you can use your camping knife to sharpen a hard wooden twig to a very fine point or use a clean fishbone.

Wilderness Hair and Face Care

Washing Your Hair and Face

Any saponin or soap can be used to wash your face and hair. However, using soap on your hair or face long-term can dry them out, so soaps are best used only once weekly. Saponins are milder and can be used more often, but they clean a bit less effectively.

Alternatively, if you have baking soda, make a paste, rub it on your hair, leave it for a few minutes, and then rinse well. Diluted vinegar, especially apple cider, also works well on both your hair and face.

Those with short hair will have an easier time; simply wash and rinse. If you have long hair, don't despair; there are ways to tame those gnarly knots.

Making Hair Rinses and Conditioners in the Wilderness

If you have long hair, follow your wash with a rinse of diluted vinegar or an herbal infusion to soften your hair and help get the tangles out. Herbal infusions (teas) can include chamomile, burdock, comfrey, stinging nettle, mint, horsetail, yarrow, chickweed, mallow, sage, plantain, elderflower, sunflower, birch, even nopal cactus or any other plants you have available (avoiding very resinous or unpleasant smelling plants). These hair rinses can also be used on your face after or in place of washing with soap.

Getting a brush through your hair can still be difficult if you have particularly knotty hair. In this case, you can create a moisturizing conditioner using oil and an herbal infusion.

A hair conditioner is simply a mixture of oil and water, an emulsifier to hold the two together, and additional vitamins, fragrances, etc. The emulsifier makes it look better as a product, as it keeps it from separating, and is completely unnecessary for your hair.

To make your own, mix your warm herbal infusion (strong tea) with a small amount of warm oil or melted fat and shake VERY WELL. Then, add a small amount of this to your hair after washing and brush it through.

If all you have is solid fats, you must heat your mixture with each use since the fat will likely re-solidify. With liquid oils, simply shake vigorously before each use. Since there are no preservatives, you may need to make a new batch every 1 - 4 weeks, depending on storage temperature.

Wilderness Brushes and Combs

No comb or brush? No problem. You can get that from the wild, too. Fish vertebrae can be made into a great comb. Other options are to bind together a small handful of fibers from grass, fine twigs, yucca leaves (pounded to remove the plant matter), or whatever else you have in your environment to make a mini old-fashioned broom-like brush that can be used on your hair. The key is to use smooth fibers that don't have knots or small protrusions that can get caught in your hair.

Once cleaned and brushed, keeping your long hair in braids will keep it cleaner and prevent future tangling while living in the wilderness.

Wilderness Toilet Etiquette and Natural Toilet Paper

Nothing is more disappointing than going out to enjoy nature in all her beauty only to have to see, or worse, step on, other people's toilet paper. Please don't; instead, bring a camp shovel or a hand trowel and dig a hole. Alternatively, make a good old-fashioned digging stick from your environment.

If you have no toilet paper, many natural options are available. However, regarding nature's toilet paper, not all are created equal. Some nice choices are deciduous leaves such as maple, alder, birch, ash, hickory, etc. Mullein leaves are especially soft and luxurious and are a widely introduced species worldwide. You can also use grasses (run your hand along them first; some have very sharp edges!) and mosses, but they do tend to leave bits behind.

This is trickier if you are in the desert since many plants have spines. Creosote bush is often abundant and has no spines; it's not soft but will work. Otherwise, somewhat smooth rocks or sticks with spines removed can work. Washing afterwards also helps.

Nail Hygiene

Cleaning Your Hands and Nails

When you are in the wilderness, nail hygiene is far more important than you realize. If you are hunting, fishing, using the toilet, etc., you can get bacteria, fungi, and/or parasites trapped in your nails and then get sick after preparing your food.

Use soap to wash your hands regularly. Then, use a knife tip (carefully) or a sharpened twig to scrape the dirt out from under your nails. You can also use a large thorn or spine; just avoid sharp ones that can easily stab the tender flesh under the nail. Then, wash your hands again to ensure they are sanitary before handling your food.

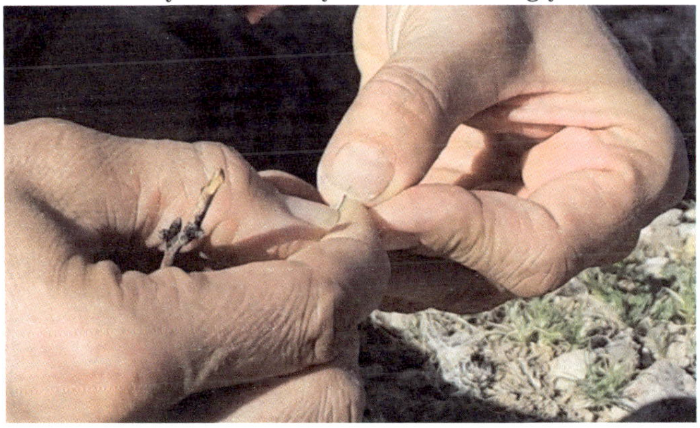

Cutting and Filing Your Nails

If your nails have grown and you have no clippers, do not bite your nails since you will put pathogens directly in your mouth. You can use a sharp knife to cut them, but the edges won't be smooth. A safer and more effective way is to find an abrasive stone and use this to file your nails down. Some rocks work better than others - rocks with the texture of fine sandpaper work best. Too smooth and it won't work, but too coarse and rough will leave the edges torn and jagged. The size of the rock doesn't matter as long as it is comfortable to use.

KEEPING YOUR BODY AND CLOTHES CLEAN IN THE WILD

In the wild, staying clean is a key part of survival, as it allows you to keep safe from the harmful microbes that build up on your skin, over time.

Issues like heat rash, jungle rot, and fungal infections can easily become a problem when hygiene is ignored. These small problems can quickly become life threatening many miles away from civilization, regardless of how insignificant they seemed at first.

Fortunately, there are easy ways to take care of personal hygiene while out in the wild.

Basic Hygiene

Basic hygiene in the wilderness simply refers to keeping your body free of microbes that can reproduce and result in disease.

In reality, this isn't going to be much different than being at home, however there will be no warm showers or lavender-scented soaps to use on hand. Practicing basic hygiene in the wilderness requires a bit of creativity and recognizing that you still won't be the best smelling person, but you'll be clean.

It's primarily about cleaning your body, including your teeth, and cleaning the clothes that you'll be wearing just about every day. Even on shows like *Alone*, contestants are allowed to bring a toothbrush with them, demonstrating just how important basic hygiene is.

Natural Soaps

Likely, you won't have any soap with you in the wild, but that doesn't mean you can't improvise. Plants are often used as additives to soaps, but many can be used alone.

Mountain lilac, soapberry, and yucca are three of the most common plants that can be used when available. For mountain lilac, simply rub it in between your hands with water and it will leave behind a pleasant fragrance. Soapberries, which contain saponins for cleaning, may be dried or mixed with water for a good lather.

Mountain lilac

Yucca leaves

Yucca roots and leaves can be shredded and mixed with water to produce a saponin-rich soap. This works incredibly well for cleaning just about everything, including your clothes and body.

Yucca root

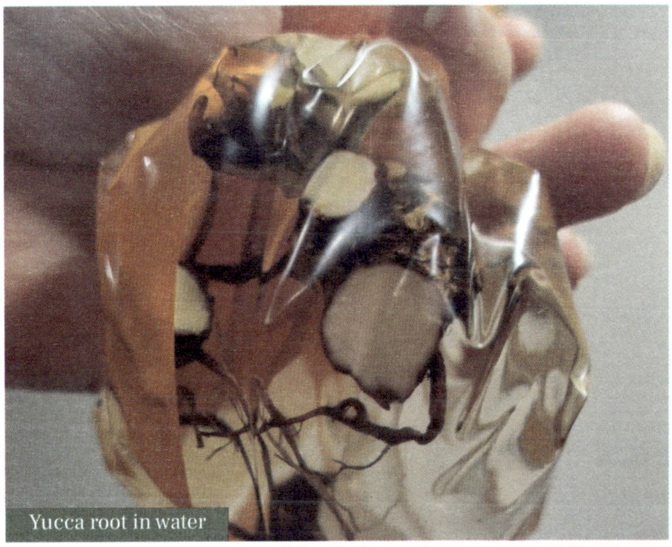
Yucca root in water

In most scenarios, you'll be left to clean yourself without any soap at all, so it's important to know how to take care of grime without your everyday cleaning products.

Sponge Bath and a Scrub Down

Friction alone is a powerful form of removing microbes and grime. When you're without soap, you are often relying on friction to do most of the work for you. One of the best ways to do this is by taking a wilderness sponge bath.

You probably don't have a sponge along in your survival scenario, but any absorbent material will work. An old piece of cloth or a bandana is perfect for scrubbing your body down, especially when you don't have much water available.

When the grime is really bad, you may need something tougher. Sand and ash from your fire are two great materials that are easily found in the wilderness to help scrub away dirt and grime from your skin.

Charcoal has the ability to pull toxins from the skin, which is why you see more and more products incorporating it into their formulas. If you're in survival mode, you're likely producing a lot of charcoal and ash, so put it to good use.

Simply grind the charcoal down and lather a paste all over your body. Pay particular attention to all of the body parts that are likely to get dirtier faster, like the armpits, feet, and groin. These are spots you'll need to clean often and thoroughly when in the wild.

Even without any scrubbing, a water bath is far better than nothing. If you have access to a source of running water, try to bathe as frequently as possible.

Taking an Air Bath

This method is exactly as it sounds. When you don't have access to water, fresh air and sunlight are going to be your next best option.

Strip down and take an air or sun bath. The UV rays from the sun are a powerful cleaner. A breeze will help move clean air over your body as the sun works to kill germs. Sometimes the body just needs to breathe.

While you're "bathing", spread all of your clothes out in the sun so they get the same treatment. The more time they spend in the sun, the cleaner they'll get. The more wind you have, the better. Try to set your clothes up in a way that will allow for air to pass through them while the sun is strongest.

Taking a Smoke Bath

When I spend a long time in the wilderness in colder months, I often smoke both my body and my clothes clean. I first learned this hygiene tool when with a Himba community in Namibia, who have very limited access to water. They smoke themselves clean every day. The smoke helps kill both bacteria and parasites, and kills the odor-producing bacteria that make us stinky. I also smoke my clothes clean – hanging them on a tripod over the smoke from my fire. It works well.

The Wilderness Washing Machine

Washing clothes in the wilderness is nowhere near as simple as throwing everything into the washing machine and pressing a few buttons. There are a few ways you can wash your clothes, including using what I like to call a "wilderness washing machine".

The wilderness washing machine is a simple concept. All you need is a vessel to hold your clothes, water, several small stones, and yucca soap.

Start off by rinsing your clothes in running water to help get all of the surface-level grime out before throwing it into the washing machine. Then, set your clothes into whatever container you have. This could be the pot you use for cooking, a birch bowl, a plastic bag you have with you or found, or even a depression in a large rock with enough space for your clothes and water.

Fill the container up with water and add the small rocks and yucca soap. Instead of how a normal washing machine shakes back and forth, you'll need to create the agitation in your "machine". Move your hands quickly back and forth to shake the clothes amongst the rocks. This motion will allow for the rocks to beat dirt out of the clothing into the water.

If you have a plastic bag, or a pot with a lid, simply hold it closed and shake vigorously to get the dirt out.

This process is usually done several times in order to get as much dirt out as possible. Once the water starts pouring out clear, your clothes will be as clean as they can get in the wild.

Wool vs. Synthetics

One of the best ways to take care of your personal hygiene is to take preventative measures. Some fabrics are much better at fighting bacteria than others. For example, wool is well-known for its antimicrobial properties. This means you can go much longer without needing to wash your clothing and they won't start smelling as soon.

Synthetic clothing, like polyester and fleece, start to smell and get dirty much quicker than fabrics like wool (or even cotton). If you prepare by wearing the right clothing, you won't need to worry about laundry as frequently and will stay cleaner longer.

Oral Hygiene

Keeping your teeth clean is another incredibly important part of taking care of yourself in the wild. The small bits of bacteria and plaque that build up in your mouth can lead to a long-term buildup of bacteria in your gut. This can be harmful in both short and long-term survival scenarios.

While you can't plug in your electric toothbrush and brush for two minutes with ultra-bright whitening toothpaste, you can still get your teeth semi-clean.

One of the best ways to do this in the wild is to use a frayed chewing stick for a toothbrush and/or use herbs to chew on for positive dental hygiene. Many people chew on wild chamomile, spearmint, eucalyptus, and others to keep their teeth clean in the wild. You may even throw in a small bit of charcoal to help clean your teeth at least once a day.

FEMININE HYGIENE TIPS IN THE WILD

Living life out in the wild means sacrificing certain city comforts, including modern ideas of cleanliness. But this doesn't have to be the case with personal feminine hygiene and care. Some women use disposable feminine hygiene products, such as tampons or pads, for convenience. While it's possible to use disposable products for long-term wilderness living— there are extra challenges, such as proper disposal so as to not attract wildlife, when outdoors.

Another big challenge is keeping an adequate supply during your time in the wild without returning to urban centers to replenish your supply. Non-disposable products are often a better option.

Using Disposable Feminine Hygiene Products in The Wild

While use of feminine hygiene products in the wild is identical to that in city life, it's the disposal, maintenance, and cleanup of these convenient products that you'll need to worry about. This is especially the case with the "classic" disposable feminine products most women use: tampons, pads, and pantyliners. Because of this, products designed to be "convenient" in the city might not be so convenient in the wild. They can also negatively impact wildlife: it takes a lot more time and effort to manage these products to protect your surrounding environment. This may tempt you to skip to the next section altogether.

Even tampons, the "least messy" of disposable products, can quickly become the opposite of convenient if you don't know how to dispose of them properly while camping or living outdoors long-term. Smell and potential bug issues can get out of hand, along with larger wildlife than insects.

Here's some guidance on how to avoid common issues with tampons, pads, and pantyliners in a wilderness setting— if you choose to use them.

For wildlife kindness purposes, use only 100% cotton products.

Choose 100% cotton disposable feminine hygiene products over other types. These are biodegradable and thus much more environmentally friendly to use in a wilderness setting. If you have a composting toilet, for example (please refer to the chapter "Latrine and Hygiene" on page 215), you can dispose of them there without much worry about wildlife or other interference— and they will completely break down...eventually. They are NOT to be disposed of in a compost pile used for growing your own food or gardening, as they are almost certain to attract wildlife.

Any tampon, pantyliner, or pad that is not 100% cotton will not biodegrade. They may also contain chemicals that can leach into the surrounding soil or water, harming plant and animal life. Even though 100% cotton products do eventually break down, keep in mind that they break down very slowly— which can open you up to possible problems with wildlife, smell, and the like.

Keep / dispose of tampons only in an airtight container.

This is only for the duration / course of the days around your period. If you don't use a composting toilet for immediate disposal, or you don't yet have time / readiness to dispose of your used products right away (which many women don't— busy dealing with the actual symptoms and issues of their period), this is a good transitional practice between product use and "final" disposal.

Preferably wrap used tampons in some used plastic wrap or a baggie (if you have one available) or in a dry cloth or unused /unusable clothing before placing in a container to manage moisture and smell. If you have access to Usnea lichen, or large dock or mullein leaves in the wild, these work quite well for wrapping. In a pinch, these can act as "plant-based" short-term emergency replacements for pads or pantyliners (and toilet paper— if you don't have it) though they are nowhere near as effective or absorbent as paper or cotton products.

If using tampons with plastic applicators, store these somewhere separate.

Unfortunately, though we may wish to stay in the wild forever, these will eventually need to be taken to an urban center to be disposed of properly. These should never be disposed of in the wild— unless your tampon applicators are made of a paper or cardboard that is 100% biodegradable.

Concealing or covering scent

This is not always called for— only if you are concerned about lingering scent following disposable product use, and if you have the right tools to do so. Before wrapping up used products apply a natural perfume or essential oil— one spray, or one drop— to each product before stowing away pre-disposal. Oils like eucalyptus or tea tree are great choices for scent concealment.

If you don't have these products available and scent is a concern: wild-harvested aromatic plants can be successfully used to keep down smell. Harvest wild plants like bee balm/bergamot, river mint, wild mint, spearmint, or crushed evergreens like juniper. If you brought spices with you for cooking in the wild long-term, herbs and seasonings like clove, lavender, or oregano can also help mask scent. They also help repel insects. Crush or grind these in your container before stowaway.

Empty your container following every period.

A bottomless container for product disposal would be great, but this is not possible in the wild. This is what makes disposable products the most challenging for menstruation in the wild: "emptying the trash" is not easy.

If you still prefer using these products, have a way of disposing them that doesn't impede too much on your wilderness existence or harm wildlife: such as measured trips to urban areas. If you've found yourself in a pinch having to use them, you may burn them using a very hot fire or bury them deeply far away from your camp.

This is another reason why disposable products are not desirable. You will have to bury them a good measure deeper than other types of human waste to fully deter wildlife from finding them— which can be a lot of work. All the same, it is good to know how to dispose of these products if you are absolutely pushed to (and don't use a composting toilet), and in a way that is not harmful to the environment if you cannot find better alternatives. This next section will help instruct you— and I emphasize again that, if you can, pack out any non-100% cotton products for urban disposal. Do NOT dispose of them in the wild.

Adequate Disposal of Feminine Products in The Wild

If you've ever followed wilderness living guidelines for going to the bathroom outdoors (whether #1 or #2), consider that these same guidelines will apply to disposing of your feminine hygiene products responsibly— if you do not have a way to compost them. Awareness of the surrounding wildlife, waterways, and your own well-being (and that of other humans nearby) is essential.

Position your disposal site strategically: always at least 200 feet (60 m) away from paths or human-trafficked areas, your own wild living area, and most importantly— away from water: lakes, creeks, rivers, and more. Also be mindful of slope. Avoid choosing a site that is uphill from any of these areas.

For the most optimal and environmentally friendly site for hygiene products, create your own. Choose a special site that meets all the above requirements and put (or build) a shelter overhead: such as canvas, tarp, tent, or other structure to mark it as a human-influenced site for discouraging plant growth or animal activity nearby the site.

While human waste disposal only requires digging around ½ foot (15 cm) deep, for feminine hygiene products, this must be a depth of 3-5 feet (1-1.5 m)— even deeper is optimal. This cuts your chances of hungry wildlife (such as raccoons, possums, or bears) digging for it. Again, all the work and details above are why disposable feminine hygiene products are possibly harmful and far less preferred.

Using Non-Disposable Feminine Hygiene Products in the Wild

The following is what you really want to have lined up for your time in the wild. Unlike disposable products, these reusable (also called multi-use) feminine hygiene and menstruation products are simple and straightforward: they don't need a whole lot of cautionary instruction to be effective, comfortable, and ultimately the more convenient and environmentally friendly of the two choices for your time in the wild. When used correctly, they don't smell or attract bugs and wildlife.

Reusable and Washable Pads

Like disposable pads or pantyliners, these products are designed to meet the same purpose, but be re-used multiple times per day or through the days of your period. They are washed and cleaned once (or more) daily then very thoroughly deep cleaned before the next menstruation cycle.

Most women are likely to purchase more than one of these so they can switch between fresh, clean pads within one period for cleanliness and comfort, and save themselves cleaning work and labor while dealing with period symptoms. These are safe options for rinsing and cleaning in creeks, rivers, or springs— much in the same manner as washing clothing.

Menstrual Underwear

These are more or less identical to the concept of reusable and washable pads, only these come in a convenient and wearable underwear form. When it comes to "external products" for feminine hygiene, menstrual panties are one of the most popular choices nowadays.

Just like with pads, it is advisable to purchase more than

one pair for comfort and cleanliness during the days of your period and in-between washings.

Menstrual Cups

Menstrual cups are highly clean and convenient internal reusable feminine hygiene products. The cup is inserted and catches flow; it is then emptied and cleaned at multiple points during the day.

One possible hurdle with menstrual cups is disposing of its contents in a way that does not create smell or attract animals. In a wildlife situation it is advised not to dispose of menstrual cup contents all in one spot— have multiple spots spread out so that a regular "smell" isn't established to wildlife nearby.

Alternately, if you have the water resources and you happen to be growing food or other plant life nearby to sustain yourself, you can dilute menstrual cup contents with water and use that as a root fertilizer for your plants (not for root veggie crops), as menstrual blood is high in nutrients plants like. Watering down the contents also helps offset any smell that could attract wildlife—though there is always a risk.

If you are 100% set on keeping wildlife away, you can bury menstrual cup contents around ½ foot deep (15 centimeters) in human disposal safe areas in the wild, much like other human waste. You can also wash your menstrual cup out in a nearby stream, river, or creek—only if it is not upstream from other human activity for drinking water, etc.

Used Clothing, Pillows, Towels, Bedding

If none of the above products are available to you, you can use any undesired clothing, towels, or other cotton or flannel materials in your possession for menstruation. These can be crudely wrapped around the lower portion of your body during activities during the day—or, placed between the legs while sleeping to catch any flow.

Afterwards however, these must be cleaned or disposed of like other feminine hygiene products. Depending on whether you plan on tossing them permanently or reusing them, follow the above instructions in the applicable section for guidance on disposal or cleaning.

Herbs for Feminine Hygiene Support

Managing feminine hygiene in the wild doesn't only focus on cleanliness, comfort, and convenience issues with products. There are also the symptoms of menstruation or other aspects of feminine health to deal with—below are some common and easy-to-access natural remedies in the wild that may help during your primitive living situation.

Cranberry
(Bloating / U.T.I. Issues)

Both leaf and berry (and twigs/stems) of cranberry are considered helpful for feminine health discomfort symptoms. Wild cranberry can be harvested and made into a tea for such purposes.

Raspberry Leaf
(Uterine Toning / Female Health Support)

You're likely to find some form of raspberry growing in the wild in most parts of the world. When not available, blackberry leaves work in a similar fashion. Harvest and dry the leaves of this plant (or use them fresh) for tea and drink regularly during menstruation, or during crucial times of your cycle when not menstruating, to enhance overall female health. It's also advisable to drink it as a daily tea. Raspberry is traditionally a "uterine tonic," known to increase and strengthen uterine health. This can holistically lead to less heavy and more pain-free periods.

Angelica
(Cramping and Pain)

It's also likely you'll find some variety of wild angelica near you. A warning: this plant can look like a lot of other wild, poisonous plants around the world, such as poison hemlock. Be sure you are 100% confident in identifying it or have a wildlife expert or herbalist with you to make sure. Once you are confident, use the root in tea to help allay cramps and pain— it can be highly effective in a pinch, and its seeds have a pleasant licorice or anise-like flavor.

Plant	Plant Appearance	Toxicity
Angelica	Tall with hollow stems, large toothed leaves, and greenish-yellow clustered flowers.	**Not toxic**; used in herbal medicine and cooking.
Poison Hemlock	Tall with finely divided, fern-like leaves, smooth stems with purple spots, and small white umbel-shaped flowers.	**Highly toxic**; contains coniine, which can be deadly if ingested.
Cow Parsnip	Large, hairy stems, deeply lobed leaves, and flat-topped clusters of white or cream-colored flowers	**Mildly irritant sap**; can cause skin reactions in some people.

Cow parsnip umbel (*Heracleum maximum*). Danielle Langlois, at Cap Bon-Ami in the Forillon National Park of Canada, Québec, CC BY-SA 3.0

Pacific Hemlock-parsley, Walter Siegmund (talk) - Own work, CC BY-SA 3.0

Dandelion
(Bloating)

Where *doesn't* dandelion grow? Use the sweet flowers or bitter roots— cleaned, and then dried, or fresh— of this sunny plant for tea if you find it growing near you in the wild. In a pinch the leaves can also work. Dandelion helps with bloating since it is a diuretic. It's also known for supporting overall female health as a regular tonic.

Goldenrod (Bloating, Inflammation, UTIs)

Herbalists know this plant well and it is found almost everywhere in some form in the wild. Goldenrod tea (made from its yellow flowers) could be thought of as a combination of dandelion and chamomile in terms of its natural remedy "usefulness." Like dandelion, it can help with bloating, but it also has a calming / soothing quality much like chamomile. It is also known to help support inflammation when consumed regularly, which may help with cramping.

Goldenrod
(Bloating, Inflammation, UTIs)

Herbalists know this plant well and it is found almost everywhere in some form in the wild. Goldenrod tea (made from its yellow flowers) could be thought of as a combination of dandelion and chamomile in terms of its natural remedy "usefulness." Like dandelion, it can help with bloating, but it also has a calming / soothing quality much like chamomile. It is also known to help support inflammation when consumed regularly, which may help with cramping.

Stinging Nettle
(Bloating and Nutrient Support)

If heavy bleeding and anemia are issues for you, learn how to harvest and make tea with stinging nettle leaves. This wild plant usually grows near water and is very high in vitamins and minerals: a great tea or cooking green to help you through the fatigue and bloated feeling of menstruation. Don't be deterred by the sting! Once it is even slightly dried, it no longer stings. Stinging nettle is both extremely nutritious and healing.

LATRINE AND HYGIENE

When you're in a survival situation, keeping a clean latrine can be the difference between staying healthy during a long-term stay and getting severely sick in a short time span.

Before you start building a latrine, it's a good idea to have a general understanding of what you need in order to keep yourself safe and healthy. This chapter covers everything from where to build your latrine, how to set it up, covering it up, keeping animals away, and differences in latrine practices throughout the winter.

The Best Spot for Your Latrine

Often it can be a difficult trip to go far from home to use the bathroom, especially when you're feeling sick or have an emergency situation. Defecating close to where you sleep is an obvious hazard for both health and safety.

Typically, in the wild you can choose a spot far from your camp and dig a trench or individual cat holes. When you stay in one spot for a longer time, you need to spread out your waste even further as you run out of spots. An easy fix to this is building a latrine closer to camp so you don't need to travel far, nor do you need to hunt for a new spot every time you have to go.

There are a few primary considerations to choosing the best spot to build your latrine. First, it needs to be far enough from your camp that you won't constantly smell the waste while in your shelter. This needs to be considered both in terms of distance and wind direction. If the latrine is far enough away in the right direction, you should never have a problem with the smell of waste in your home.

Next, it's necessary to think about the land that you are placing the latrine on. This needs to be a spot that won't flood, carrying waste away with it, nor should it be on a spot that's prone to landslides, like the side of a hill.

You also need to take into consideration where any other latrines may have been and where your drinking water comes from. If you are using a well, you need to build the latrine so it goes no deeper than 7 feet (2 m) above the water table. If you are drawing from a fresh source, you need to be over 330 feet (100 m) from this water source.

When possible, try to find a spot with stable soil so you can avoid building extra supports around the latrine pit. In unstable soil, additional brick supports can help keep the latrine in position.

Setting Up the Latrine

Once you've chosen the right spot for your latrine near camp, you can start the process of building.

The first step in setting up a latrine is measuring and digging the hole. If you plan on using this latrine for a long time, it's easiest to dig a uniform hole that is about 3 feet (1 m) in diameter. A circular hole will provide you with the most stability in the walls of the latrine.

To dig a uniform hole, you can build a simple tool of two long sticks that are each 3 feet (1 m) in length, lashed together to form a large cross. This can be used to measure the latrine as you dig downwards, ensuring that you maintain a consistent diameter of one meter.

Keeping the walls vertical is important for the structural integrity of the latrine. It will provide the most support, whereas a latrine with walls that lean inwards or outwards will have small dirt slides or can potentially fully collapse.

The hole should be at least 7 feet (2 m) deep if you are planning on using it for a long time. For short term use, you can stop digging after 3 feet (1 m) or so, but this all influences how long you can use the latrine for. Once you've reached this depth, you may need to provide additional support for the walls.

If the soil is stable, you can support the unstable portions with hardened clay bricks or stones that are built into the surrounding walls. If you have fully unstable soil, you'll need to create a wall out of stones and clay that will help provide strength to the walls over time.

Finally, the latrine will need a cover with a platform that is strong enough to hold your weight, with a hole in the center for your waste. A platform can be easily built by lashing sticks together with a tight weave. Support on the side of the platform can be helpful to help you stabilize yourself when using the latrine.

Keeping the Latrine Covered

Building a system that helps keep the latrine covered is important to keep the scent to a minimum and to help keep animals out.

Building a small structure that can cover the latrine is also an opportunity to build a privacy screen if you are in a group survival situation. This can be easily done by weaving branches together with leaves and other brush in between them.

The cover to the latrine can be built in the same way. Lashing sticks together for a larger frame and then fastening smaller branches together will provide a solid frame to hold leaves and duff that can be effective in both keeping scent in and everything else out.

Latrines that are built as a more permanent waste solution will have more durable coverings that are highly effective at keeping the latrine covered.

These covers can be built by lashing long, straight logs together tightly over the hole and then packing the top with clay and thick mud. This will build a small mound over the latrine, but also leaves a small space carved out in the middle of the covering for use. This option tends to be best when you are using the latrine for a long period of time as it will stay structurally sound for longer than a branch and leaf covering.

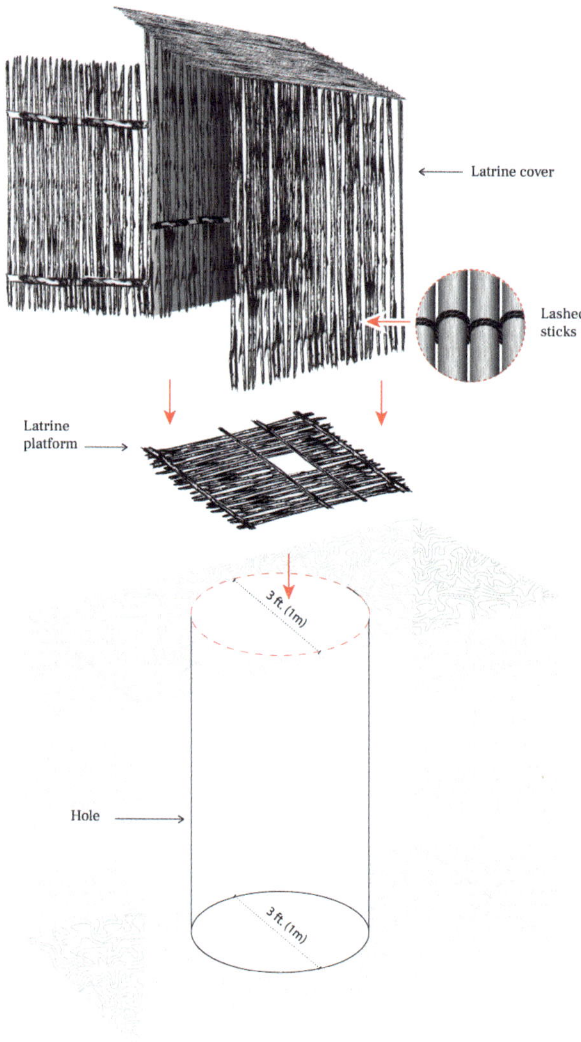

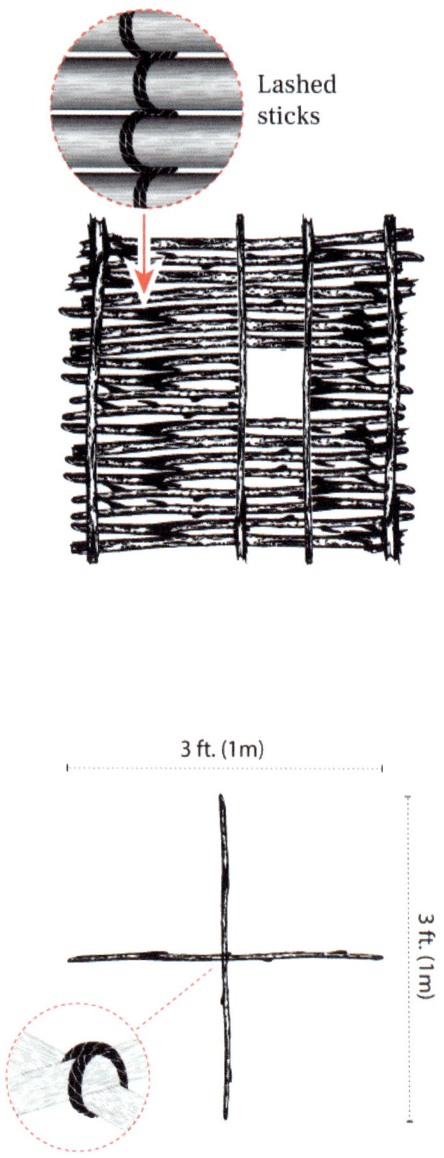

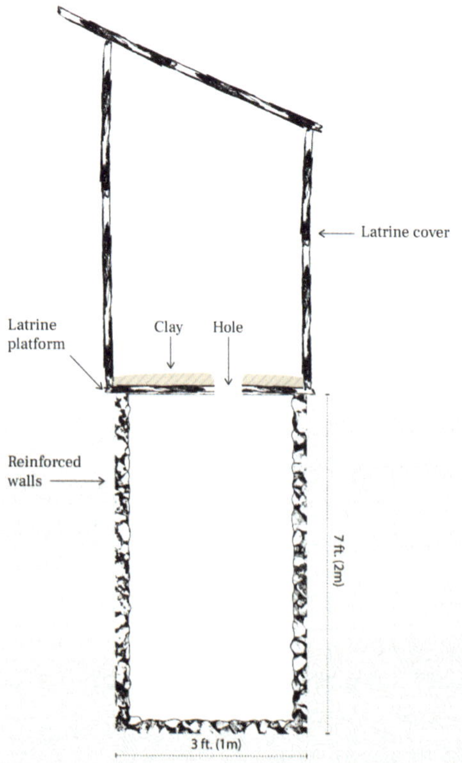

Keeping Animals Away

Keeping animals away from the latrine can be difficult, but is incredibly important to keep your campsite clean and hygienic.

If you've built a solid covering system and some small walls or blinds around the latrine, animals should have a tough time getting in. However, when animals are determined, they'll start digging and finding their way in no matter what. To stop this from being a problem, you need to address the different attractants that bring animals toward you in the first place.

One of the main attractants for animals is the strong scent of your latrine; keeping the scent to a minimum is the best way to keep animals out. This is mitigated well by providing proper ventilation and covering your feces after use.

Keep a small pile of dried leaves and dirt nearby the latrine so when you're finished, you can throw some organic material on top. This helps trap scent and add more organic material for compost if you are planning on using your latrine for that purpose later on.

The other important piece is to provide proper ventilation. If you are building a structure on top of the pit, make sure to provide a space where the air can flow and circulate through the latrine, rather than trapping it and having the scent build up.

Keep your latrine covered and as scent-free as possible to keep the number of animal visitors you have to a minimum.

Using the Latrine in the Winter

Peeing in the winter time is a long-debated topic amongst survivalists. Many people say that emptying your bladder will give your body more energy to keep warm, or that the stress created by needing to pee is enough to waste important energy.

Regardless, you'll need to pee at night at some point if you're in a survival situation in the winter. The important piece here is where to pee. If there's a lot of snow around, you don't want to contaminate it, especially if you are using snowmelt as a water source.

The best thing to do is create a small path to a single spot and pee there. Keeping one general area as your "bathroom" to pee in and your latrine for defecating, you can keep a clean camp. The winter tends to make fluids freeze and stick around longer than the summer when rains can wash everything away quickly.

Final Thoughts

A latrine is one of the most hygienic ways to take care of human waste in a survival situation if you are setting up a long-term camp. It helps consolidate all of the waste in one spot, is effective at trapping scent and keeping animals away, and can be used in the future for compost if you end up staying at your site for a long time.

Building the best latrine for survival isn't a task to be taken lightly, nor will it be done quickly. It can be a tough job to complete, but is well worth taking the time and putting in the energy to get it right. With the right latrine, you'll never need to move camp because of poor wilderness bathroom hygiene.

KEEPING YOUR FEET HEALTHY

When you are in the wild, it is helpful to establish a foot care routine that includes washing and drying your feet, frequently resting, and familiarizing yourself with possible injuries, as well as strategies for their prevention. It is important to keep your feet clean and dry in order to avoid infection and wounds that can compromise your comfort when standing and walking.

Foot Care Routine

Feet and socks should be rinsed daily, ideally in a downstream, moving water source. Avoid using soap in the wild unless it is completely biodegradable and natural (please see our chapter "Crafting Wild Soap, Toothpaste, and Other Items" on page 202), as it can contaminate water resources. When you rinse your socks, turn them inside out and remove any grit or organic matter. Additionally, keep shoes free of any debris, no matter how small; even the tiniest of rocks can damage shoes and socks, or cause sores on your feet.

Along with rinsing your feet and footwear, keeping your feet, socks, and shoes completely dry is an essential part of a successful care routine in the wild. After rinsing your feet, let them fully dry before putting socks on. Socks that have been rinsed can be pinned to your pack while you walk or hung from a tree while you rest or sleep.

Likewise, your feet should be dry at night when you go to bed. Dry feet can be coated with an oil-based, herbal salve to prevent skin from cracking and to create a barrier between the skin and water. By following these basic foot rinsing and drying practices, your feet will be better protected from discomfort and injury.

Tips and Tricks

When we spend time in the wild, we must remind ourselves to rest. A healthy wilderness lifestyle includes frequently elevating and resting your feet to improve circulation and reduce swelling. To successfully incorporate this habit into your daily routine, try taking off your socks and shoes during mealtimes and elevating your legs and feet before going to sleep. If your feet feel particularly fatigued, painful, or swollen, seek out a natural source of cold water to soak them in. Cold water helps alleviate inflammation and minimize pain.

When you rest your feet, be sure to massage them. If your feet become too fatigued and painful at any point during your stay in the wild, don't be ashamed to take a couple of days off to rest and walk as little as possible.

Despite the best of intentions, discomfort and injury does happen in the wild. The key is addressing it immediately. A common injury that happens when spending time on your feet is blisters. Addressing blisters right away will prevent them from becoming a larger issue, causing excessive pain, and hindering the ability to stand and walk. Herbal salves, poultices, and bandages can be applied (please see our chapter "Wilderness Basic First Aid" on page 113). Bandages, tape, or moleskin can also be used on areas that are prone to blisters.

One of the many advantages of living in the wild is that you have access to a plethora of medicinal plants that are beneficial for the feet.

Comfrey

Comfrey, *Symphytum officinale*

Comfrey is a plant with a long history of use for topical injuries. Its latin name, *Symphytum officinal*e, comes from the Greek word, sympho, which means 'grow together'. There are many varieties of comfrey, but this species can be found growing in North America and Europe. Comfrey can grow up to 3 feet (90 cm) high and 2 ½ feet (60 cm) wide. It has large basal leaves that are pointed and hairy.

Comfrey leaves and roots can be prepared for medicinal use and have analgesic (pain-relieving), emollient (soothing), and vulnerary (wound-healing) properties. Comfrey can be made into a poultice or infused into water or oil and applied to small cuts, bruises, sprains, breaks, sores, and rashes. The leaves can be moistened with water and applied to the skin. Comfrey heals very quickly, so don't use it on deep wounds or puncture wounds, as you want them to heal from the inside out.

Rose

Rosa multiflora, Qwert1234, CC BY-SA 3.0

Rosa virginiana, magnolia1000 from Canada, CC BY 2.0

Rose leaves and flowers can be of use when living in the wilderness. Although most people are more familiar with garden roses, there are a variety of rose species that grow abundantly in the wild across the globe. Depending on your location, you may come across *Rosa multiflora, Rosa rugosa, Rosa virginiana, Rosa canina, Rosa gallica*, and more. Wild roses tend to have smaller flowers than their cultivated counterparts and are usually pink or white in color. The leaves grow as leaflets on a single, thorny stem and have serrated edges.

Rose flowers and leaves have anti-inflammatory, antimicrobial, and astringent properties that are beneficial for topical use and first-aid needs. Rose flowers and leaves can be prepared as rosewater by adding the leaves and flowers to a pot and covering with water. Cover and simmer for 20-30 minutes and then strain the plant matter from the water. This rosewater can be applied to small wounds, rashes, and burns.

Blackberry

Rubus fruticosus, H. Zell - Own work, CC BY-SA 3.0

Like rose, blackberry is in the Rosaceae family and shares many of the same medicinal properties. In many areas, blackberries are considered an invasive plant and grow prolifically. *Rubus fruticosus* is a blackberry species native to Europe that now grows on all continents except Antarctica. It is a deciduous shrub that can quickly grow up to 9 feet (2.7 m) high by 9 feet (2.7 m) wide. The stems, also called canes, are long, thorny, and arching. The alternate leaves have serrated edges and are dark green on top with a lighter underside. The plants produce clusters of white or pink flowers that give way to the black fruit. You can generally find blackberry plants growing in woodlands or along hedges.

The leaves, stems, and roots are antimicrobial and strongly astringent. They can be prepared as an infusion or poultice and applied to burns, inflamed skin, rashes, and wounds.

Gotu Kola

Gotu kola, *Centella asiatica*

Gotu kola, or *Centella asiatica*, is a low-growing, herbaceous plant that is native to India, China, Indonesia, Australia, the South Pacific Islands, Madagascar, and parts of Africa. It is well known for its wound-healing properties and is an excellent plant to forage for and use medicinally in the wild. Gotu kola creeps along the ground and at most, grows 18 inches (46 cm) in height. Its green leaves are fan-shaped and odorless. It is commonly found growing in damp, swampy areas.

Gotu kola is anti-inflammatory and skin-supportive; it can be applied to wounds and achy joints and muscles. Fresh gotu kola leaves can quickly be transformed into a poultice by crushing the leaves and applying to the feet wherever needed.

Other common herbaceous plants that can be used as a poultice by applying the crushed leaves directly to the skin are: Yarrow (*Achillea millefolium*) as a coagulant (stops bleeding) and antibacterial, Plantain (*Plantago major* and *P. lanceolata*) for stings and bites, and Violet (*Viola odorata*) for inflammation. Yarrow can also be infused into water and used as a rinse on the feet; Violet leaves and flowers can be used as a compress, infused oil or salve for dry or chafed skin, insect bites, and rashes.

Yarrow
(*Achillea millefolium*)

Plantain
(*Plantago major*)

Violet
(*Viola odorata*)

Pine Tree

Ponderosa pine (*Pinus ponderosa*)

Beyond herbaceous plants, there are many trees that can help you care for your feet while living in the wild.

The *Pinus* genus contains over 100 pine species that can be found worldwide. Most pine trees can be used medicinally and their benefits have been enjoyed by various cultures for thousands of years. Traditionally, the needles, inner bark, and resin are used as medicine. When identifying a pine tree, look for two to five pine needles growing together in a bundle with a paper-like sheath at the base.

To utilize pine for foot care, try simmering the pine bark and needles in water, letting it cool, and then soaking your feet in the water. Pine bark and needles are antimicrobial and astringent. Pine resin can also be used topically and is often applied as an antimicrobial dressing to wounds.

Black Walnut Tree

Black Walnut Tree, *Juglans nigra*

The black walnut tree, or *Juglans nigra*, is a deciduous tree that can quickly grow up to 100 feet (30 m) high. Black walnut trees can be found growing in woods and along hillsides in rich, fertile soil. Black walnut bark is fissured, sharply-ridged, and dark gray in color. Its leaves are pinnate and strongly aromatic when crushed. Black walnut trees produce an edible nut that is surrounded by a yellow-green husk.

An infusion of the leaves can be used to cleanse the feet and wash wounds. The leaves and bark can be made into a poultice and applied to injuries and inflammation. The green husk of the nut is strongly antifungal and can be used in a foot soak.

Tea Tree

Melaleuca alternifolia, Murray Fagg, CC BY 3.0

Melaleuca alternifolia, commonly known as tea tree, is an evergreen shrub native to Australia that grows in swamps near the coast. Tea tree has a bushy crown and white, papery bark. It is in bloom from spring to summer when it showcases its fluffy white flowers. The essential oil in tea tree leaves is antimicrobial and commonly used in skin products. To use this plant in the wild, simmer the leaves or twigs in water and use the cooled and strained liquid as a foot wash. When used externally, tea tree can soothe bites, burns, infection, and rashes.

In addition to a healthy foot care routine and taking advantage of the medicinal plants that nature provides us, it is also wise to consider the shoes, if any, that you will wear while living in the wild. Every individual is unique and requires different footwear in order to have a comfortable and injury-free experience. The appropriate set of shoes will offer you physical ease and stability. In order to assess what type of shoes will be most beneficial for you, think about the type of terrain you will be traversing, the typical weather conditions of the area you will be in, and the weight you will be carrying.

Wilderness shoes range from primitive sandals, to heavy, sturdy hiking boots, and everything in between. Sandals have the advantage of allowing the feet more freedom and access to fresh air. A lightweight shoe may be preferred if you plan on walking long distances, although lighter shoes tend to have less stability than a heavier shoe. A heavy hiking boot generally provides the ankles and feet with the most support. You may also want to consider the tread of your shoe and how much traction you think you will need. A wet area calls for a good set of rubber boots with good traction. No matter what type of shoe you decide to bring with you, be sure to frequently clean your shoes and keep them dry.

If you desire an authentic experience while you live in the wild, you may choose to build your own sandals out of the natural resources surrounding you. Tree bark or roots can be collected and woven into a flat, lattice shape that is the size of your footprint. Be sure to choose bark or roots that do not break easily and that have a relatively smooth surface. Once you have the sole of the sandals made, you can use additional roots or paracord to create straps that will hold your feet in place when they are in the sandals.

THE RIGHT MENTAL ATTITUDE TO HAVE IN THE WILD

In the unforgiving realm of the wilderness, where nature reigns supreme, and the unexpected lurks around every corner, a survival mindset is not just a valuable asset—it is the key to enduring and thriving in the face of adversity. This chapter delves into the core principles that define this mindset, from maintaining emotional composure and heeding one's instincts to embracing resilience and seeking spiritual strength. Whether you're an intrepid adventurer or in an unexpected survival situation, these guiding principles will equip you with the mental fortitude and strategies essential to navigate the challenges of the wild.

Staying in Control - of Yourself

When facing the unpredictability of nature, it becomes clear that our ability to manipulate external circumstances is limited. Mountains, rivers, and forests have followed their rhythms for eons, indifferent to our presence. However, in the face of this awe-inspiring power of nature, an essential understanding must be embraced—the control we maintain over our internal emotions, thoughts, and actions. The wilderness can be unforgiving, and succumbing to fear, panic, or despair in such an environment can be life-threatening.

This mindset is one of humility. It is the acknowledgment of our smallness compared to the vastness and power of the natural world. Yet, it is also a mindset of awe—a deep appreciation for the intricate web of life, the beauty of the wilderness, and the humbling realization of our place within it.

Simultaneously, it's asserting the self as a being equipped with the capacity to endure and thrive in nature's embrace. It believes in our ability to adapt, problem-solve, and make informed decisions, even in the most challenging circumstances. This mental attitude is a source of inner strength—a beacon guiding us through the wilderness, reminding us that while nature's forces are formidable, the human spirit is equally resilient.

In this balance of humility and self-assuredness, we find the core of the survival mindset. It's an analytical recognition of the external environment's uncontrollable nature and a steadfast commitment to maintaining control over our internal responses. It is, ultimately, the harmony between the reverence for nature's power and the unwavering belief in our capacity to navigate its challenges.

Listening to Your Instincts

Listening to your instincts is a critical skill when navigating the unpredictable terrain of the wilderness. While rational and analytical thinking plays a vital role in decision-making, there are moments when the intuitive power of your mind takes center stage. Nature communicates subtly, and your instincts often act as the interpreter, offering valuable insights that can mean the difference between success and adversity.

Our instincts have been honed through millennia of evolution, finely tuned to detect danger or opportunity even before your conscious mind can process it. In the wild, these instincts serve as an early warning system, alerting you to potential threats—a rustle in the underbrush, a change in the wind's direction, or an inexplicable feeling of unease. Trusting these intuitive signals can be a lifeline, guiding you away from danger and toward safety.

The Importance of Intuition

Intuition, often called the brain's probability calculator, is a remarkable yet often underappreciated facet of decision-making that begins in your gut. It operates in the background, sifting through a vast repository of experiences and information and rapidly arriving at conclusions that might otherwise take time-consuming analysis. Intuition becomes an invaluable asset in the wilderness, where decisions can be a matter of life or death.

What sets intuition apart is its ability to thrive in moments when time is scarce—those split-second or brief windows of opportunity or peril. There is no room for ponderous analysis or exhaustive evaluation in these instances. Instead, intuition steps in, offering a swift and often accurate assessment of the situation.

Wilderness enthusiasts must recognize that nature's challenges don't always afford the luxury of ample time for contemplation. There are moments when split-second decisions are the only option, and in these instances, the counsel of your intuition should be heeded with the utmost seriousness.

Keeping Your Emotions in Check

Maintaining emotional composure in the wilderness is a paramount aspect of survival. Fear, panic, anxiety, and anger are natural responses to stressful situations, but allowing them to dominate your decision-making can be dangerous. These emotions often prioritize short-term reactions over long-term, rational thinking, potentially leading to poor choices in high-stress environments.

It's vital to recognize the signs of rising emotions and implement strategies to keep them in check. Deep breathing exercises can help stabilize your emotional state and clear your mind. Meditation or closing your eyes for introspection can provide clarity and restore focus. Taking a break to center yourself amid adversity is not a sign of weakness but a demonstration of wisdom.

Understanding that negative emotions can become your worst enemy in survival situations is crucial. They can disrupt your ability to think, problem-solve, and make rational choices. By mastering the art of emotional self-regulation, you equip yourself with the mental resilience necessary to navigate the wilderness with a level head and ensure your long-term survival. In nature's unforgiving embrace, emotional control can be the difference between succumbing to despair and emerging victorious.

The Importance of Situational Awareness

Situational awareness, the keen perception of one's surroundings, is an indispensable skill for wilderness survival. It encompasses a multifaceted awareness beyond immediate threats and opportunities; it's a holistic understanding of your environment and place.

First and foremost, situational awareness involves being acutely aware of your inventory. Knowing what supplies and tools you have on hand can be the key to making informed decisions. It ensures you have the resources needed to adapt and overcome challenges.

Listening to the sounds of the wilderness is another dimension of situational awareness. The rustle of leaves, the calls of distant animals, bird language (see "How to Track and Use Bird Language in the Wild" at page 187), the rush of water—these auditory cues offer vital information about your surroundings. They can alert you to potential dangers or lead you to valuable resources like water sources or wildlife.

Observing the terrain and the wind patterns is equally crucial. Changes in topography can guide you to shelter, water, or safety. Understanding wind direction can help you detect the scent of predators or locate distant fires or other signs of human activity.

Situational awareness also extends to the behavior of wildlife. Animals often react to changes in their environment before humans can perceive them. Observing their movements, alarm calls, or sudden stillness can provide valuable insights into nearby threats or changing weather.

In the wilderness, threats and opportunities can emerge suddenly and without warning. Maintaining heightened situational awareness is your shield against unforeseen dangers and your compass to discovering hidden resources. It's the skill that keeps you attuned to the ever-changing symphony of the wild and equips you to thrive amidst its challenges.

The Importance of Routines

Maintaining routines is a cornerstone of wilderness survival, providing structure and order in an environment characterized by chaos and unpredictability. Routines extend beyond mere habits; they are lifelines that ensure your physical and mental well-being, enhance efficiency, and increase your chances of thriving in the wild.

A structured routine begins with essential daily activities, including regular sleep and wake times. Adequate rest is crucial, as it helps preserve energy and mental clarity. Hygiene routines, such as maintaining cleanliness and addressing minor injuries promptly, are equally vital to prevent infections and ensure overall health.

Dietary routines, which involve planning and rationing your food supplies, help sustain your energy levels. Maintaining a consistent eating schedule prevents unnecessary depletion of resources and sustains your physical strength.

In the wilderness, flexibility is essential, but routines provide a framework for survival. Regularly checking the weather can alert you to approaching storms or temperature drops, allowing you to prepare accordingly. Monitoring traps set for catching animals, gathering wood for fires, and waterproofing and maintaining shelters are all routine tasks that contribute to long-term wilderness living.

Routines include maintaining and cleaning your clothing, preserving your gear, and performing essential repairs. These tasks not only ensure the longevity of your equipment but also bolster your overall preparedness.

In the unpredictable world of survival, routines are a safety net ensuring structure and keeping you proactive. They instill discipline, keep you organized, and ultimately increase your chances of facing each day in the wilderness with a structured, purposeful approach that fosters your well-being and survival.

Resilience, Grit, and Perseverance

Resilience, grit, and perseverance are the bedrock of a survival mindset in the wilderness. They constitute the unwavering determination to face adversity head-on and emerge stronger on the other side. This mindset is a beacon of hope in the darkest moments, believing that positive outcomes are attainable, even when the path ahead seems fraught with obstacles.

Resilience becomes your most reliable companion in the wild, where the journey is often treacherous and the terrain unforgiving. It's the understanding that setbacks and dead ends are part of the journey, not roadblocks to defeat. Each challenge encountered is a lesson, a chance to adapt, learn, and grow. Acknowledge that the more attempts you make, the greater your odds of success.